THE CORPORATION MANUAL

*The Entrepreneur's Passport
To Financial Security*

By: Aaron Young

Published by
LAUGHLIN ASSOCIATES, INC.

9120 Double Diamond Pkwy.
Reno, NV 89521
Phone: 775-525-2892 1-800-648-0966
FAX: 775-525-2898
E-Mail: info@laughlinusa.com
Web: www.laughlinusa.com

John F. Kennedy said, "In a time of turbulence and change, it is more true than ever that knowledge is power". As we go to press with this 7th edition of the Corporation Manual, we certainly are living in a time of turbulence and change. Everything seems unsure and people are worried how to move forward with their lives let alone their businesses. It is at such a time that people need straight forward information that is easy to deploy in order to get predictable results. This manual provides you with the knowledge and power you need to transform today's challenges into growth opportunities.

For over 40 years, Laughlin Associates has been working with owners of closely held companies. Most of these are small business people who don't have a deep bench of lawyers, CPAs and other specialized advisors readily available to answer every little question. As a matter of fact, most of these owners can't afford to pay several hundred dollars an hour for basic advice. For this reason many business owner have turned to Laughlin Associates for free consulting, education and cost effective implementation of business strategies. Our value proposition has always been to empower entrepreneurs to proactively protect their business. Tens of thousands of business owners have entrusted us to provide that guidance which has led to the formation of nearly 80,000 entities. We are humbled by such trust and confidence.

Small business owners are the life blood of the U.S. economy. They create the amazing products, provide vital services, and do the majority of job creation. These American heroes deserve to be appreciated and supported. Unfortunately, they more often than not get little more than lip service from federal and state government and are never the ones getting "bailed out" when times are tough. The good news is that small businesses are nimble and can make course corrections quickly. They adjust to the changes in the mood of the country. They adapt and survive. This book is designed to help them do even better than that. It is designed to help them thrive. And to do that, you need knowledge.

The pages of the Corporation Manual are filled with tried and true strategies, clear and concise business education, and are a quick and easy guide to help you understand how to get the most from your corporation or LLC. Take some time to read through these pages and you will discover that your corporation is an amazingly powerful tool that can help you gain advantages that you probably don't even know exist.

We hope that you enjoy and feel empowered by the information offered here. If you want to dig even deeper, we are always available to answer your question, help you organize a plan, and then support you as that plan takes flight.

To those of you who have been our clients over the years let me say thank you for sharing your insights. Thank you for your courage. Thank you for showing up day after day. And mostly, thanks for your business.

Scott,

EXCITED FOR THE FUTURE. LOVE BEING YOUR FRIEND

Printed in America by Laughlin Associates, Inc.
9120 Double Diamond Pkwy., Reno, NV 89521
1-800-648-0966
www.laughlinusa.com

All that we do is submitted and performed with the understanding that we
are not engaged in rendering legal, accounting or other such professional
service. If legal advice or other expert assistance is required, the services of a
person in those professions should be sought.

LET'S GET ACQUAINTED

LAUGHLIN ASSOCIATES, INC.

We have been in this business since 1972. We provide newly-formed corporations, resident agent representation, and the Nevada headquarters for those seeking to profitably locate corporate offices in Nevada. We also provide training courses and management consulting. Education is our only sales tool — when people learn what they can have through our products and services, they generally retain our services or obtain our products.

All we do is submitted and performed with the understanding that we are not engaged in rendering legal, accounting or other such services. If legal advice or other technical assistance is required, the services of a professional in that area should be sought.

We are the oldest and most reliable company of this type in Nevada. We have formed more than 80,000 corporations. Our clients trust us for stability, dependability and reliability. These are items of basic importance in the corporation area.

Many try to imitate us and we consider it the highest form of flattery. Others copy our material and documents, which we accept as evidence that we offer and produce the best. Our "would-be" competitors soon learn that this, like a lot of businesses, is not as easy as they thought it might appear.

We respectfully suggest it is prudent to beware of whom you deal with in the field of corporations and statutory representation. You need a firm that will be there when needed- a year, 10 years, or 50 years from now. You need a firm that won't head you in the wrong direction. We'd like to be your firm. We are the only firm of this type with a proven 40-year track record upon which you can rely. You can count on us when you need us. We are here to serve you.

Table Of Contents

SECRETS of FINANCIAL SECURITY

Introduction

The Secrets of Financial Security will cover many topics but two of the subjects that you should pay special attention to are the tax and asset protection strategies.

You take a dollar and give it to the government and you just did a magic trick. You made a dollar disappear. It's gone and it produces nothing. Government doesn't create wealth and I suppose in it's defense, it really isn't supposed to.

But take the same dollar and invest it in the private sector and you get what is commonly known as the ripple effect — economists call it waves. A dollar becomes savings, a loan, an investment; it creates employment, opportunity, a larger taxpayer base; it takes tax burdens, in fact, and turns them into taxpayers. What happens? Everyone pays less taxes which creates more taxpayers, who create more dollars and the wave continues. It grows geometrically and really without end and what is then created is prosperity, value — what economists call wealth.

So let's remember that there is not a more magnanimous gesture that you can make to help our society as a whole but to make available more of your hard earned dollars for investment in the private sector and your own business.

How much do you pay in taxes?

Let's look more closely at what we pay in taxes. The highest federal tax rate is 39.6 percent along with an additional 8 to 12 percent incurred by state taxes. That means around 50 percent of your income goes to pay taxes. Most Americans will work until June just to cover their tax liability for one year.

Now if you are wondering why they allow you to keep the other half, the answer is easy. You need the other half to pay sales tax, excise tax, use tax, franchise tax, gross receipts tax, inventory tax — there is no end. There is not a serious student of economics in this country that would suggest to you that you pay less than 60 percent of your hard earned money in taxes.

How would you like to pay less taxes?

"Anyone may arrange his affairs that his

taxes shall be as low as possible. He is not bound to choose the pattern which best pays the treasury, there is not even a patriotic duty to increase one's taxes. Over and over again courts have said that there is nothing sinister in so arranging affairs as to keep taxes as low as possible. Everyone does it, rich and poor alike, and all do it right, for nobody owes public duty to pay more than the law demands."

Judge Learned Hand
Gregory vs. Helvering 293 U.S 465

Now anybody, including the IRS will tell you, "You don't have to pay more taxes than the law requires. The maximum rate is 39.6 percent. What is the minimum individual tax rate? 10 percent! Well if you are able to cut your state taxes on your money to zero and you are able to keep your federal tax burden down to 10 percent — you have just effectively cut your state and federal taxes by a healthy 60 percent. Or in other words, you have just given yourself more than a 100 percent raise in take home pay.

Let's do the math. If you are paying about 60 percent of your income in taxes every year and you cut federal from 39 to 10 percent and you cut state income taxes from 10 to 0 percent, you are now only paying 35 percent. You just went from retaining 40 percent of your hard earned money to keeping 75 percent.

Now add the savings from the insurance or self-employment taxes you pay and you could effectively add another 15.3 percent to this amount. Wouldn't you agree that keeping 90 percent of what you earn is a lot more attractive than being left with a measly 40 percent of what you earn.

The Need For Asset Protection

Now let's briefly discuss the other side of building and retaining wealth. Outside of taxes the single greatest threat to your success are future risks that you face personally and in business. Many of these risks can land you in court where you could face a lawsuit and then a judgment.

A lawsuit is filed in America every one and a half seconds. In the time you've been reading this book 400 lawsuits have been filed.

NBC News said the average American will be sued an average of 5 times in his or her life. Well you are different. You are not the average person, you are in business. Because if you are any of the following four things, any one, an entrepreneur, an investor, self-employed, or if you operate a small business you have a one in four chance of being sued in the next twelve months.

Picture this, you get sued, in a rather mundane case of routine business litigation. Expect it to occupy 5 years until you dispose of it. An antitrust case — 30 years. What can you expect during the 5 years? The cost of a rather modest legal defense today is $80,000 to $100,000, including attorney's fees, additional fees, your time, travel — I mean discovery alone can be $100,000. In addition to the cost, what else can you expect? Statistically, the business in which you're trying to protect will suffer severely from neglect, it might even fail. Families are torn apart, people lose their homes and guess what? It turns out that being sued is not good for your health. The incident of stroke and heart attack goes up 500 percent during a lawsuit. So the business suffered, marriage is gone, home's gone, health's gone, but you win the lawsuit. I still have faith in the system. But it costs you everything to win. You didn't do anything wrong and ultimately prevailed in the lawsuit. The person that sues you moves on to their next victim with no consequences.

Why? Because ours is the only modern and industrial nation on earth that does not employ a "loser pays" legal system. If someone sues you and loses they have to compensate you for your time and expenses. Without it you have cases happening like this everyday. "I sued Diane because she worked hard for 35 years, and she's got a nice business, and I'd like to take it away from her."

The United States is the only country in the world, which permits contingency fee litigation. In all other countries it is unethical for an attorney to take a case on a contingency fee basis.

"The new American dream, as you know, is to slip and fall and win it all!"

I read about a figure that will just astound you. At first I thought it was impossible. It said the cost of our legal system to American business exceeds $350 billion a year. That's almost the national deficit. Most of these costs are derived from the big 3 — product liability, malpractice and tort law, but there's plenty more.

There are over 1 million lawyers in the United States, all looking to make a living. They know that once they serve you with papers it is easier and cheaper for you to pay a settlement than to go to court.

Summary

When you go into business or you've been in business for a while it doesn't take too long for you to realize that nobody cares about your business as much as you. You are the one person that is ultimately responsible for your success. That means you are the one person who needs to be informed on all aspects of your business, the taxes, the risks, the preventions and the wealth building opportunities that are available to you.

This book will provide you with the insight to get you going in the right direction. This book contains the information your attorney and CPA never seem to mention. You have the

Introduction

right to know as much as you can to
drive your business toward success.

This book will provide you with the
foundation you need to make the right
choices. At the end of each chapter we
have included a notes section. As you
are reading along and come up with
questions or ideas, write them down. As
part of our service we will answer those
questions and assist you with taking the
steps necessary to get you going in the
right direction.

1 Business in America!

- *Our Business Environment*
- *What You're Up Against*

Times are changing, more and more individuals are taking it upon themselves to start their own businesses. In fact, 25 million Americans will report some form of self-employment income to the IRS this year. These individuals want to be in charge of their own financial destiny. But, as anybody knows who's either in business or looking to start a business, there are inherent risks that must be dealt with before you take one more step.

The road to true success is never easy. In small business, we have a high profile, people know we have a business and therefore it, makes us more of a target for lawsuits.

Running your own business is a risky proposition. It doesn't matter if you work out of your house, buy investment property, start a store, take on a profession or provide consulting services. While all these occupations are distinct in their own way, many of the hazards that exist for small business owners are very similar.

When you start your own business you face risks that fall into two categories: the first category contains things you have control over: taxes, litigation, creditors and employee. The second category contains things you have no control over, natural disasters, terrorist attacks, suppliers and illness.

From the moment you open up your doors, see your first patient, start selling your product or rent your first house you become a target. Why? Because everybody knows that if you own your own business you must be rich, if you are rich you must have something to take.

True asset protection comes from removing the incentive for someone to sue you. The "incentive," comes from how much they think you have and how much of that they can take in a lawsuit. Establishing a level of privacy between you and your assets isn't about hiding, or covering up, it's about having a structure in place that legally allows you to control those assets without the liability of ownership.

Privacy Does Matter

Some argue that if they have nothing to hide why does privacy matter. I can assure you that it does matter a great deal! My guess is that you close your drapes at night, not because you have anything criminal to hide, but simply because someone looking through your window may not have honorable intentions.

Another challenge that we have as entrepreneurs is the everyday invasion of our privacy. It's very difficult in today's public age to keep anything private, or confidential. It's not very hard for a computer hacker or somebody with a credit reporting agency to find out everything there is about you. To find out your spending habits, what assets you own, your income, from where you get your income, where you live and have lived. Your life tends to be an open book in today's computer information age.

Many people think they don't need privacy because they are not doing, and never will do, anything wrong. I don't think anybody reading this book, is doing anything wrong or has anything to hide. I would certainly hope that each and every one of us is conducting business in an aboveboard, honest fashion.

Unfortunately, in today's litigious society, people who can be directly associated with their assets, become favorable targets for litigation. Establishing a level of privacy is about lessening your risk of a lawsuit.

Controlling Your Taxes

The United States was built on the backbone of the small business owner and while you are not required to pay more in taxes than the law requires, you are required to pay taxes.

Everybody knows that there are two things in life that are certain, death and taxes.

Paying taxes is like paying dues for living in such a wonderful country, but many people fall into the trap of overpaying their taxes. In fact 70% of small business owners will over-pay their taxes this year. According to the U.S. Department of Treasury, they are holding 4 billion dollars in a trust for people who overpaid their taxes.

Overpaying your taxes doesn't help grow the economy. The government had supplied us with 11,760 pages in the tax code to assist us in decreasing our tax burden. What would you do if you could save $5,000 a year in taxes? Would you reinvest in your business, buy stocks, go shopping, or put it toward your retirement? What does that mean to the government, that means you are helping to grow the economy.

14

As we go though some of the different strategies available to you we will spend a little time discussing the tax ramifications or different business entities but always be sure to check with your CPA or other financial professional. The strategies discussed are in general terms and might not fit your exact scenario.

Summary

As a small business owner, it's all about risk verses reward. The ultimate goal of this book is to reduce your risk and increase your reward. While running a business is risky, you have in your hands the tools necessary to reduce those risks. Taxes, litigation and regulation are all part of the daily world of a business owner.

This book is your resource guide to understanding the steps you can take now to reduce your taxable burden and reinvest that money saved to grow your business. We will show you how to secure your assets and structure your affairs to provide for financial privacy.

You don't have to risk it all to start a business. You don't have to wait until it's too late. To be successful in business as well as in life you must prepare. Prepare for the worst and hope for the best. Everything requires preparation. By reading this book you are preparing for the future, to protect your assets, to secure your financial privacy and to lower your taxable burden.

NOTES

2 The Building Blocks of Business

- *Sole Proprietorships*
- *Partnerships*
- *Limited Partnerships*
- *Limited Liability Companies*
- *Corporations*
- *S-Corporations*

No discussion of corporate operation would be complete without a brief overview of other business entities. In the context of all business entities, it becomes quickly evident that the corporation is far and away the most versatile, most powerful and most beneficial business entity of them all. We will discuss the sole proprietorship, both general and limited partnerships, and the limited liability companies. With each entity, we will describe what it is, how it is formed, and its advantages and disadvantages.

SOLE-PROPRIETORSHIP

A sole proprietorship is the simplest and most risky form of doing business. The easiest way to understand the sole proprietorship is simply to understand that it is you. All you need to do is to begin doing business. In most areas you will need to obtain a business license, and if your business operates under a name other than your own, you usually need to file a fictitious name statement, and that is it. The business and you are one and the same. There is no protection from liability, and as a result, your personal assets are always at risk.

There is nothing to form, no papers to file, no agreements to sign. When you have decided to go into business you are a sole proprietor, and so you tack up a shingle and you start selling widgets. The primary benefit of a sole proprietorship is it's simple, it's easy, there's nothing to form, and it has a single level of taxation. This is both the great advantage of the sole proprietorship, and its Achilles heel. Because the business is you, its money is your money and the liability can fall only on you.

What does one level of tax mean? Well, since it's just you earning the money and spending the money, it's only you that has to worry about paying taxes. The income or loss from the business is reported on your personal tax return by attaching a Schedule C form.

Disadvantages Of A Sole Proprietorship

What about the disadvantages? In my opinion, the liability exposure is reason enough for anybody not to be a sole proprietorship. If someone were to file a claim against your business, not only your businesses assets, but your personal assets, like your house, your car, your child's college fund, etc. are all directly at risk as well.

Not to mention, you also would be required to pay self-employment tax of 15.3 percent.

PARTNERSHIPS

Partnerships take two forms, general partnerships and limited partnerships, so let's take them one at a time. The general partnership is the second most common method of doing business. Like the sole proprietorship, it is simple to form and has one level of taxation.

A general partnership consists of two or more people who agree to enter into business together. They should see an attorney to draw up what is usually a simple partnership agreement, although very often they do not. They agree on how much money each will contribute to the business and who will be responsible for what.

Disadvantages of Partnerships

From a liability point of view, general partnerships are a high risk proposition. Not only are you taking on personal liability for the business but you are taking on the liability for your partners actions. Suppose one partner gets into an auto accident while driving to a movie. There is a lawsuit. The plaintiff's go after your partner's share of the business. If that party wins the lawsuit, you may find yourself with a new partner. This new partner may well decide that he or she wants nothing to do with the successful operation of the business, and may want to force its liquidation. Now if that person has just as much decision-making authority as you do, they can make your life an utter nightmare.

A situation such as this is bad enough if that were the only problem with general partnerships, but it's not the end of the story. Most business people who have been involved in partnerships of this type in the past will tell you that they would never do it again, because of the management difficulties they experience. Who makes decision? If two partners share 50% of the business, they must agree on everything and this is not realistic. In fact, most partners who enter into business as friends leave the business as enemies.

Tax wise, the partnership is quite similar to proprietorships in that the partner's share of the profit or loss is reported on their individual tax return by attaching a form K-1. Again, the deductions and tax rates are personal, and there is self-employment tax to be dealt with.

LIMITED PARTNERSHIPS

The limited partnership, on the other hand, offers some solutions to the problems that the general partnership has. In this entity, there are two different types of partners; general partners and limited partners. The general partner has unlimited personal liability for the actions of the partnership. To compensate for this, the general partner also has full management and decision-making power. The limited partner, on the other hand, has no liability for the actions of the partnership, and has no management or decision-making capacity.

They have another great advantage over general partnerships in liability. If there is more than one partner, and if a partner is sued individually, a judgment creditor cannot normally take away the interest of the partner in the partnership. In this case they are limited to a charging order, which entitles the judgment creditor to receive any partnership distributions that would have gone to the partner in question. Since the partnership usually has no obligation to make distributions of profits, the judgment creditor may have a long wait to be paid. During this waiting period they will be receiving the K-1 for the debtor partner, and if the partnership is making money, the judgment creditor must pay the tax of the debtor, while not receiving the money.

In many cases, this feature can motivate the judgment creditor to either settle with the debtor, or simply to leave the partnership interest alone.

Disadvantages of Limited Partnerships

From the point of view of formation, a limited partnership is much more complicated and expensive than the previous two entities discussed. An attorney normally prepares the Partnership Agreement, which sets forth the structure of the entity as well as its governing rules. In addition, a filing with the Secretary of State must also be made, listing the general partner(s). While limited partnerships are not usually used for operating businesses, if they are, they will also need the usual licenses and permits.

LIMITED LIABILITY COMPANIES

The limited liability company (LLC) is a hybrid between the limited partnership and the corporation. It is also one of the newest forms of doing business in the United States. It combines the limited liability aspects of corporations with the partnership taxation of a limited partnership in a flexible and workable way that has caught the eye of many business people, and is becoming more popular everyday.

Rather than having partners or stockholders, the LLC has Members, who own an interest in the company.

LLCs can either be managed by members or they can choose to hire a manager. "Member Managed LLCs" require votes of the members to make decisions. Like a corporation, they can also have officers. Another LLC option is to create "Manager Managed LLCs" wherein the members elect a manager, who exercises all management authority, thus acting as the general partner in a limited partnership, leaving the members acting as limited partners. Unlike the limited partnership, however, all parties within an LLC maintain limited liability for personal protection from business liability.

This flexibility gives the LLC a great advantage when you are considering a form of doing business. Partnership taxation can be a great thing if the company loses money, or makes certain types of investments where personal capital gains treatment would be preferable to corporate treatment, such as in real estate investment. In addition, because any person or entity may be a member in an LLC, an LLC offers advantages for income splitting which an S-corporation cannot offer.

Disadvantages of Limited Liability Companies

Even with these advantages, however, LLC's have their share of problems. The biggest problem that they currently have is the fact that they are so new. The first LLC statute in the US was passed in the state of Wyoming in 1976. Nevada passed one in 1991, California in 1995, and the last state joined the fold in 1997. Because of this, there is simply a lack of case law to determine how LLCs will be treated in certain instances. In addition, tax treatment is not entirely carved in stone, and the IRS and certain states have from time to time made changes that could be adverse to people in particular situations. For instance, in Texas an LLC is taxed as a corporation no matter if the IRS views you as a partnership or not. In California, if you are a single member LLC you are not protected by a charging order and they require LLCs to pay an annual $800 franchise tax. Questions as basic as whether or not an LLC needs to have corporate style formalities are not yet clear. Some experts claim that LLCs do not need to worry about formalities, others claim that they do. If in doubt it is always better to maintain corporate formalities. Sooner or later a court will decide the issue, but for the near future no one knows for certain.

CORPORATIONS

For over one hundred years, corporations have been the kings of business entities. Like an LLC, they offer limited liability for all involved, be they stockholders, directors or officers. They offer not only protection from lawsuits, but they offer many more opportunities for deductions, as well as the ability to income split.

Unlike LLCs, corporations have literally hundreds of years of case law. Your attorney can reasonably predict how courts will treat them in most situations, so you will know how to operate for asset protection and tax savings. No wonder most business experts would never enter into a business with any other form of doing business than a corporation. As you read on, you will learn the reasons that people incorporate, how corporations work, what things you need to do to keep your corporation healthy, what you can achieve by using multiple corporations, asset protection strategies, tax strategies and much more!

A corporation, unlike all the other entities that we discussed, is really a separate legal person. There's a doctrine of separateness between the corporation and the individuals associated with it. It's actually held to be a separate legal entity, a separate legal person, separate and apart from you as its owner, director, officer or employee. It's really easy, but it's also really hard for people to get of mindset of their business not being them. For most of us, we are our businesses. They're not separate things, they just go together, like jam and bread, and we can't quite get the concept of those things being separate in our head.

Your liability is limited to the extent of your investment in the corporation. So if you invest $10,000 into the corporation, then the corporation gets sued and a judgment is entered against it, all you stand to lose is the $10,000 that the corporation now holds as your

investment. This is the main reason people incorporate.

The main benefit incorporating provides you is limited liability and personal protection from the risks and hazards that your business faces.

S-CORPORATIONS

An S-corporation is a regular corporation that files an election with the IRS to become an S-corporation. The election turns the regular C-corporation into an S-corporation making it a "pass through entity". That means all profits and losses are passed directly onto the shareholders. The S-corporation is not considered a separate taxable entity like a regular C-corporation.

As a shareholder of an S-corporation you still receive all the same liability protection that you would as a shareholder of a regular corporation.

S-corporations must follow the same rules and regulations as regular corporations, which means they need to follow corporate formalities, hold meetings, elect a board of directors, write resolutions and document company decisions.

An S-corporation election does have to be filed within a certain time frame and according to certain time limits if you want to take advantage of the pass through tax treatment for the current tax year. If the corporation is new it must file form 2553 within 75 days of the date of incorporation.

Disadvantages of an S-Corporation

S-Corporations are very inflexible when it comes to shareholders and taxing issues. An S-corporation can only have 75 shareholders, and they are limited to individuals, estates or certain types of trusts, they cannot be corporations or partnerships. This eliminates the opportunity to use income splitting strategies. Shareholders must also be resident aliens of the United States.

S-corporations are limited to one class of stock, though one can be voting and nonvoting of the same type. Losses from an S-corporation can only be shared with shareholders to their proportion of debt. That means that S-corporation shareholders can't increase their basis in the S-corporation without either guaranteeing a loan or loaning the company money.

S-corporations don't allow for as many benefits as a regular corporation. In fact, as you will see at the end of Chapter 16, S-corporations aren't the business entity for you if you are looking to take advantage of additional fringe benefits. If you own 2% or more of an S-corporation, you can't be treated like an employee, and being an employee with earned income is what generates most of your benefits.

Summary

It's important to understand your options when choosing to form a business entity. One size does not fit all and you should take the time to do the due diligence necessary to make sure you are making the right decision based on your current and future goals.

There are various questions to be answered in the incorporating process such as where, when, and how to get started. Also, how easy is the structure to set-up, who controls the structure, what are the levels of liability, and what are the tax consequences?

On the next four pages we have inserted an easy to read comparison chart of corporations vs. S-corporations, limited liability companies, limited partnerships and partnerships.

CHART I
NON-TAX COMPARISONS OF
DIFFERENT BUSINESS STRUCTURES

Factor	Regular Corporation	S-corporation	Limited Liability Company	Limited Partnership	Partnership
Brief Description	A business entity established by the recording of Articles of Incorporation with the state. It is considered an association that is responsible for paying its own taxes.	A regular corporation that has elected to be treated as a "pass-through" entity that passes its profits and losses through to the shareholders for taxation at a personal level.	A business entity established by the recording of Articles of Organization with the state. It may structure itself to be treated as an association like a regular corporation or as a "pass-through" entity like an S-corporation.	A business entity established by the recording of a partnership agreement with the state. It is always considered a "pass-through" entity.	A business entity established by the agreement between its partners and licensing to do business as a partnership. It is always considered a "pass-through" entity.
Continuity of Life	Unlimited or perpetual unless limited by state law or by its own Articles of Incorporation.	Same as a regular corporation. Election of S-corporation status may be changed without affecting its continuity of life.	Same as a regular corporation. Its election of being treated as an association or "pass through" entity does not affect its continuity of life.	Can be limited to a set period as stated in its agreement, or as long as the partners wish to continue their business relationship. The death, legal disability or withdrawal of a partner will terminate the entity.	Can be limited to a set period as stated in its agreement, or as long as the partners wish to continue their business relationship. The death, legal disability or withdrawal of a partner will terminate the entity.
Entity Status	A corporation is considered to be completely separate from its owners.	Same as a regular corporation.	Same as a regular corporation.	Same as a regular corporation.	Generally recognized as being separate from its owners, but not for all purposes, such as liability.
Ownership and management structure and the personal liability of the Owners and Managers. (The limited liability that owners enjoy is limited to actions of the business entity not caused by fraudulent actions of the owners.)	Owners are shareholders while management consists of elected or appointed Directors and Officers. While shareholders enjoy limited liability for the actions of the corporation, the Directors and Officers may be indemnified by the corporation for actions of the corporation.	Same as a regular corporation.	Owners are Members while management can be either elected Manager(s) or Manager Members(s). Members enjoy limited liability while managers may be indemnified from actions taken against the LLC by the LLC itself, not unlike the indemnification a corporation can offer its Directors and Officers.	Owners are partners. The General Partner(s) manage the company with full personal liability for the actions of the partnership while Limited Partner(s) have no part in the management of the partnership but enjoy limited personal liability for the actions of the partnership.	Owners and managers are partners in the partnership and share personal liability for the partnership's actions.
Ease and effect of transfer of ownership interest.	General stock is easily and readily transferable along with any voting rights associated with that stock. Transfer of stock has no effect on the corporate entity.	S-corporations are limited on the number of stockholders and who can be stockholders. Transfer is the same as regular corporations, except that the transfer of stock cannot break these limitations if the S-corporation wishes to maintain its "pass-through" status.	All members must approve any transfer of interests by any members. They can allow the transfer of ownership with or without voting rights, or deny the transfer of ownership entirely.	Transfer of ownership in a partnership is overseen by the Partnership Agreement and may require the approval of all partners. The transfer of ownership may require the termination of the old partnership and creation of a new one.	Same as a Limited Partnership.

CHART I
NON-TAX CONSIDERATIONS FOR COMPARISONS OF DIFFERENT BUSINESS STRUCTURES

Factor	Regular Corporation	S-corporation	Limited Liability Company	Limited Partnership	Partnership
Availability of outside capital or financing.	May sell stock or bonds to the public. There is no state set limit on the number of shareholders a regular corporation may have, and so it may raise capital through stock issuance. A corporation may also enter into contracts establishing debt so it can borrow money with the corporation itself as the debtor.	Same as regular corporations except that they have a limit on the number of shareholders (75) to whom they can sell stock to raise capital.	Same as regular corporations with no limits on the number of members. However, limitations may be imposed by the members right to deny potential members membership.	Same as regular corporations, but all loans are backed personally by the General Partner(s) and new partners may be limited by the partnership agreement.	All loans to the partnership are backed personally by one or more of the partners and the addition of new partners may be limited by the partnership agreement.

CHART II
INCOME TAX CONSIDERATIONS FOR COMPARISONS OF DIFFERENT BUSINESS STRUCTURES

Factor	Regular Corporation	S-corporation	Limited Liability Company	Limited Partnership	Partnership
Who pays the tax?	The corporation is taxed on its taxable income before dividends are paid, whether or not dividends are distributed to the shareholders. The shareholders are taxed personally on any dividends they receive.	The owners are taxed on their share of the profits the business generated, regardless of whether they actually received the cash or it was retained by the business.	Same as a regular corporation if LLC elects to be taxed as an association, and the same as an S-corporation if LLC elects to be taxed as a "pass-through" entity.	The owners are taxed on their share of the profits the business generated, regardless of whether they actually received the cash or it was retained by the business.	The owners are taxed on their share of the profits the business generated, regardless of whether they actually received the cash or it was retained by the business.
Salaries paid to owners.	Where owners are employees, salaries are taxable to the owners and deductible by the corporation. Salaries must remain reasonable for services rendered.	Same as a regular corporation, except that residual profit of the corporation (after salaries and overhead) is passed through as unearned income to the owners.	Same as a regular corporation if LLC elects to be taxed as an association, and the same as an S-corporation if LLC elects to be taxed as a "pass-through" entity.	Same as S-corporation except limited partners may not be employed by the Limited Partnership in any fashion.	Same as S-corporation.
Liquidation of the business.	Amount received by owners in excess of their original investment is usually taxable as capital gain.	Same as a regular corporation.	Same as a regular corporation.	Same as a regular corporation.	Same as a regular corporation.
Pension or profit sharing plan.	Owners who are employees can be included in a regular qualified plan.	Same as a regular corporation.	Same as a regular corporation.	Same as a regular corporation, except that limited partners cannot be classified as employees.	Partners may participate only in a qualified self-employment plan.
Capital gains and losses.	Taxed to the corporation; there are no capital gains deduction.	Capital gains and losses normally flow through to the owners as such.	Same as a regular corporation if LLC elects to be taxed as an association, and the same as an S-corporation if LLC elects to be taxed as a "pass-through" entity.	Same as an S-corporation.	Same as an S-corporation.
Can business determine amounts of profits to pay its individual owners regardless of their percentage of ownership?	No.	No.	Yes, if LLC elects to be taxed as a "pass-through" entity and prior agreements have been made by the members and are reasonable.	Yes, if prior agreements have been made by the partners and are reasonable.	Yes, if prior agreements have been made by the partners and are reasonable.
Limits and taxation of after-tax earnings accumulated by the business.	May be subject to a penalty tax if amount of accumulation is unreasonable.	No limit since all income is taxed to the owners whether it is distributed or not.	Same as a regular corporation if LLC elects to be taxed as an association, and the same as an S-corporation if LLC elects to be taxed as a "pass-through" entity.	Same as an S-corporation.	Same as an S-corporation.

CHART II
INCOME TAX CONSIDERATIONS FOR COMPARISONS OF DIFFERENT BUSINESS STRUCTURES

Factor	Regular Corporation	S-corporation	Limited Liability Company	Limited Partnership	Partnership
Passive investment income.	Excessive passive income may cause the regular corporation to be classified as a holding company with a penalty tax imposed on its earnings.	If it has excessive passive income for three consecutive years, the S-corporation may lose its status as a "pass-through" entity and revert to a regular corporation, when it may be classified as a holding company.	Same as a regular corporation if LLC elects to be taxed as an association, and the same as an S-corporation if LLC elects to be taxed as a "pass-through" entity.	No effect.	No effect.
Selection of taxable year ends.	No restriction.	Limited to Dec. 31, or what is commonly referred to as a calendar year. Exceptions are occasionally allowed when calendar year causes undue duress or unwarranted business disadvantage.	Same as a regular corporation if LLC elects to be taxed as an association, and the same as an S-corporation if LLC elects to be taxed as a "pass-through" entity.	Same as an S-corporation.	Same as an S-corporation.

NOTES

3 When and Where to Form Your Business Entity

- *When to Form a Business Entity*
- *Where Should You Form Your Business Entity?*
- *Preferred States*
- *The Corporate Citizen*
- *When Can a State Tax a Foreign Corporation*

When To Form a Business Entity

If you're in business or going into business, the time to form a business entity is now. Actually, yesterday would not have been too soon. If you get sued tomorrow, the amount of money you would have spent to incorporate will seem like peanuts.

Where Should You Form Your Business Entity?

When we refer to a business entity we are referring to corporations and LLCs. We will use the term corporation to reference both entities throughout this chapter. Both entities fall under the same rules and regulations when it comes to qualifying to do business.

Where you form your business entity is just as important as when to form your business entity. You are free to incorporate anywhere, no matter where your operating business is currently located, but you need to be aware of the fees, rules and regulations of any state you plan to form a business entity in. You need to ask yourself a few questions like; What are your long term goals? Where do you plan to do a majority of your business? Are you looking for asset protection? Is this going to be an operating business or is it simply going to hold real estate?

If you choose to incorporate in a preferred state such as Delaware, Nevada or Wyoming but you plan to operate your business out of a different state, you will need to qualify that corporation to do business in that state and pay fees and some taxes in that state. The company formed in the preferred state would be considered a "foreign corporation" in the eyes of the state in which it is doing business and must adhere to the taxes and fees of that state.

As you read through this book and discover a variety of strategies you can accomplish by having one company in a preferred state and another in your home state you might just decide that the additional expense more than justifies the end result.

Preferred State

When should you form a business entity outside of your home state (the main state in which you do business)? You may be surprised to find that most of the companies with whom you are doing business in your home state are not incorporated in your home state! The reason is that some people realize the benefits of incorporating in a state with the most advantageous business and tax laws.

In the past Delaware was the state of choice but Nevada and Wyoming have taken the lead. Delaware is great for publicly traded company's because it offers a tremendous amount of case history, but it also requires additional reporting.

Nevada has come forward as the number one pro-business state in the nation. This is due to legislation passed that protects officers and directors from frivolous lawsuits. Nevada also has no corporate income tax, no franchise tax and no unitary tax.

Nevada also offers a simple layer of privacy for corporate shareholders. In Nevada only the officers have to

be listed on public record. Nevada is also one of the few states who doesn't share information with the IRS. There is a preferred state chart showing the difference between Nevada, Wyoming and Delaware at the end of this chapter.

The Corporate Citizen

A corporation is a citizen of the state where it is created or incorporated. A corporation does not cease to be a citizen of the state in which it is incorporated by engaging in business or acquiring property in another state.

One of the benefits to incorporating in a preferred state is that regardless of where the corporation does business, its inner-workings are governed by the state of incorporation. You'll find the inner-workings Nevada prescribes to be very advantageous to the person who runs the company, generally you.

If, for example, you started a small retail business in your home state and you never intend the business to become involved in interstate operations or sales, then you are probably well-advised simply to incorporate in your home state.

Many persons mistakenly believe that they can form a corporation in Nevada or elsewhere, and then simply proceed to do business in their home state. That is usually not true. Each state has exceptions to its legal definition of "doing business within that state."

You should ask your attorney or possibly your secretary of state's office what constitutes doing business in your state. For example, a Nevada corporation can own property in any state without having to qualify or be incorporated in that state. Although if you generate income with this real property by selling, renting or leasing the property then you could be considered doing business in most states.

If activities of your business require you to qualify in your home state, then you must make the decision whether it is best to incorporate in your home state, or to incorporate in Nevada and qualify to do business in your state. It is an important decision and you should consider it carefully.

When are you required to qualify or register as an out-of-state or foreign corporation in your home state or any other state? Before we attempt to answer this question, let's be sure you clearly understand the meaning of the terms and definitions as used here.

Foreign Corporation: The word or term "foreign" as used in the various state corporation codes can be misleading and confusing until we realize and isolate the fact that the word "foreign" is always used by a single specific state. Corporations formed or incorporated in foreign countries or nations are referred to as "offshore" corporations.

Any corporation formed in a given state is a domestic corporation to that specific state. Any corporation incorporated in any other state jurisdiction is a "foreign" corporation insofar as any other state is concerned.

For example: *If you form a corporation in Nevada, your corporation is a domestic corporation in the eyes of the state of Nevada. In the eyes of any other state, your corporation is a foreign corporation.*

A corporation is authorized (licensed) or allowed to do business only in the state in which it is incorporated unless and until it is qualified (or exempt from qualifying) to do business in another state.

To qualify a foreign corporation in a state is often referred to as registering or licensing the corporation to do business in that state. The terms mean the same thing and are usually referred to as "to qualify" or "to register."

To qualify or to register in a particular state usually requires that the state be paid a one-time qualification or registration fee. When the fee is paid, the foreign corporation is then recorded in that state and is qualified or registered to do business in that state.

A requirement in practically every state is that before the corporation can be registered or qualified, it must have a resident or statutory agent appointed (which is for service of process only).

That resident or statutory agent has to be duly appointed and accept that appointment on the papers filed in the particular state for qualification.

The other requirement for qualification or registration in any state (in addition to paying the required fees and having a resident agent) is that the name of the corporation desiring to be registered may not already be in use in that state by some other corporation. If the name is already taken or in use in that state, then the corporation cannot qualify with the real name assigned to it by a "foreign" state. However, the corporation in question is still allowed to qualify by registering a DBA (doing business as), a name NOT already taken or in use in that particular state.

Now that we clearly understand the meaning of foreign and qualifying, we have a basis or foundation on which to build an understanding of what is meant by the term, "doing business." Most of the time this is the term that causes the greatest confusion. This is because it is usually legally defined differently in each state. "Doing business" legally means one thing in one state and at times something different in another state. It is important that you understand what the legal definition is of "doing business" in the state(s) you are concerned with.

If your activities legally constitute doing business in a state, your corporation has to qualify in that state. If the definition does not legally define your corporation's activities as doing business in that state, then you do not have to qualify your foreign corporation to do business in that state.

When Can A State Assert Taxing Authority Over A Foreign Corporation?

Public Law 86272 really governs when a state can and when a state cannot assert taxing authority over a foreign corporation. The United States Constitution grants the exclusive authority to regulate interstate commerce transactions between states to the U. S. Congress.

Public Law 86272 says that a tax state may not exert taxing authority over a foreign corporation unless the foreign corporation has a sufficient nexus with that state in order for it to do so.

To have a nexus means there has to be a sufficient connection between the tax state and the foreign corporation in order for the tax state to assert taxing authority over the foreign corporation. Based upon these rulings, states made laws within the frameworks of the rulings.

One good case that sums up the generalities pretty well is the Wrigley case. Essentially, the Supreme Court said here, that a foreign corporation can conduct any activity that is purely sales related, or entirely ancillary, to the sales of its products within the state, and the state cannot assert taxing authority over it.

But the Supreme Court really cleared up some examples of what the company can't do. The company can't maintain an office in the state or maintain a presence. That would make it a resident. The state would therefore have a sufficient connection with the company in order to assert taxing authority over it. Secondly, the company cannot actually provide services in the tax state, and it makes sense when you think about it, because what we're really trying to determine is, "Okay, where did the corporation earn the money? Did it earn it in the tax state, or did is earn it in the tax free state?"

If I have a company that's located in Nevada, and it performs a service in Nevada, and you're in your home state and you send a check to Nevada for that service, the service is provided in Nevada, or a product is manufactured in Nevada and shipped to you in your home state, that's obviously, purely an interstate transaction. It wasn't completed in one state. It was completed across state lines.

A Nevada corporation could sell you a washing machine in California, ship the washing machine into California, and that's fine. The Nevada corporation has not engaged in an intrastate transaction in California. You send them a check — they send you a washing machine. Now, if the Nevada corporation sends a guy out to hook up your washing machine,

fix your washing machine, and move your washing machine, so all activity was completed in California. It was an "intrastate" or in-state transaction inside the state of California, and is therefore taxable in California.

The main thing is whatever the corporation is doing to earn the money, it cannot be done in the tax state. It should be done in a preferred state like Nevada, and the Nevada corporation cannot have an office within the tax state. Its office, or its base of operations where it earns the money needs to be in the tax free state of Nevada.

Now the specific rules that were developed are all adopted to comply with Federal law and Supreme Court rulings. In two pages, you will see a Newsgram. It says, "Is a Nevada Corp good in California?" And it defines what California says is a sufficient nexus with California for it to assert taxing authority over a Nevada corporation.

Summary

It's very important to review the advantages and disadvantages of forming a corporation in a preferred state and the steps you would need to take to qualify to do business in your home state. If you qualify a "foreign" corporation to do business in your home state, you will most likely incur additional fees. But the end usually justifies the means if you are putting together a strategy that will

not only protect your assets but possible
generate tax savings.

Newsgram
IS A NEVADA CORP.
GOOD IN CALIFORNIA?

The answer is unequivocally, YES! (Study our Newsgram sheet entitled, "HOW CAN I DO THAT?") However, you may or may not be required to qualify your NEVADA corporation to do business in California.

Following is a quote from the "Handbook of Corporation (California) Law", by Stewart J. Faber, California attorney and member of the California bar. Also, be advised that a Nevada corporation or any other corporation other than a California corporation in this instance is legally referred to as a "foreign corporation".

"THE RIGHT OF A FOREIGN CORPORATION TO TRANSACT BUSINESS IN CALIFORNIA."

A foreign corporation may not transact business in California unless it first obtains a certificate of qualification. To obtain such a certificate, it shall file a statement signed by the corporate officers stating:
1. Its name and the state of, or place of its incorporation or oganization.
2. The address of its principal executive office.
3. The address of its principal office within the state.
4. The name of an agent upon whom process directed to the corporation may be served within the state.
5. The irrevocable consent to service of process directed to it upon the agent designated, and to service of process directed to it upon the agent designated, and to service of process on the Secretary of State of the agent so designated or the agent's successor is no longer authorized to act or cannot be found at the address given. Corp. C 2105(a).

The statement shall have next to it a certificate by a public official of the state of incorporation to the effect that the corporation is an existing corporation and is in good standing in that state. Corp. C 2105(b). Before it may be designated as an agent for service of process, any corporate agent must comply with Corp. C 1505. See Chapter 15.

The statement reflecting the certificate shall be filed on a form prescribed by the Secretary of State.

DEFINITION OF TRANSACTING BUSINESS IN CALIFORNIA

The activities constituting the transaction of intrastate business are set forth in Corp. C. 191.

1) Corp. C. 191(b) provides that a foreign corporation shall not be considered to be transacting business in California merely because its subsidiary transacts intrastate business.

Transacting business in California means entering into repeated and successive transaction of its business in this state other than interstate or foreign commerce.

2) Without excluding other activities which may constitute transacting business, a foreign corporation shall not be considered to be transacting business solely by reason of carrying in any one or more of the following activities:

E X E M P T I O N S

1. Maintaining or defending any action or suit or administrative action.
2. Holding meetings of its board or shareholders or carrying out other activities concerning its internal affairs.
3. Maintaining bank accounts.
4. Maintaining offices or agencies for the transfer, exchange or registration of its securities.
5. Effecting sales through independent contractors.
6. Soliciting or procuring orders either by mail or through employees or agents or otherwise where such orders require acceptance without this state before becoming binding contracts.
7. **Creating evidences of debt or mortgages on real or personal property.**
8. Conducting an isolated transaction completed within a period of 180 days and not in the course of a number of repeated transactions of like nature.

EXCLUSION OF LENDING INSTITUTIONS.

A foreign corporation engaging in the business of making or investing in loans should not be considered to be transacting intrastate business if in the course of the business, the corporation participates in such activities as making loan commitments, making inspections or appraisals on property, enforcing loans, modifying, renewing, transferring or selling loans, acquiring property, making contracts to collect payments on loans or engaging in any activity necessary to carry out its loan activities.

It would appear that the loan institution may engage in virtually every loan connected activity as long as it does not maintain an office in the state. Corp. C. 191(d). (End of quote.)

PREFERRED BUSINESS STATES COMPARISON CHART

Attributes	Nevada	Wyoming	Delaware
State Corporate Tax	No	No	Yes
State Personal Income Tax	No	No	Yes
Annual Filing List of Officers	Yes	No	Yes
Franchise Tax	No	Yes*	Yes
Minimum Capital Required to Incorporate	No	No	No
Minimum Number-Board of Directors	1	0...if less than 50 Shareholders	No
Annual Filing of Assets	No	Yes	No
Officers and Directors Protected from Judgment Against Corporation	Yes	Yes	Yes
State Shares Tax Information with IRS	No	Yes	Yes
Shareholders Names Filed with State	No	No	No
Requirement to report number of shares issued and outstanding	No	No	Yes
Requirement to report places of business outside state of incorporation	No	No	Yes
Requirement to report dates and times of annual Stockholders and Directors meeting	No	No	Yes

*Minimal tax based on assets located within the state of Wyoming.

NOTES

 Tackling The Myths About Incorporating

- *Not unless you're making $50,000 or more*

- *Double Taxation*

- *Retained Earnings*

Myth: *"Don't incorporate until you've reached a certain point in your business, like making $50,000 per year."*

Advice such as that totally ignores the possibility that anybody going into business is placing their personal assets at risk. It only takes taxes into consideration and taxes pale in comparison to the possibility of losing everything.

One should consider both taxes and liability when thinking of incorporating. The sad part about all of this is such advice isn't even good tax advice. It's true that you have to earn some revenue before you can reap all of the tax benefits of incorporating, but it's only fair to mention that there are tax benefits from losing money with the corporation too. When you look at the tax benefits available to you through incorporating, even if you never make a profit, you will see that advice such as

the above is actually a disservice to the one receiving it.

When someone says don't incorporate now, they are generally coming from one of the following positions:

1. If you incorporate and lose money, you lose your personal tax loss deduction on your personal return so the corporation would have the tax loss, not you.

2. You shouldn't spend the money on incorporating until you are sure you are going to succeed. If you don't succeed, you won't benefit from lower corporate tax brackets, pension and medical reimbursement plans, and passive loss deductions available to corporations.

Consider, however, these points: In the first situation, if you are worried about taking personal tax deductions for your business losses, consider that the law allows you to create what is commonly called an S-corporation. The S-corporation will pass through the losses to you and you can take advantage of personal tax losses.

Further, even if you don't elect "S" status for your corporation and your business becomes worthless, Section 1244 of the Internal Revenue Code allows you to write off those losses on your personal tax return. (We will discuss this in the next chapter.) That's up to $50,000 if you're single and up to $100,000 if you're married and filing a joint return. You simply do not lose personal tax loss benefits if you do things correctly.

Now let's consider the second position, which is that you don't benefit from corporate perks and lower tax rates up to certain income levels if you're not making money. That may be true but you can benefit from the losses now and the lower rates later. Not only can you get the personal benefits from losses like we've talked about above, but a regular corporation, as contrasted to an S-corporation, can carry forward its losses for 15 years. That's right, if a corporation loses money this year and goes into the hole, for $20,000, then it has a $20,000 loss going into next year. If it makes $20,000 next year it pays no tax.

Avoiding Double Taxation

Many will say, sure corporations pay less tax up to $110,656 in net taxable income but the income that corporations receive is double-taxed, so this benefit is really no benefit at all. Well, that is true provided you do everything wrong. If you form a corporation, earn income in

it, take advantage of only a handful of deductions available to it, take advantage of no fringe benefits, and declare all income that the corporation receives as a dividend to the shareholders, then it is probably true.

Let's take a look at what happens when you do a few things right.

First, people who say the income a corporation receives is double-taxed assumes that the shareholders are going to take the income out in the form of dividends. A corporation pays taxes separately from its shareholders, assuming it's not an S-corporation. An S-corporation generally doesn't pay taxes, its shareholders do, so there is no double tax problem in an S-corporation. When a regular corporation earns money, it pays taxes on its net income. When it pays a dividend to its shareholders, it cannot deduct that dividend. However, when a shareholder receives a dividend he must pay taxes on it. That means that the same income was taxed once at the corporate level and then taxed again at the individual level.

There's no law that says that a corporation must distribute its profits out to its shareholders in the form of dividends, but with the new Tax Reconciliation Act of 2003, dividends are only taxed at a maximum of 15%. The corporation is not required to declare a dividend, the corporation can simply retain the earnings in the corporation. That way the money is only taxed once. Plus, since a corporation pays less tax on its income up to $110,656 net, the income is not only taxed once, it is taxed once and pays less than you would if you earned the money in the first place.

Furthermore, the corporation offers more deductions than a sole proprietorship. So, a corporation can earn more than an individual and still pay less tax.

Retained Earnings

Maybe you've heard your accountant say that there is a limitation on how much money a corporation can retain without declaring a dividend. Well, yes and no. The corporation can retain up to $250,000 without ever having to declare a dividend. Many people will tell you that when a corporation reaches $250,000 of retained income that it has to declare a dividend, but that is not true. The corporation can retain far in excess of $250,000, provided it is retaining that income for growth and has a corporate resolution to that effect.

People operate under the assumption that they have to take money out of their corporation. When you have a corporation, you have a corporate checkbook. It is just as easy to write a check on the corporation as it is to write one out of your personal checkbook. Many things that a person wants to write a check for are actually business expenses. The corporation can buy a car, pay medical expenses, provide for

the individual's retirement, buy real estate and the corporation can even buy an airplane.

If you do need to take money out of the corporation, one method is to simply have the corporation loan you the money. You may have loaned the corporation some money when you first started out and then the corporation can pay you interest payments. In the case of the corporation loaning you money, there is no tax. Of course, you would have to pay the corporation interest on any money you borrow and the corporation would have to claim that as taxable income, but the tax effects are usually minimal. With the lower corporate tax rates and higher corporate deductions, you still have quite a tax benefit.

Also, the corporation is probably going to pay you a salary of some sort. That salary is an expense to the corporation and is income to you. It is not double taxed except to the extent that the corporation and you must contribute 7.65% in Social Security taxes, and the corporation's contribution is a deductible payroll tax expense on the corporation's books. The rest is only taxed once, and the tax benefits that the corporation provides make up for the Social Security tax.

Summary

So there you have it. First, there's no law that says the corporation has to declare a dividend to begin with. Second, you probably don't need to take that much money out of the corporation. Third, if you do need to take money out of your corporation, there are much better ways than dividends. As you can see, double taxation is really an overblown problem. In fact, in most closely-held corporations it is no problem at all.

Even if the corporation loses money, there are tax benefits and this translates into benefits for you. Even if you did not take advantage personally under subchapter S of the corporation's losses while it was losing money, you still get to write off the value of the money you put into the business by claiming a stock loss under Section 1244. Thus, you still get personal tax benefits from corporate losses. In addition, while trying to make money with the business, you've been doing it with the personal protection of a corporation and your personal assets have not been put in jeopardy.

NOTES

Chapter 5: Taking Money Out of the Corporation

5 Taking Money Out of the Corporation

Contributed by Bert Seither, Director of Operations at Corporate Tax Network.

I. Not the Same as Personal Taxes

II. How Businesses Are Taxed

III. Pay Yourself & Your Employees

IV. Living the Corporate Lifestyle

V. Business Deductions

VI. Tax Strategies of the Wealthy

VII. Proactive Tax Planning

VIII. Finding a Qualified Accountant

IX. Summary

Taxes can be an intimidating process for many people, especially if you are starting a new business. For the past eight years I've had the pleasure of assisting more than 10,000 small business owners get a handle on their business taxes working for Corporate Tax Network. What I've recognized is that many people are intimidated by the thought of taxes and the subject leaves a sour taste in many people's mouths. Most of the people I've talked to over the years have had a good understanding of how they were going to generate income for the business, but when I asked them how they were going to keep that money, well, let's just say there is normally a moment or two of silence. For most of us in the United States our taxes are our biggest expense every year. Once you understand that taxes play a significant role in how much money you take home, you can do something to attack the issue head on. There are two approaches you can take when it comes to your business taxes. One, you can reactively prepare your taxes, cross your fingers and hope for the best, or two, you can proactively plan by understanding your filing deadlines, the deductions you qualify for and tax strategies you can implement. By understanding and planning out your finances you're likely to keep more of your money. After all, that's why you're in business, right – to make money. Figuring out ways to keep it is equally important and starts with educating yourself.

I. Not the Same as Personal Taxes

A Continuous Activity

In contrast to personal taxes, business

42

taxes must be tracked and paid throughout the year. Specifically, businesses must pay out four types of taxes: income, self-employment or employment, and excise tax. 1

Each year businesses must file annual tax returns, accounting for their tax liability incurred throughout the course of the year. The filing form required depends on the structure of the entity (see III. How Businesses are Taxed.) In addition, each business must pay out federal income taxes. Referred to as a "pay-as-you-go tax," these taxes are incurred as income is earned. Often income taxes are automatically taken out of the employees' paychecks via withholding. As a business owner it is your responsibility to withhold, file and pay taxes throughout the year.

Self-employment taxes are paid out for self-employed business owners. Encompassing social security and Medicare taxes, you must pay out what would be traditionally taken out if you worked for someone else's business.

If the business has a hired workforce then it is required to pay out employment taxes on behalf of the employees. Employment taxes include social security and Medicare taxes, federal income tax withholding, and federal unemployment (FUTA)." 2

Lastly, excise taxes are derived from certain business activities such as manufacturing, equipment operation,

and payment methods.

Paying out the proper amount in taxes is essential to creating a profitable business. Failure to do so will result in fines and punishments by the IRS. Overall, proper categorization of taxes will help you understand where to look for deductions and in turn save money.

Following Federal and State Taxes

Tax collection at the federal level is overseen by the Internal Revenue Service. Anyone who earns income within the United States is subject to tax liability. It is essential to follow taxes at both the federal and state levels. Incurred taxes are transferred to the government and received via paycheck withholding and income tax returns. 3

In addition, each state, county and municipality in the United States has the right to impose additional income taxes at their respective level. Most states exercise this right, whereas few counties or municipalities do so. While the rules vary from state to state, they usually follow the same principles as the federal tax system and often mimic it in format or use it as a starting point in their own calculations. Taxes at the state level include "transaction taxes, such as sales tax; income taxes, the money withheld from your paycheck; and property taxes from homeowners." 4

Proper adherence to both federal and state tax requirements is necessary by law. The tax rate and filing requirements will differ based upon the location of interest, so if in doubt, consult a certified accountant.

II. How Businesses are Taxed

Tax Liability

After setting up your entity it is important to think about taxes right away – even if you're not making money. Setting up and gaining approval for your legal structure is different from establishing your federal tax structure. Businesses are taxed differently based on their entity and in many cases you are given the ability to choose what tax paperwork your business files on. The chosen entity structure drastically affects the amount of money paid out in taxes. With time, the tax structure that is ideal for your business can change. It is extremely important to stay up to date with the various tax structures. This will ensure that your business is set up to maximize your profits.

Sole Proprietorship

As a sole proprietor your profits or losses pass down to your personal tax return. This often results in the highest tax liability, as you must pay self-employment taxes on top of your regular federal or state income tax at an US average of 25 to 28 percent. This can increase your tax liability sometimes higher than 40 percent, reducing your profits to only 60 percent of the original value. Additionally, sole proprietorships have the highest audit rate by the IRS. You must be able to prove your business is a real business that is properly tracking and paying out the amount of taxes the IRS holds you liable for.

To reduce tax liability sole proprietors want to reduce their profit. As counter intuitive as that sounds you must remember you are taxed on the profit not the income. Thus, to reduce your overall tax bill, you will want to take the handful of deductions offered through the sole proprietor entity structure. With time, as you reach higher profits, you may want to consider switching to a more formal structure that will enable you to keep more of your money.

Limited Liability Company, LLC

Without an inherent tax structure, the business owner of an LLC must choose their liability by selecting from one of four sets of paperwork. Choosing the proper tax form is incredibly time sensitive and must be done within 75 days after forming the LLC rather than when it's time to file the annual return. Businesses' taxes are done throughout the year, and without choosing your tax structure at the beginning, you wouldn't know how to pay yourself or what taxes to withold. Additionally, without knowing what tax forms you will be using, your entity wouldn't know what deductions to track for claims. If the LLC does not choose a tax structure, the IRS will choose for you and likely choose the highest tax liability of a sole proprietorship. Again, this subjects your business to your regular state or federal income tax plus the self-employment tax.

C-Corporations & S-Corporations

The C-Corp is the standard setup for a corporation, while the S-Corp provides you with a special tax election. C-Corps and S-Corps are required to follow the same corporate formalities and obligations, such as the adoption of company bylaws, the issuance of stock, and the filing of annual reports. The main difference between the two relates to how you will pay out taxes.

With a C-Corp you always hear the term double taxation which intimidates many new entrepreneurs. Double taxation means that your corporation's profit is taxed at corporate tax rates, which are different than personal income tax rates, and then the shareholders are taxed on the money that the corporation pays out as dividends. [5] Distribution of dividends does not provide the corporation with any tax deduction nor can shareholders deduct the losses incurred by the corporation. However, setting up as a C-Corp does extend the owners limited liability protection with taxes filed separately from the owners' personal taxes. [6]

An S-Corp is a pass-through structure in which the profit or loss is passed through to the shareholders' personal tax return. In order to pay yourself throughout the year the S-Corp must have a payroll system set up. The IRS evaluates the tax liability of the corporation at the individual tax rates for each shareholder. This enables the S-Corp to avoid the double taxation present with a C-Corp.

S-Corps that pay too high of distributions and too low of a salary are increasing the likelihood of an IRS audit.

Nonprofits

Operated for the good of the public interest, creating a nonprofit can be a very rewarding experience. Many nonprofit organizations are eligible for full tax exemption. To receive tax exemption benefits the nonprofit must apply for 501(c)(3) status. Receiving approval will help bring in donors while lowering your tax liability.

The most common types of nonprofit organizations classified under 501(c)(3) status are charitable, educational, and religious organizations. If your organization is classified as tax exempt you are eligible to receive tax-deductible charitable contributions. This is very appealing to businesses who are seeking to lower their tax liability. Individual and corporate donors are more likely to support organizations with 501(c)(3) status, as the larger their donation, the larger their tax write off amount.

To qualify for tax-deductible charitable contributions your nonprofit must be registered and recognized by the IRS. Recognition of exemption under 501(c)(3) assures foundations and other grant-making institutions that they are issuing grants or sponsorships to permitted beneficiaries. It is important to file your tax exemption paperwork with the IRS as soon as possible. Most organizations must file their nonprofit application by the end of the 15th month after they were created. However a 12-month extension is available. In all, you'll want to file before the 27th month mark as filing before the deadline ensures your organization will be recognized as tax exempt starting on the day of creation. If your application is filed after 27 months of incorporating, your tax exemption will only become effective the day the IRS approves your nonprofit. If this occurs your business will have to pay taxes on all the activities you completed between your first steps of incorporation and the long process of waiting to hear back from the IRS.

A private foundation earning less than $5,000 a year is not required to file. However, if they exceeded $5,000 within 90 days of the end of the year, the private foundation will have exceeded the threshold and will be required to file.

By receiving 501(c)(3) status your nonprofit organization can reinvest its profits to help support your cause! Properly categorizing your business and filing for tax exemption status before the deadline is essential to success.

III. Pay Yourself and Your Employees

As an employer, it is your responsibility to oversee the payment of payroll to your employees and to properly take out taxes. You must report and deposit payroll taxes to the appropriate agency in an accurate and timely manner. Late or inaccurate deposits will result in penalties and interest charges, so it's extremely important to pay close attention to the dates. The complex payroll tax requirements may seem intimidating but by learning a few simple concepts, you can utilize payroll software or an accountant to maximize your efficiency.

Payroll Management

First, payroll management is comprised of two major activities – payroll accounting and payroll administration. Payroll accounting consists of: 1) calculating the earnings of employees and the related withholding for taxes and other deductions, 2) recording the results of payroll activities, and 3) preparing required tax returns. This includes adherence to tax requirements at the federal, state and local tax levels. Payroll administration deals with the managerial aspects of maintaining a payroll, many of which are distinct from the accounting aspect of payroll. Payroll administration includes 1) managing employee personnel and payroll information and 2) compliance with federal, state and local employment laws.

When you're building up your business you must first determine the cost of hiring a workforce. To do so, you'll want to weigh the costs of salary with the benefits and payroll taxes for each employee. Depending on your state and local laws, payroll taxes can increase the total cost of hiring an employee by as much as 20%.

Keeping a Payroll Register

You next must set up a payroll register, a spreadsheet that lists the total information from each payroll. Specifically, the total gross pay, totals for each deduction, and total net pay is set out in a payroll register. An employee earnings record is used to keep track of each employee's total gross pay, withholding and deduction amounts, and total net pay. The totals from all of the employee earnings records are the source of the totals for your payroll register. The summation of information in your payroll register will be used to make payroll deposits, submit quarterly payroll tax reports to the IRS, and provide annual wage and tax reports to employees and to the Social Security Administration.

Tracking Payroll

Each business entity has an associated cost structure that business owners must use to pay themselves and their employees. Overall, the IRS does not set a monetary value to reasonable compensation, but if the IRS deems it excessive you will need records to defend it.

Sole Proprietorship

Operating as a sole proprietorship, you will have pass-through taxation. As mentioned, you should expect to pay the most in taxes at the personal income level. You will be required to pay out income tax plus the 13.3% self employment tax.

Limited Liability Company, LLC

As previously mentioned, the LLC does not come with a tax benefit - it's about liability protection, hence the name. The way you elect to pay your taxes will also impact how you are paid. To receive a tax benefit under an LLC you must apply for it by making an entity classification election. You will complete this form within 75 days after forming your entity. If approved, the entity classification election can reduce your self-employment taxes by potentially half which is an extremely significant level of savings.

A good portion of your compensation will be paid out in owner's distribution and you will be able to circumvent the 13.3 percent self employment tax. As the owner of an LLC you are required by law to pay yourself a "fair and reasonable" salary. This salary is a deductible expense for your business.

Operating under the hybrid entity of an LLC will provide tax benefits while offering limited liability for business debts. Overall this will create flexibility for the business owners and help guide them towards long-term profitability.

C-Corporations and S-Corporations

Operating a C-Corp or S-Corp, compensation is divided into two categories - distribution and salary. These types of corporations often have shareholders and thus they must pay out shareholder distributions. These distributions are treated differently than wages because they are deemed to be a return on the investor or employee's investment. Distributions to a shareholder must be included in the shareholder's taxable income.

To review, the profit or loss of S-Corps pass through to your personal tax return where as C-Corps are subject to double taxation – taxed at the corporate tax rate and then wages are taxed at the individual level. Just like the LLC, you are required to pay yourself a "fair and reasonable" salary if you operate an S or C-Corp, as you cannot pay 100 percent of your compensation in distributions and dividends.

Nonprofits

Determining the proper compensation for non-profit employees requires business owners to consider reasonable compensation, due diligence, and arms length. [7] The nonprofit board of directors must conduct due diligence to determine the value of reasonable compensation. To do so, they can reference census data, the salaries paid out by similar charities, and so on. The owners and employees of a nonprofit cannot play a direct role in setting their personal salary – this is referred to as arms length. In total, it is important that nonprofit employees are valued with paychecks matching their workload.

Regardless of the entity type, it is important that companies strive to satisfy their employees. Having a valued workforce will transfer into a more productive environment and help to foster prosperity for the company.

Business Bookkeeping

Bookkeeping is the first step in the accounting process and the most time consuming thing you will do on the back end of your business that unfortunately doesn't make you any money. Your time and best use will be spent on the income-generating activities you probably enjoy doing such as product or service development, marketing, or sales. However, the law says bookkeeping must be done, leaving you to decide how and who will be in charge of it.

Bookkeepers are responsible for organizing and tracking receipts, canceled checks and other records generated by financial transactions. Additionally, bookkeepers chronologically record all transactions — cash disbursements, cash receipts, sales and purchases, and so on — in a journal and post the journal entries to a general ledger of accounts, which accountants use to prepare monthly, quarterly, and annual financial statements.

As a business owner you aim to maximize profit. You may forget expenses when you file your tax return, unless you record them as they occur. By tracking your deductions you can save more of your hard earned income. In addition, bookkeeping accounting will help you meet deadlines and make timely payments on loans, rents, bills, taxes and so forth.

If you were planning on using a simple Excel spreadsheet or ledger on paper to keep track of your books, it is wise to reconsider a more advanced option. There are many technology products out on the market that help simplify business bookkeeping. By synching online banking with an online business management system you can export all of your bank information into the program where deduction categories are automatically listed and updated throughout the year. You only have to set up your business entity once (and then maintain it,) so why not leverage technology to your advantage in regards to your books? This will simplify the process every three months when you must stop your income generating activities to address your quarterlies, referencing the IRS's website to see how deductions have changed since the previous quarter, etc.

While concentrating on your core business, financial record keeping can easily become overwhelming. However, well-kept books provide business owners with an accurate financial picture and enable better decision making, in turn increasing profitability. Forecasting your business needs and planning ahead for purchases and other miscellaneous business needs will become easier with business bookkeeping.

IV. Living the Corporate Lifestyle

As we all know, businesses incur expenses. Some expenses may be quite obvious, such as the cost of setting up your new entity. However, other expenses may not be quite as obvious – such as consistent business lunches or transportation. These small regular expenses generally add up to thousands of dollars over the course of the year and in turn raise your tax liability if they aren't claimed as deductions. In fact, more than 90 percent of the United States population pays out more in taxes each year versus any other expense –

mortgage or rent, food, insurance, and so on. In other words, your taxes are often your single biggest expense each year.

Taxed on Profit, Not Income

When it comes to tax filings, you are taxed in accordance to your profit recorded rather than your income. By owning a business you can use your entity to cover business-related expenses such as meals and entertainment, travel expenses, and so forth, enabling you to deduct as much as possible to offset your regular tax bill. This is the essence of "living the corporate lifestyle."

V. Business Deductions

Choosing Deductions

To be deductible, a business expense must be both ordinary and necessary. An ordinary expense is one that is common and accepted in your trade or business. A necessary expense is one that is helpful and appropriate for your trade or business. When recorded together, debits and credits must equal out in order to reconcile for tax purposes. Important deductions to consider include the home office deduction, meals and entertainment, and the vehicle deduction.

Home Office Deductions

Home office deductions can be utilized when your business is run out of your home. Such deductions must meet some pretty strict tests, though when claimed, allow you to write off a portion of your bills associated with the business which is consuming the homes' resources. You may be able to write off the cost of rent or mortgage interest, utilities including electric and internet, insurance, repairs, and depreciation. [8] Specifically, the home office deduction is calculated by determining what percentage of your home is utilized to run the business. To claim it, you must be able to calculate this percentage.

Furthermore, to be eligible for this deduction you must meet two requirements. First, your home office must be utilized regularly and exclusively for business activities. [9] Secondly, you must be able to prove that you conduct the majority of your business from your home office. You can additionally extend this deduction to include free-standing buildings on your property, such as a studio or garage, where you may meet with business clients or work on projects.

Whether you own or rent your primary residence makes a big difference when claiming this deduction. If you do own your home and claim the home office deduction, you'll have to come back and pay a recapture tax if you later choose to sell your residence. This can be very painful for those who didn't budget for it.

Business Meals and Entertainment

Meals and entertainment can be deducted as long as they are an ordinary and necessary expense, directly related to or associated with a business activity.

To be deductible, you must have the proper records in place outlining the business purpose, bill amount, date and location of the dining experience, and a listing of the people present with the applicable business relationship recorded. 10 It is wise to record these details on the back of your receipts. You must keep track of this information and receipts in order to ensure an accurate tax claim.

Generally speaking, the value of the deduction is 50 percent of the cost of business meals (including food and beverage) plus entertainment expenses. 11 This is especially useful if you have high profit margins, such as in the business consulting industry. With high profit margins comes high taxable income, so keep track of your expenses so you won't be left kicking yourself at the end of the year wishing you had more deductions. Make sure your numbers match up to avoid an investigation.

Vehicle

If you use your vehicle for exclusive business use you may be eligible to deduct its entire operational cost.

Otherwise, if you use your vehicle for a mix of business and personal, you can

still claim the deduction but only for the value of business purposes.

To determine the value of your deduction you must choose from one of two approaches – the mileage rate or authentic expenses. Once you select a method you must obtain IRS approval to switch, thus it's wise to calculate the deduction underneath both options and then choose the deduction that produces higher savings.

The mileage rate system is a cost per mile driven deduction. You must set this system up the first year you begin using a car for your business. Additionally, your business must possess less than 5 cars in order to qualify.

To use the actual expenses system you must determine the operational costs of using the car(s). Here you can include the costs of gas, oil changes, tolls, repairs, maintenance, and insurance.

Overall, the more deductions you claim the lower your tax liability. Once you understand tax compliance requirements – such as your filing date, deadlines, form recipients and addresses, and so forth- you can get into your deductions or what you can and cannot write off.

If you have already set up your business it is likely that you have gone through a list of deductions with your accountant. As you may already know, choosing deductions is contingent upon the company's unique financial situation. You'll want to look through all the deductions and pick and choose your deductions wisely. Claiming one deduction someplace may disallow a deduction offered elsewhere that could have saved you more money. So overall, be careful when choosing your deductions and, if in doubt, consult a professional.

VI. Tax Strategies of the Wealthy

Wealthy individuals recognize that the more strategies incorporated into a financial plan, the lower the tax liability. To qualify for many of these strategies all you must do is own a business. You can utilize tax strategies of the wealthy to find a way to shelter your money from the IRS.

Self-Insured Medical Reimbursement Plans

As a W2 wage earner you're unable to write off your medical costs, unless your medical costs exceed 7.5 percent of your annual gross income. This leaves most people unable to qualify to write off their medical costs each year. But if you have a corporation, you can utilize self-insured medical reimbursement plans. This is not a plan that you're paying an actual monthly premium on, but rather verbiage in the by-laws of a corporation that states any of the out-of-pocket medical costs that the owners, employees, or dependents incur

may be reimbursed to you through the business (and termed reimbursements deductions.) Effectively, it's a way to circumvent the 7.5 percent annual gross income rule.

Multiple Entity Structures

Multiple entity structuring strategies are used when you have multiple entities structured together for asset protection or tax benefits. For example, assume you are a business owner operating an air ambulance, transferring sick individuals from hospital to hospital by jet. You are running a one-man operation, owning the corporation and simultaneously flying the jet. On paperwork however, neither you nor your corporation own the jet but instead lease it from an LLC. Coincidentally, you own that LLC and in effect, are protecting your investment of the jet, as your corporation is the only customer conducting business with that LLC. The value of this arrangement is that if someone sues your corporation, your jet is still protected.

It's also very common to utilize multiple entity structuring in real estate. For example, C-Corps are often used to run property management companies. They will own associated LLCs and the LLCs own the properties. Their rental properties may include residential properties, such as houses, apartments and multi-family units, as well as commercial property, which can be office buildings, retail stores, hospitality facilities, and so forth. In a properly structured and managed company, owners will have limited liability for business debts and obligations. If something goes wrong with one of their properties, the rest will be kept safe. Additionally, the C-Corp cannot be held personally liable for business debts and lawsuits against the business.

Overall, multiple entity structures are incredibly attractive for the asset protection and tax benefits they provide.

Retirement Plans

If you plan to retire one day it is a good idea to come up with alternative methods of saving rather than relying on our faltering social security system. Each year you are taxed on all of the money that you make. To save some of this money, you can establish a pre-taxed retirement plan, delaying taxes on this income. The year that you make withdrawals from your retirement funds you should come up with a strategy to offset the taxes you must pay on them.

VII. Proactive Tax Planning

Staying Up-to-Date with Changing Tax Laws

There are more than 300 legal business deductions with additional deductions introduced or altered each time a new tax law is established. Business credits and deductions are constantly changing, so staying up to date with the system is imperative to save money!

The Benefit of Proactive Tax Planning

A tax credit is a dollar for dollar situation that returns to your pocket the equivalency of the value you are eligible to claim. However, tax credits are not always directly listed on your tax refund. You must know about the credit, fill out the appropriate paperwork, and reflect that credit on your personal or business return and submit it when due. If you do not use a tax credit, you lose it, so it's important to stay up to date with the changing tax laws. The only way you can go back and reclaim a credit or deduction for that matter, would be to amend a return. An amendment is a refilling and when you amend a return, you are increasing the likelihood of being audited by the IRS.

VIII. Finding a Qualified Accountant

The Benefits of Outsourcing

To put it quite simply, if you're not an expert, outsource it! You can outsource your taxes, accounting, bookkeeping, payroll, and so on. Outsourcing will free up your time as a business owner, enabling you to focus on the core functional activities of your business. If you're spending an hour a day documenting your business activity that comes out to roughly six weeks a year spent completing your bookkeeping. Wouldn't you rather spend that time generating another 10 percent worth of revenue?

Outsourcing results in cost savings by freeing up office space and computers and eliminating the need to purchase or upgrade software. Additionally, it ensures proper financial statements. Having access to accounting expertise not available in-house can provide you with peace of mind in knowing your paperwork is done correctly. Certified accountants can help you understand your financial statements and learn how to use them to run your business more effectively.

Questions You Should Ask Potential Accountants
Before selecting an accountant you should ask questions to ensure a proper fit for your unique situation. Questions you may want to ask include:

1.   Are you experienced within my specific industry?
2.   How are your fees structured? Is there an additional fee for filing?
3.   How often do you review a client's tax liability?
4.   How many clients do you have like me?
5.   What are your hours? How accessible are you?
6.   What tax preparation software do you utilize?
7.   What services are offered by your firm?

To find an accountant you can trust, it is wise to consult friends, family, and most importantly, other business owners. [12] Make sure that you go through the list of questions before choosing an accountant. Aim to find an accountant who will suit your unique situation, with expertise in taxes and experience in your industry.

IX. Summary

Overall, owning your own business is an extremely rewarding venture. Proper tax planning is essential – by reducing your tax liability you can keep more of your hard-earned income. Be prepared to commit more time to devote to your business taxes than you would normally for personal taxes. But complete your taxes right and ahead of time, and this will transfer into savings.

Constantly refer back to your entity structure and research the latest tax changes, looking for opportunities that could translate into savings. Remember, it may be wise to switch your entity structure in time, taking advantage of tax and payroll options.

Aim to live the corporate lifestyle, claiming deductions and properly tracking them. Search for a qualified accountant that matches your unique business environment. Work alongside this accountant, making sure you are up to date with the most recent tax changes. By employing a proactive tax planning strategy you can maximize your returns and enjoy the benefits of a fruitful business entity.

1 *Business Taxes. IRS. (accessed on Nov. 4, 2012). http://www.irs.gov/Businesses/Small-Businesses-&-Self-Employed/Business-Taxes*

2 *Business Taxes, id.*

3 *File Your Taxes. USA.gov. (Oct. 17, 2012) http://www.usa.gov/Citizen/Topics/Money/Taxes.shtml*

4 *File Your Taxes, id.*

5 *Corporations. IRS. (accessed on Nov. 4, 2012). http://www.irs.gov/Businesses/Small-Businesses-&-Self-Employed/Corporations*

6 *Pros and Cons of a C-Corporation, All Business. (accessed on Nov. 5, 2012). http://www.allbusiness.com/business-planning/business-structures-corporations/2515-1.html#axzz2BS3qPKeG*

7 *Nonprofit Executive Compensation, Foundation Group, (accessed on Nov. 5, 2012) http://www.501c3.org/blog/nonprofit-executive-compensation/*

8 *Home Office Deduction. IRS. (accessed on Nov. 5, 2012). http://www.irs.gov/Businesses/Small-Businesses-&-Self-Employed/Home-Office-Deduction*

9 *Home Office Deduction, id.*

10 *Business Entertainment Expenses, IRS. (accessed on Nov. 6, 2012). http://www.irs.gov/taxtopics/tc512.html*

11 *Business Entertainment Expenses, id.*

12 *How to Find an Accountant Who Can Help Your Small Business over the Long Haul. Small Business Association. (accessed on Nov. 8, 2012). http://www.sba.gov/community/blogs/how-find-accountant-who-can-help-your-small-business*

-over-long-haul

NOTES

Bringing Your Company to Life

- *Laying The Foundation For Your Corporation*

Bringing Your Company to Life

While corporations and LLC's have differences in the benefits they offer, they also have similarities in the way they are structured. Both forms of business entities must file documentation with the Secretary of State and pay a fee in the state in which they are forming the business.

Both business structures must decide how they are going to be managed and how profits are going to be distributed to the shareholders or members.

Make sure you have taken the time to read and understand the documents that make up your company. They will provide the guidance you need to operate your company with minimal problems.

Corporations

Corporations are not as difficult to establish as some people might think.

Forming a corporation is as simple as filing Articles of Incorporation with the Secretary of State and paying a fee. Corporations do require a little more work in the structuring and maintaining of the company than an LLC.

But the benefits offered by a corporation far out weigh the additional documentation you must keep. The biggest benefit to forming a corporation is asset protection. But many people, especially people who have been operating a sole proprietorship or a partnership, seem to forget that the corporation is a separate legal entity, separate and apart from them and must be treated as such. The primary principle in corporate operations is the separation of the corporate identity from the individual shareholders. Always remember that...........

The corporation is not you, and you are not the corporation.

A corporation, as a separate, artificial person, must maintain its own separate identity, entirely distinct from that of its principals. This established through corporate formalities. Corporate formalities, which will be covered in depth later on, are the way that a corporation's activities are documented, to show separation between the corporation and the individual.

The corporation's identity is established by its Articles and Bylaws. Each of these documents has its own purpose and function, and should be read and understood by the principals of the corporation to ensure that they do not inadvertently violate, not only the corporation's rules, but its distinct identity.

Strategy Briefing

In organizing your new corporation, care must be given to ensuring that you carefully consider how the corporation will be used. If your corporation is to be a primary business operation, you will do things one way, if the corporation is a second corporation, designed for privacy, and asset protection, an entirely different set of operational rules will usually apply. Care has been given throughout this work to explain possible different courses of action, depending on what you are trying to accomplish.

The Basis of Corporate Operation

The basis of corporate operation is really a matter that results from the reasons people incorporate in the first place. The main (textbook) reason for incorporating

a business is to establish a corporate veil of protection between your business operations and yourself.

You probably remember sitting in a classroom at some point in your education. The instructor may have said that in a corporation, business people are limiting their risk to the money they actually invest in a corporation, whereas a sole proprietor can lose everything they have in the world, if things go wrong. If you purchase stock in a corporation that you are going to use to operate your business, let's say for $10,000, then, in the worst case, you could lose the $10,000. No one could force you to pay any more money out of your pocket to cover the company's debts. Clearly, this is an important factor in the corporate form of doing business. The difficult question is, "Is this really all I could lose?"

Since this is really a legal question, I'll give a "lawyerly" answer: "It all depends..."

"On what?," you ask. It all depends on how well you do at keeping the corporation and your own activities separate. The whole legal premise of a corporation is that you and the corporation are separate. You are not the corporation, and the corporation is not you. Unfortunately, however, this is not the way that most of us operate. In most cases, an outsider looking in cannot tell the difference between our corporations and ourselves. Think about it. What do you call your business? You call it "your" business.

If someone from the outside was looking at the corporation's records to establish what the corporation did and thought, as opposed to what you did and thought, how could they tell? These are the sorts of questions that put into danger the distinction between the corporation and you, the questions that can put the corporate veil upon which you are depending to protect you from liability at serious risk.

In a courtroom situation if an adverse party can establish that you and the corporation are the same, or that your corporation is your alter ego (your other self), then they can ask the court to pierce the corporate veil. This means to disregard the corporation, and put your personal assets on the table, to satisfy the debts and liabilities of the company, just as though you were doing business as a sole proprietor.

To avoid this, you must ensure that you maintain an appropriate level of separation between your affairs and assets, and those of the corporation. One of the ways that this is accomplished is by maintaining proper corporate records, which will document the fact that the corporation's activities are separate from your own. Let's face facts, nobody is going to question the corporate identity of General Motors, asserting that it is the alter ego of an individual. But anybody in litigation or collections against Joe

Blow, Inc. is going to try.

The purpose of carefully setting up your corporation is to get off to the right start. From there, you must continue to work at maintaining a separate existence between yourself and the company.

Articles of Incorporation

The articles of incorporation is the document which brings the corporation to life, literally. By filing the articles with the appropriate authority in your state, the corporation comes into existence. Generally, the articles set forth the structure of the corporation include its name, period of life, and list of players. They also set forth the type, or types, of stock, its limitations, if any, and the total number of shares which are allowed to be issued. They even cite the actual purpose for which the corporation is being formed, either in a very general way, or in a very limited way. Because of the fundamental importance of the articles and their function, you would be well advised to peruse your articles carefully. While you are looking them over, there are several issues you should be considering, which are listed and discussed briefly below.

Name

Your articles should clearly state the exact name of your corporation. This is its legal name, just as your legal name is recorded on your birth certificate. If you are going to expect other people to recognize that they are transacting business with your corporation, and not with you personally, then they will need to know the corporation's legal name. While this may sound too basic, or even silly, please understand that my research files are loaded with court cases where business people lost everything because they failed in this one, obvious area. It is vitally important to your future!

Period of Existence

Most of the time, corporate articles will indicate that the period of existence of the corporation in question will be perpetual. As this would imply, that means that the corporation is immortal, and will never die on its own, or at least not of natural causes. This is one of the major factors in the doctrine of separateness alluded to above. Perpetual existence is not the only possibility, however. The corporate life span may also be limited to a certain number of years. This is often referred to as a collapsible corporation. It will die, or collapse, on a pre-specified date in the future; often thirty years.

Imagine how thrilled you would be, after buying an existing corporation from someone, anticipating that its lifetime is perpetual, only to discover that it ceased to exist already. Looking over the articles could have eliminated this disaster. It is important to note that a collapsible corporation can be amended, under most circumstances, before the

termination date arrives.

Purpose

Another important matter covered in the articles is the purpose for which the corporation is being formed. Most of the time, the purpose will be to conduct any lawful business activity. This allows the greatest flexibility, and is sometimes referred to as the elastic clause. It is elastic because you are permitted to do anything you want to with the corporation, as long as it's legal. While this may be the most common feature, it is not the only way that purpose can be handled.

In some cases, an incorporate may wish to limit the potential activities of the corporation, and may so indicate in the articles. In other cases, a franchise or other business relationship with another entity may result in a limitation of activity to that approved by the franchiser, or other party. In any event, you need to be sure that your corporate operation does not violate any limitation contained in your articles, as this could result in a loss of your protection by the corporate veil.

More and more, as America careens into the litigation explosion, attorneys and others will add more descriptive material, along with the time honored language of the elastic clause, spelling out all of the possible activities they can imagine, to augment the declaration that the corporation is being formed to engage in any lawful activity. This is designed to circumvent those who would attempt to claim that any lawful activity doesn't necessarily include such and such. While it may seem silly, this long form of describing the business purpose of the corporation seems to be the wave of the future and is, after all, a reflection of our times.

Authorized Shares

Another important characteristic of the articles of incorporation is a listing of the number and types of authorized shares. The number of shares authorized means the number of shares of a particular class of stock which may be issued by the corporation. Any shares which are issued in excess of this number are in violation of law and are, at best, invalid, and at worst are fraudulent. This number offers protection to the potential shareholder, who is trying to determine what his or her percentage of ownership will be. The number of authorized shares in many states is also the basis of calculating fees and taxes. A few states, such as Wyoming, have no provision at all for authorized stock and will allow a corporation to authorize any amount of stock, or an unlimited number of authorized shares. This provision can be quite convenient for its flexibility, but can be a little scary for investors.

Once a certain number of shares is authorized, a corporation need not worry about having to issue all of the shares at once. They can issue as few as

they desire, as long as they don't exceed the authorized limit.

Classes of stock

Usually, a corporation will have common stock. This is what most of us are thinking about when we talk about stock; voting shares, usually at no par, purchased for capital contributions of cash, property or services. There can be many other types and classes of stock as well. These types of stock, and their restrictions, are typically stated in the articles of incorporation, allowing a public record access to the entire picture, for the protection of potential investors, as well as for the edification of the corporate directors and officers. More discussion of stock types and features will be provided in the chapter on stock.

Other typical provisions

The particulars contained in articles will vary, depending on many circumstances, such as the state of incorporation, who is drafting the articles, and the needs and circumstances of the parties. This volume is not intended to be a definitive legal reference, but rather to provide general guidelines. For a definitive reference on all of the possibilities, and their various ramifications, you should consult your attorney who can also make specific recommendations to suit your particular situation.

In addition to the issues covered above,

typical articles will contain the names and addresses of the Incorporate, the first Director and the Resident Agent. There may also be provisions pertaining to liability by state law and, in many cases, other issues regarding the relationship between the principals of the corporation. Some states, such as California, seldom have articles of more than one page of length as a way of controlling the volume of material contained in the public record. Corporations in these states will usually cover more of these issues in the Bylaws.

Bylaws

While the articles of incorporation are the actual document which brings the corporation into existence, and contains the basic structure of the corporation, the bylaws are much more specific, and contain more information on how the specific players and entities within the corporation will function and interrelate. For example, the articles will ordain a Board of Directors for the corporation. The bylaws will establish how their meetings will operate, how they will be notified of meetings, and what their specific function in the corporation will be.

In the same way, the bylaws will specifically state what the duties and functions of each officer will be. It is extremely important for anyone who is operating a business within the corporate framework to understand what these requirements and rules are,

as they must be followed. Failure to do so can cause severe problems to the corporation and its owners in the event of a lawsuit, or other peril, because an adversary will usually examine the corporation's records to determine if you have treated the corporation as a separate entity. If you have not, then the adversary will attempt to have the court set the corporation aside so the adverse party can attack your personal assets, otherwise known as piercing the corporate veil.

Some of the issues that are usually covered by the bylaws are procedures for meetings, proxies, stock certificates, what constitutes a quorum in meetings, provisions to allow for written consents (such as free standing resolutions), the number of directors, the terms of officers, and so on.

The Players in a Corporation

If you are like most people who are starting a small, closely-held corporation, where you are responsible for holding many positions, you will sometimes have to stop yourself and ask, "Which hat am I wearing in the corporation right now?" Don't feel bad, this is a common question. If you are stopping to wonder, then you are ahead of the game! The reason for the common confusion is that most people are not used to playing different roles in their businesses. If you have been either a sole proprietor or a partner, you are used to the idea that the

CORPORATE ORGANIZATIONAL STRUCTURE

THE PLAYERS — THE CHAIN OF COMMAND!

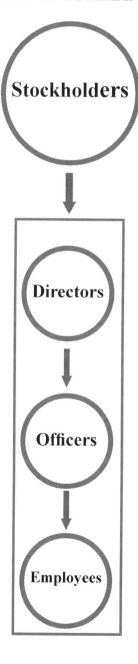

owner of the business is the boss, the one who rules the roost and calls the shots. You may be used to putting "owner" on your business card, or using that title when signing contracts. If this is the case, be careful with your corporation!

A corporation, on the other hand, has several different roles that must be acted out at specific times. There are four players within the corporation. They are the shareholders, the directors, the officers, and the employees. To fully understand the concept of corporate structure, you need to have a good feel for what these players do and what they don't do.

The person who controls the majority of the voting stock has control of the corporation, but this control is indirect. In the corporate form of doing business, shareholders are not the people who sign contracts and usually are not the ones who make day to day decisions. A look at the history of corporations will reveal why this is.

Corporations were originally invented as a way to pool capital, and provide centralized management. This idea assumes that there will be numerous investors, and several different persons in the management and decision making capacities within the company.

Today, this is usually the case with large organizations. Publicly traded firms, such as General Motors, are examples of this concept, but this is usually not the case with small and medium sized companies. In fact, there is often one person who controls the stock and provides all of the decision making and management functions within a small or medium sized corporation. Such small corporations constitute the backbone of our modern economy, providing the greatest amount of growth, jobs, and new products for the American economy. They also provide the area of greatest danger for business people who are not entirely clear on the roles that they are playing.

Shareholders exercise their control by electing directors, who are the thinking branch of the corporate structure. Here is where the decisions and policies are actually made. The directors are the ones who oversee the direction that a corporation will take as well as determine what is and what is not to be a corporate act.

To put these directives and decisions into action, the directors elect officers. The officers are the ones who actually sign contracts, negotiate with the world outside of the corporation, and hire employees to do the day to day work of the business. If you are in a small corporation where you will perform many or all of these functions, then it is of vital importance that you recognize which function you are performing at any given time and follow recognized procedures for getting the job done.

As you can see, simply using the title of "owner" isn't going to cut it with a corporation and, in fact, is going to invite an adversary to treat you as if you were a sole proprietor. And, since you would be acting like a sole proprietor, you would also be begging to have your corporate veil pierced; the last thing you really want.

As we proceed with the operation of the corporation, you will become more familiar with the differences between the players, and much will be explained as we go.

How Directors Are Appointed

When your corporation is filed with the state, you will, in most cases, have to list an Incorporator and first Director in your Articles. If this is the case in your state, you already have a Director. If you wish to add Directors or change Directors, the procedure is simple. The first Director, because he or she is serving in the absence of shareholders, can simply appoint Directors to assist in the organization of the corporation, until the first meeting of the shareholders, which will typically take place much later. In addition, if you wish to replace the first Director with someone else, you can do so by having the first Director appoint someone else as an additional Director, and then resign. Be sure that this resignation is done in writing. If you are concerned about the first Director making a claim to the position later, then have the resignation notarized, which will make it quite difficult for the person to assert that he or she did not, in fact actually resign the post.

After the shareholders hold their first meeting, they will be electing Directors to serve for specified periods of time (terms are stated in the Bylaws).

Corporate Officers

Another important player in the corporation game, is the corporate officer. Officers are in charge of the day to day affairs of the corporation. In so doing, they will make decisions, and take action on behalf of the corporation, and for most people, this is the role you will play most often. It is important to note, however, that corporate officers only make decisions that fall within the scope allowed by the Board of Directors. In some cases, when the corporation is closely held and there are only a few people involved the officer's duties can be very broad. Officers sign contracts, sign notes, hire and fire employees, and represent the corporation in meetings, proceedings, and with customers. These are not the normal activities of directors or shareholders. Again, their actions in these circumstances are limited by their Directors' authorization for their actions. If you are looking for a place to give someone a title, this is a better place than on the Board of Directors.

A typical small corporation will have three officers, and most states require that a corporation have these three officers: they are President, Secretary, and Treasurer. Other offices may be added, such as Vice President, Operations Officer, C.E.O. etc., but generally these three are required. The particular responsibilities will differ from corporation to corporation, but in any case, they are spelled out in the corporation's Bylaws.

Generally, the President (and in some cases C.E.O.) is the officer in charge, who is specifically responsible to the Board of Directors, and who, subject to Board authorization, will direct the activities of the other officers. The Secretary is also vital, because the corporate secretary is the one who is responsible for the corporation's minute book, which is where the Directors' decisions and authorizations are documented. The Treasurer is responsible for the accounting of the corporation's moneys and securities.

Most states will require a listing of these officers' names and addresses, as part of the public record in that state. If you are looking for anonymity, this will be an important consideration.

Electing Officers

The initial group of officers will be elected by the directors in their first meeting, to serve until their term expires, or until the Board shall choose their successors. Generally, they will serve one-year terms, and election for the offices will be held during the annual directors meeting.

Nominee Directors and Officers

When you are concerned with matters of privacy, or when you have established a corporation that you don't wish to be personally associated with for whatever reason, you may wish to consider the possibility of hiring a professional nominee to serve as director and officer in your place. When you hire a professional nominee, you will have a contract with that person which limits their actions to those, which you have authorized, and nothing else. In addition, that other person is the one who appears on the public record.

Shareholders

Holding shares of stock is where the ultimate control of the corporation comes in. This is not because shareholders are necessarily closely involved with the day to day operation of the corporation, but because they hire and fire directors. It is often the practice of small business people to give shares of their corporations to certain people; key employees, family members, and so on. If this is beginning to sound like the scenarios discussed briefly in the director's section; it's no coincidence. Often these same people give shares to the ones they confer a "title" upon, again with less than desirable results. Careful consideration

should be given to how to structure such stock sharing. There are ways to compensate key people with corporate stock, without giving them voting power in your corporation, if you do some advance planning and study.

I must relate here a brief story about a client who came to us after the fact, wanting to try and save his situation, after it was much too late. He had started a construction business a number of years earlier and successfully completed a number of projects before a friend of his came to him with a proposal for a new development. The idea sounded good, so they joined forces for the new project. My client felt that in order to cement their relationship, he would give his friend 40% of the stock in his corporation, making him a "partner". Another reason for doing this was that they agreed to pay the friend a smaller salary than might otherwise be the case. In addition, the friend was named as the new President of the corporation, a move that was supposed to be strictly a "title".

Two years into the project, they were the victims of fraud, which stemmed from a fraudulent financing scheme perpetrated by a mortgage company that was providing construction financing. The scheme will, no doubt, result in several principals in the Mortgage Company going to prison; it was no small matter, no matter how you look at it. As this situation resulted in a major setback for the project, and a terrible cash shortage, subcontractors and vendors were not paid on time. While my client was attempting to get things straightened out, and back on target, his friend was nowhere to be found, because he was running scared when creditors were calling for their money. All of a sudden, the "friend" filed an action in court to have himself appointed receiver of the corporation. The friend claiming that the man who had set it up years before, put all of the money into the corporation, and whose business it really was, was not really a principal! Now you may be wondering how he could do such a thing, and guessing that no court in America would go along with such a ridiculous assertion.

Actually, the court bought the whole idea, and appointed the "friend" receiver of the corporation, giving him total control, entirely disregarding the wishes of the majority shareholder, whose business this had been for many years before the "friend" ever came along. What follows is a brief description of various types of stock, which may give you some ideas relating to how you can retain control of your business.

Who Should Own the Stock in Your Corporation?

Who the shareholders should be in your corporation, depends largely on the purpose for your corporation. If the corporation in question is your own operating business, with which you are

identified, then you should probably own it. Should you give stock to other key players in your organization in exchange for sweat equity, or their position in the family? Only you can answer that one, but keep in mind how you are going to handle things when trouble arises.

Summary

When you first receive your corporate record book your job does not end there. To bring your company to life you need to have your initial meeting. This will establish the foundation for your first year of business. It's where you elect your officers, issue stock, sign your bylaws, file for an employee identification number and established a tax year.

These are the preliminary steps to bring your company to life. Without these steps you have nothing more than a shell so be sure you take the time to review your articles of incorporation and the bylaws.

NOTES

7 Starting Your LLC Off Right

Forming an LLC is as simple as filing your Articles of Organization with the Secretary of State in which you plan to do business. But, before you take that step, you need to make a few decisions like; who are the members going to be, what will you accept as consideration for buying interest in the LLC, how will the LLC be managed?

Before forming an LLC be sure to take into consideration the business laws of the state in which you wish to operate. Most states will accept one member LLC and some states require you to post a notice in the local paper when forming a new LLC. In some cases if you are converting an existing business into an LLC you must notify current creditors, lenders and leasers before you can convert to an LLC.

Also, if you are a CPA, engineer, doctor, lawyer, or other licensed professional, many states don't allow you to use an LLC. The states worry that you would use the entity as a way to shield personal liability.

The Players in an LLC

LLCs are made up of members who act in similar capacity to shareholders in a corporation. Anybody can be a member of an LLC, unlike the limitations of shareholders in an S corporation. In fact corporations could even be member. There can be one member or multiple members, it's really up to you.

The members buy interest in the LLC with cash, property, services or the promise of payment. In exchange for their investment the members receive ownership interest. In most cases the investment of cash is not a taxable event. In the case of property, services, equipment or promise to pay there are tax issues that should be looked at.

There can be different designations of members based on active decision makers or passive investors. This is a decision that must be made when outlining the operating agreement. If the LLC is managed by its members then it is considered "member managed". If the LLC chooses to hire an outside manager or designate the position to a member, then the LLC is considered "manager managed".

How the LLC is going to be managed usually depends on the long term outlook for the company. If you are planning to only allow a few people to participate in the LLC and you are all on the same page, then you might want to look at having the LLC member managed. If you are operating multiple ventures out of one company with active and passive investors then you might be better off hiring a professional manager or electing an active member to be the manager to avoid any unnecessary conflict when it comes to decisions made by the LLC. How an LLC is managed is outlined in the articles of organization before it is filed with the state and in the operating agreement.

Some people will choose to have a corporation as the manager of the LLC. This allows income to be split between the LLC and the corporation usually causing a favorable tax outcome. Then you could pay management fees to the corporation for overseeing the LLC.

If payments to a managing member are outlined in the operating agreement and documented as a wage to the manager then it would be treated like a salary and become a deduction to the LLC. If the manager is paid on a percentage of profit and loss of the LLC, then the payment would not be considered a deduction to the company.

Officers

An LLC may elect officers just like a corporation. You can have a president, secretary and treasurer. The officers are voted on by the members and elected once a year.

Officers in an LLC play the same role as officers in a corporation as discussed on page 56.

Articles of Organization

The Articles of Organization is simply a form you file with the state in which you wish to form the LLC. The articles of organization contain the names of the members and/or manager, the business address and who the resident agent will be for the LLC.

The resident agent is the location where any legal documents for the LLC can be delivered. In most states you can be your own resident agent or you can hire a service to act as your resident agent. It is usually recommended to hire a service to act as your resident agent. They will accept service of process at their offices versus having a process server come into your place of business and serve you with papers. It's usually a nominal fee and many resident agent services offer priceless information on how to operate your company and keep you informed of changing rules and regulations imposed by the state.

Operating Agreement

One of the first things you need to develop after you file your articles of organization with the state is the Operating Agreement. While operating agreements are not required by all states, it's important to take the time and develop a working operating agreement that fits the needs of the LLC.

The operating agreement outlines the inner workings of the LLC. It defines ownership, if the LLC will be member managed or manager managed. The operating agreement also outlines how distributions will be handled and who has voting rights. Developing an operating agreement allows the parties involved to sit down and agree on a course of action for the company. It's a great tool to start looking at the long term goals of the company with everybody having input on how the company will be run. It also prevents any disputes over ownership and distribution rights as all the members should participate in completing the operating agreement.

Federal Tax Classification

One of the great flexibilities of an LLC is the ability to select how you want the entity to be taxed. If you are a single member LLC the IRS will automatically tax you as a partnership, which means the profits and losses of the company will flow through to you personally. You also have the option to be taxed as

a corporation. This makes the LLC its own taxable entity and you are taxed on dividends and/or salary received from the LLC.

The form you use will depend on what kind of entity your business is for federal tax purposes. Following are some general guidelines and the forms which go with each entity:

If your business has only one owner, it will automatically be considered to be a sole proprietorship (referred to as an entity to be disregarded as separate from its owner) unless an election is made to be treated as a corporation. A sole proprietorship files Form 1040 (PDF), *U.S. Individual Income Tax Return* and will include Form 1040, Schedule C (PDF), *Profit or Loss from Business*, or Form 1040, Schedule C-EZ (PDF) and Form 1040, Schedule SE (PDF), if net income $400.00. If an election is made to be treated as a corporation, Form 1120 (PDF), *U.S. Corporation Income Tax Return*, is filed.

If your business has two or more owners, it will automatically be considered to be a partnership unless an election is made to be treated as a corporation. A partnership files Form 1065 (PDF), *U.S. Partnership Return of Income.* If an election is made to be treated as a corporation, Form 1120 (PDF), *U.S. Corporation Income Tax Return*, is filed. The election referred to is made by filing Form 8832 (PDF), *Entity Classification Election.*

Members List

Just like a corporation keeps a stock ledger, LLC's need to keep a record of whom their members are along with names and addresses. This list needs to be available for review by any member of the LLC.

Tax Identification Number

If the LLC is going to have multiple owners or employees you will need to obtain an Employer Tax Identification Number (E.I.N) for the LLC. You will be required to obtain an EIN number before you can open up a bank account and if you are accepting payments from an outside service, many times they will request the company's EIN number so they can report payments to the IRS.

The IRS uses the number to identify taxpayers that are required to file various business tax returns. EINs are used by employers, sole proprietorships, corporations, partnerships, nonprofit associations, trusts, estates, or decedents, government agencies, certain individuals, and other business entities.

You will not need a new EIN if you change the name of your business or change the location of your business. If you purchased the business from another party you cannot use their EIN number, you will need to file for a new one.

You can apply for an EIN number by phone, fax or by mail. If you apply by phone you can have an EIN number right away. Simply have the person authorized to sign the SS-4 form call 1-888-816-2065 and you will receive an EIN number within minutes.

Company Name

When deciding on a company name most secretary of state web sites allow you to go on-line and make sure that the name you are looking for is available. Nobody else in the state can be using the name that you want. If the name you want is not available sometimes just altering the name slightly will make it available. When you designate a name be sure to include LLC or LTD at the end of the company name. This lets the secretary of state know you are forming an LLC and it lets people you are doing business with know your company is an LLC.

Buy Sell Agreement

You should also look at including a buy/sell agreement in the operating agreement. The buy/sell agreement outlines the steps a member has to go through to sell their ownership interest, or if a member dies or becomes ill. It lays the ground work to avoid future legal battles over control and ownership.

Acts of the Limited Liability Company

The premise of using and documenting

company decisions for an LLC are the same as a corporation. A resolution is a formal record showing a decision was made based on a majority of the members. Many times the LLC will have a meeting and the resolution is the documentation that shows what decisions were finalized and approved at the meeting.

Because LLC's are still being defined as far as their requirements for corporate formalities you may find that certain states have enacted different regulations when it comes to documenting business decisions made by the LLC. Different states have their own requirements as outlined by the Model Business Corporation Act or the LLC Act. They are trying to come to a formal decision that governs all the states but until they do it is always recommended to treat your LLC like a corporation when it comes to maintaining corporate records.

The "brain" of the LLC are the members. Many times when important business decisions need to be made concerning the financial obligations of the LLC the members will pass a resolution. Resolutions are passed based on a majority vote of the members or in some states a unanimous vote of the members.

While LLC's don't have directors they can have officers, members and a manager. You can think of the manger as the President of the LLC.

Resolutions are also used to set the level of decision making authority for members and or the manager of the LLC. If you have members who want to be active in the decision making process of the LLC but can't be involved with the day-to-day operations they might pass a resolution restricting the authority of the manager. This would require the members to come together at formal meetings to pass written resolutions before the manager can make certain business decisions.

If this was the case and the members didn't have the confidence in the manger they selected to make business decisions then maybe they should look at getting a new manager.

The documentation can also be a great tool to use when disputes arise between members. If all important business decisions were presented to the members and a vote was received and documented it would be hard for a member to come back later and say that a decision was not disclosed to them.

Especially when you are using a manager and you have members who have a financial interest in the company you would be better off to document all major business decisions. Especially if a decision is made not to issue a distribution.

For example: *You decide to get a few family members together and start an LLC as a way to buy and sell real estate. The members have other obligations so nobody is in a position to manage the new company but they still want to have some control because it was their money they invested. The LLC would hire a manger to handle the day to day operations of running the business but due to the fact that the members want some control, they could pass a resolution restricting the authority of the manager. Maybe the manager can only manage current properties and lead the negotiations for new properties but didn't have the authority to sign the final purchase agreement without the consent of the members.*

You would use resolutions to open a bank account, purchase property, sign a long term lease, or make a financial obligation for the LLC. Some business transactions that take place require a resolution showing that the decision makers of the company knew of and approved the decision: For instance some banks, leasing companies or loan companies.

Summary

If there is going to be multiple owners it's important that you take the steps to start your company off right. If you don't feel comfortable developing an operating agreement, buy/sell agreement, or you're not sure what tax selection you should make, be sure you take the time to consult with a professional. This extra step could save you extra expense and headaches in the future.

The steps you take to establish the foundation of your company is very important and should be thought out not only for the present goals of the company but looking to the future and where you see the company in 5, 10 or 20 years from now.

Some people jump into forming a business entity without realizing that there is more involved than just filing a form and putting a sign up. You are forming the entity for the additional liability protection the LLC provides, so why not take the steps to do it right.

Laughlin Associates has been assisting businesses just like yours for over 40 years. As you read through this informative book, feel free to give us a call and we will be more than happy to answer your questions at 1-800-648-0966.

NOTES

8 Organization of the Corporation

- *Directors First Meeting*
- *When To Issue A Resolution*
- *Getting Started*

The initial organization of the corporation is of vital importance. There should be a formal organizational meeting of the directors in which they authorize bank accounts, required filings, official forms of stock certificates, corporate seals, elect officers and so on.

The first time your Board of Directors meets will be the corporation's organizational meeting. In this crucial meeting, you will make many important decisions which will affect your business for years to come, such as adopting Bylaws, establishing a fiscal year, possible election of S-corporation status, opening bank accounts, and many others.

To begin with, you need to have your directors in place for the meeting. If you choose to have more directors than are named in the Articles of Incorporation, then you should appoint them prior to the first meeting, if they are to participate in this meeting. Since there are no shareholders at this point, the Board

of Directors can do this by adopting a Consent to Action Appointing Additional Directors prior to the meeting. Note that a Consent to Action is usually an action taken by the shareholders, but in this case, since there are no shareholders, the directors are acting in their place in appointing additional directors. Most states require a notice to be sent out before a meeting of the Director.

The easiest way to accomplish this is by using a *Waiver of Notice*. The waiver allows you to proceed with the business of organizing your corporation without waiting for a notice period (typically ten days). Each director who is in office at the time of the meeting must sign the waiver.

When this is accomplished, you are ready to proceed with the meeting. In the first meeting you should address the following issues:

1. Ratify the pre-incorporation actions of the Incorporator and first director.

2. Authorize the corporation to reimburse the person who paid the costs of incorporating.

3. Ratify the appointment of the

Registered Agent.

4. Adopt the corporation Bylaws.

5. Adopt a corporate seal.

6. Adopt a form of stock certificate.

7. Give authorization for the corporate secretary to make all necessary filings.

8. Elect officers, directors and shareholders.

9. If you are going to be an S Corporation, authorize the election of S status.

10. If you are not going to be an S Corporation, adopt a fiscal year.

11. Select a bank, and authorize the opening of a corporate bank account. You will also need to designate the person(s) who will be authorized to sign on the account.

12. Approve the Articles of Incorporation.

Let's discuss these items briefly, to assure that you are clear on the purpose of each part. We have also put sample documents at the end of this chapter for your review.

Ratification of Pre-Incorporation Actions

First, the ratification of the pre-incorporation actions. It is of supreme importance in the operation of your corporation that you maintain separation between your actions as an individual, and your actions on behalf of the corporation. Ultimately, this could be the difference between having your corporate veil pierced in a lawsuit, and having the corporation protect you from attack. Consequently, we begin the Corporation's life by beginning this necessary separation.

Incorporating the company is clearly an important corporate act, yet how could it be done pursuant to prior corporate authorization, if the corporation doesn't exist? Clearly, this is impossible. The answer to the dilemma is the ratification of the actions, after the fact, which has the effect of making them corporate actions, and not your personal actions.

Reimbursement of Costs of Incorporating

The second item on our list follows from the first. The cost of incorporating cannot possibly be paid for out of the Corporation's bank account, since the corporation is not yet formed. Authorizing a reimbursement in the first meeting allows you to shift the costs over to the corporation as a reasonable and ordinary business expense.

Ratification of Resident Agent

The third item is the ratification of the Resident Agent appointment. A Resident Agent for service of process is required before incorporation, yet this appointment must be authorized by the corporation, hence we again ratify it after the fact.

Adoption of the Bylaws

Adoption of Bylaws, the fourth item, is one which you should pay careful attention to. You may have purchased a corporation from an incorporating company, in which you received Bylaws with your other materials. Before you just accept the boiler plate Bylaws without thinking, be sure that you review them and understand them. The corporation bylaws are designed to provide the day to day rules and regulations for your corporation's activities and internal workings. They set forth the dates and times of the annual meetings of shareholders and directors, the method of notice for these meetings, the abilities of the differing players to make amendments, and other decisions. All of these items are important for you to consider at this point, and critical for you to follow later. In order for you to operate the corporation after this time, you will need to have Bylaws adopted, so don't put this step off.

Adoption of a Corporate Seal

Fifth is the adoption of a corporate seal. Many states, such as Nevada and Wyoming do not require one at all, but that really doesn't mean that you should simply forgo the seal. It will afford a great deal of authenticity and credibility to corporate documents which need to be shown to others if you use it consistently.

Adoption of Stock Certificates

Sixth, is the adoption of stock certificates. This is simply the official designation of a particular form or design which conforms to your state's requirements, and will make it difficult for someone to come along with just any old blank form, and claim it as evidence of ownership. The Seal should be placed on a sample certificate, and included with the minutes of the meeting as an official sample for the corporation's records.

Authorization of Required Filings

Seventh, authorizing the corporate Secretary to make all necessary filings will provide the necessary authorization to continue the organization process in compliance with applicable federal, state and local requirements for such things as Employer Identification Numbers, officers' lists, business licenses, and so on.

Election of Officers

Eighth, the election of officers is certainly important. It may seem hard to imagine, but this step is often overlooked. Any time I am asked to help someone bring their corporate records up to date, the first thing I do is to make a chart showing the shareholders, directors, and officers that show up on the various filings and documents that have been done, and compare them with the annual meetings which have (or have not) been held. The purpose for doing this is to determine if there were officers and directors for the corporation in any given year. Usually, there are years, or many years when the corporation transacted business, and didn't have any valid officers or directors. You should begin clean, and omit this fatal step now; elect officers.

Who Should Serve?

At this juncture, we need to consider two basic questions, who should serve as director and who should serve as officer? Often, business people will have others serve in these capacities who really have minor roles in the business. As is the case in all phases of corporate organizations, you need to carefully consider what the purpose of the corporation is, and who really has a role to play in that purpose. For example, if you are starting up a new corporation to conduct your primary business, who is going to make the important decisions? You? Your children or other relatives?

Often, people with family businesses will appoint their older children in officers' positions. Sometimes, they even appoint them directors. What a sad day many people have when their disgruntled adult children figure out that they can fire their parents! Is that really what you want? Another example along these lines is the person who welcomes his new son in law to the family by making

him a director or an officer. Worse yet, when he gifts his soon to be former son-in-law a large amount of stock. Let's face it, there are enough pitfalls in business without causing your own problems by awarding "honorary" titles by installing someone into a real office. Again, you must carefully consider what could eventually go wrong in the future before you make such appointments.

If it is your intention to maintain tight control over the business, then do not appoint other people to critical positions, unless you know that you can keep them under control. Always consider what could happen, even though you don't think that it will. Then and only then can you be secure in your new undertaking.

Adopt a Fiscal Year

Ninth, if you are planning to become an S Corporation, you will have to adopt a calendar year. A fiscal year for tax purposes will void your S election. If you are not planning on being an S Corporation, then give some thought to your fiscal year. Most people choose a calendar year because they are used to calendar years. If you have multiple corporations, however, a fiscal year can be an excellent tax planning device. If you have multiple corporations working together and you put them on different fiscal years, you can take certain steps to spread income between corporations, effectively differing some taxation.

Let's say that you have two corporations. One operates on a calendar year, we will call it corporation A. The other, corporation B, has a fiscal year which ends on June 30. In December, corporation A makes a large cash purchase, or enters into a large deductible services contract from corporation B. When the tax year for corporation A ends at the end of the month, its income for the year may be way down because of the transaction just completed with corporation B. This may have an impact on its taxable income, which is about to be calculated for the year. If this results in corporation A owing less in taxes for the year, would that hurt your feelings? (Most people answer "no" here). Corporation B now has six months to figure out what tax planning it will need before its year ends.

Now, just theorize that corporation B enters into a large cash transaction with corporation A in mid June. If this transaction had the effect of lowering the taxable income of corporation B, just before it had to file its taxes, would you feel bad? Take some time to think about what your various corporations can do for one another, and when would be advantageous times for them to get together before you choose a calendar year for your corporation, just because that's what you are used to.

If you authorize a particular tax year in your first meeting, and then get with your tax advisor, and wish to change your fiscal year, you can do it, as long as

you have not filed your first tax return. The corporation's first tax year must end within one year of the time it first started doing business, and must be filed seventy-five days after that ending. At any time prior to the filing of that first return, you can change your fiscal year, as long as your first fiscal year is not longer than 365 days from the date on which you started doing business. Once the first return is filed by the corporation, the fiscal year can no longer be changed.

Types of Consideration In Exchange for Stock

Stock is issued for cash, property, or services. Cash is fairly obvious as a form of consideration, but property and services will vary in form and substance. Property can take many forms, stock can be issued for tangible assets, such as office equipment, and real estate, or it can include such items as mental property, formulas, copyrights, trademarks, and so on. Services can be such things as actual work for the corporation, longevity, consulting, and service contracts. You may have a special circumstance which will fit into one of these categories which isn't mentioned, and yet could certainly be a valid consideration for the stock.

Issuance of the Stock

The actual issuance of the stock is rather simple. You issue stock by corporate resolution. First you will need a resolution to authorize issuance, and then you will need to draft a resolution issuing a specific number of shares to a specific individual or individuals (or bearer) for a type of consideration, cash, property or services. The resolution need not state how much money is involved, just the particular type of consideration. As an accounting function, you will have an equity account, usual called "paid in capital" on your books which indicates the actual amount of cash, or the cash value of the property or services performed in exchange for the stock.

All states require that corporations maintain a stock ledger as a record of share ownership. Stock ledgers usually are in two steps. First is the Register of Original Certificate Issue, which performs much the same duty as a check register. It allows the secretary to keep track of your numbered certificates, so that at any time, he or she can determine where they are. The register will indicate to whom and when each issued certificate was issued, and when combined with the remaining blank or unused certificates in the record book, will indicate if any certificates are missing. (see sample)

The second ledger that you will need to keep, is called the Shareholder Ledger. The shareholder ledger is a separate ledger for each shareholder which indicates each stock transaction the shareholder has been involved in, and shows a running total of the shares each person owns. It also has the address of the shareholder. The shareholder ledger is what is used in determining who is entitled to vote in shareholder meetings, and how many shares each shareholder is entitled to. The address on the ledger is used for providing notices of meetings to each shareholder.

States will vary on whether or not copy of the shareholder ledger must be kept by the Resident Agent. In some states, such as Nevada, only a statement stating who is the custodian of the ledger is provided to the Resident Agent. You should contact your state's Secretary of State to find out what is required in this area.

Changes of the Guard

There are several possibilities in this area. First, there is the fundamental matter of appointing officers. Next, there is the possibility that an officer may resign or be fired. Next, directors need to be appointed, they can resign and need to be replaced, and then, of course, they too can be fired. All of these actions are done through documented means. As most of these actions involve actions of the directors or shareholders, there are resolutions involved. Yet even a resignation requires some sort of written procedure, even if the officer quits verbally and stomps off in a huff, refusing to write anything down.

The reasons for this need of documentation are fairly obvious. In a corporation, everything depends on the roles we are playing at any given time, and upon our ability to prove (or disprove) it. With a partnership or sole proprietorship, this is not nearly as important, because those entities are synonymous with the individuals involved. Corporations, however are different, and anyone can claim to be an officer or director for various purposes. What we don't always consider is that people can also deny their truthful position when they want to wiggle out of something. Thus, not only is such documentation important from the simple perspective of formalities, it is critical for some very practical reasons as well.

Officers

Election or appointment of officers is done by the directors. In their annual meeting, they elect the officers for the coming year. Yet, in the event that something goes awry during that time, they may have cause to replace an officer. The procedures are relatively simple. First, let's assume that an officer resigns.

Resignations can, of course come about for a variety of reasons. Let's first of all look at what happens when a resignation is friendly. The Treasurer resigns to pursue his or her dream to travel the world. The Treasurer would then submit a brief letter of resignation (usually given to the president, could be given to the board or secretary). The directors get together and draft a resolution accepting the resignation and appointing a new person to fill the unexplored term. The new Treasurer accepts in writing the appointment (as all directors and officers should be required to do) and that is all there is to it.

Things can be a little more complicated in an unfriendly situation. Yet, if the resigning officer gives a written resignation, which is exactly what you want them to do, everything would proceed as noted. However, they may refuse to do so and just leave. In this case, it is of vital importance that the directors adopt a resolution accepting the resignation, which documents exactly how they have come to know about it, since the person in question didn't sign anything.

Here's an example. Suppose that the Treasurer became disenchanted with the management of the corporation for some reason and walked into the president's office and said," Take this job and shove it, I'm out of here!"

The president them informs the directors of the situation, and the directors adopt the following resolution:

WHEREAS, it has come to the attention of this Board that Sam Smith, the Treasurer of this corporation, has given his verbal resignation to the president of the Corporation, and

WHEREAS, the president has reported

to this Board that said verbal resignation was given to him on Tuesday, December 5, 2003 at 2:35 p.m., and **WHEREAS**, the president's secretary, Mary Jones attested that she overheard the verbal resignation of the Treasurer, therefore be it

RESOLVED, that the resignation of Sam Smith from the post of Treasurer of this Corporation, given to the president on the date and time noted above, be and is hereby accepted effective as of the date and time given.

While this resolution may seem to be longer than absolutely necessary, there is a reason for all of this. First, don't be too shocked if this person who quits in a huff turns around and sues for wrongful termination, asserting that he or she was fired. In that case, all of the official documentation possible will be necessary. Second, you need some sort of record to establish that the position was indeed vacant, so that there will be no question as to the legitimacy of the successor. This approach will work in most situations of this type. It would be followed by a resolution appointing a new Treasurer, either combined with the above resolution, or separately:

RESOLVED, that Harry A. Jackson be and is hereby appointed Treasurer of this Corporation, to fill the vacancy created by the resignation of Sam Smith, such appointment to be effective this date.

What about terminations? Termination of an officer may be done by the board of directors, and in some cases by the shareholders. There is some dispute about the degree of detail which is appropriate on a resolution terminating an officer, with some arguing that the resolution should contain all of the reasons for the action, while others disagree. Those favoring the reasons assert that this is an excellent opportunity to document those just causes for the termination, in the event there should be a lawsuit. Those on the other side argue that listing of reasons, in the event of a suit, could end up being a trap for the company, while not listing them will give the company the ability to surprise the other side with the reasons at the right time. If you are thoroughly confused by all of this, you would do well to talk it over with an attorney who is knowledgeable in employment law. For our purposes, it is sufficient to grasp the need and importance of some sort of resolution to remove an officer. A sample resolution of this type would read something like this:

RESOLVED, that Sam Smith, Treasurer of this Corporation, be and is hereby removed from the office of Treasurer, effective immediately.

Hiring and firing of employees is normally handled by the president, or by another person designated to do so such as a Human resources person. As a rule, the directors would not get involved in personnel matters dealing with employees. However, yours might be an organization where the directors would step in and become involved with a particular position, where the president's authority may have been limited in some area. If this is the case, the directors should act, or at least ratify the termination. Obviously, there could also be a case where the directors disagree with the president, and insist that an employee be terminated. In such a case, they should adopt a resolution instructing the president to make the termination.

Directors

This area becomes a little more complicated than dealing with the officers, because we must involve the stockholders. Directors are appointed by stockholders in most cases. Yet, where there are no stockholders, the directors may appoint as many additional directors as the Bylaws permit, by consent to action. A consent to action is actually the name of a resolution of the stockholders, and since there are no shareholders, and the directors are acting in their place, they would use a consent rather than a director's resolution. The consent to action uses the exact same format as a resolution, simply substituting the name.

There is another case in which the directors would elect directors, even while there are shareholders, and that is to fill an unexplored term, where a vacancy would have resulted from a termination, resignation or death. This appointment could also be made by the shareholders. I know, you are wondering which is best, having the directors fill a vacancy, or having the shareholders do it. As a practical matter, this depends upon whether you are a director or a shareholder! Since directors serve at the pleasure of the shareholders, it would be a good idea for the directors not to be overly aggressive in this area.

Procedurally, resignations of directors should be handled in the same way as resignations of officers, with a written resignation being submitted and accepted by the shareholders, prior to the appointment of a new director. If your board of directors has not fallen below the minimum number set by the Articles, you aren't required to fill a vacancy.

Termination of a director is another matter. In almost all cases, the directors do not have this authority, so it must be done by the shareholders. Additionally, most state statutes require a super majority of the voting shares of the corporation to remove a director, usually two thirds, sometimes three quarters. While removal of a director can be done either in a meeting or by consent to action, if you have several shareholders, it would be wise to hold a meeting, so that the representation of the necessary percentages of shares can be fully demonstrated. Where there is only one shareholder, this would not be a problem.

Salaries

Officers' salaries and directors' fees are also a matter for resolutions. Because officers are hired by the directors, the specifics of their compensation, including bonuses, benefits and salaries are all determined by the Board. As always, it is naturally understood that if there is no resolution, than the Board has not taken an action. This being the case, a corporation which has officers, benefits for officers and officers' salaries (or no officer salaries for that matter) needs to have documentation. A lack of documentation can make the corporation appear to be an alter ego in some cases, or in others it may appear that the officer(s) in question could be acting improperly. Some corporations also pay fees to directors for attending meetings. These fees are also documented with resolutions.

Purchasing

Resolutions relating to purchasing can be minimal in number, or very numerous, depending on the degree of latitude the directors wish to give to the officers. Normally speaking, since the officers are charged with the responsibility of conducting the day to day business of the corporation, they can make normal and necessary purchases without prior or specific Board approval. Yet in some cases, the directors may wish to limit the ability of officers to purchase. This limitation would be a matter of drafting

and adopting a resolution. Limitations may be placed on types of purchases, dollar amounts, or most anything that the directors would deem necessary.

Out of the ordinary purchases, however, should always be approved by the directors. Such purchases would include new phone systems, re-tooling of a plant, purchases of company cars which are not otherwise provided for, real estate purchases, and so on. The rule of thumb would be set by a policy resolution. Policy which allowed for purchases in the ordinary course of regular business would then require by implication, resolutions for unusual purchases. For most small to medium sized companies where the players are more or less the same people in differing roles, this arrangement is the easiest one to handle.

Establishing a Principal Place of Business

It is fair to say that in all cases, the establishing of a principal place of business is neither ordinary or regular in the course of a corporation's activities. It is something which seldom occurs, and may only occur once in the entire history of a company. Thus, an action of the Board is going to be necessary to authorize the move. In fact, it may even require a series of resolutions. Let's say that the corporation has maintained the same location for a number of years, but with the growth of the company, the current location is no longer big enough to get the job done. The Board may direct the president to look into a possible relocation. That's one resolution. Then the president reports back what he has found out. Then the Board tells the president to enter into negotiations with the landlord. Probably the Board will say that they would agree to a certain price, or certain terms. They may say that if the price and terms are met, than the president can go ahead and sign. All of this would be done by resolution. Remember that the Board's thinking and decisions are the purpose of resolutions.

Next, the president concludes successful negotiations and signs the lease. At this point he reports to the Board, and the Board ratifies the lease. Another resolution. This general process may apply to many different situations if you think about it. Real estate purchases, auto or aircraft purchases, business alliances, and many other scenarios may need to work like this. That is not to say that these steps are somehow required, because they are not. However, things may well work out this way, and if they do, you should have them covered in the corporate records. What if you have only one person holding all of the positions, do you need to have such a lengthy process? The answer is, most likely not.

Let's go over the process again with a one person corporation. You as president say to yourself, "Hey, this place isn't big enough any more." So you do some checking, and find that you can move the company to a better location. You talk to the landlord, cut a deal, and sign on the dotted line. Now, back at the office you as director look at the deal you signed and say, "Good job. You did the right thing." Your resolution would ratify the new lease. Here's some language that might be useful here:

RESOLVED, that the lease for new corporate offices by and between this Corporation, and so and so, executed on such and such a date, and attached hereto, be and is ratified and approved as if done pursuant to prior authorization.

If this is not on the contract, write it in. Otherwise, you may find yourself in a position where someone is trying to claim that you, as an individual are a party to the agreement, even though the corporation is listed as the party. This is certainly true of leases, but it is also true of other contracts that you will see in the future.

The Five Tests Your Corporation Cannot Afford to Fail

1. Does your corporation have an actual business address, and the documentation to prove it?

2. Does your corporation have a phone in its name?

3. Does your corporation have its own business license?

4. Does your corporation have a bank account in its name?

5. Does your corporation have transactions with unrelated parties?

These five tests are seldom any problem with your primary business. They usually come pretty naturally. In a secondary corporation, however, they must be given some thought, especially if it is to be located in a preferred state, such as Nevada or Wyoming. Sometimes people will move a division to the preferred state. Others will establish a home office in the home of a good friend, or relative. While this particular option has its problems, it can work in some cases. Still others will use a partial solution, such as a post office box, or a mail forwarding service. This option is fraught with peril, because it clearly fails most of the tests.

Financing

Financing is another area where the activities are usually not the normal course of business. One factor in this area is that most banks will provide you with a resolution for their protection. You need to ensure that the corporate records contain that resolution. However, all financing is not done through banks. For this reason, you should review your corporation's records to ensure that lending or borrowing money is properly documented.

A special case here is related party loans. Loans to and from stockholders, directors and officers are of particular importance, since they can come under intense scrutiny in tax audits. You should ensure that all such transactions are fully documented, contain reasonable terms, and are entirely arms length.

Summary

The initial steps you take to organize the corporation will be the foundation your company is built on. It's important that you follow the steps as outlined in this chapter.

SAMPLE

ACCEPTANCE OF APPOINTMENT AS DIRECTOR

   I, IM Director, having been appointed a Director of YOUR COMPANY, INC. a Nevada corporation, do hereby accept said position, effective as of the time of my appointment on January 1, 2014.

Effectively dated the 13th day of January, 2014.

_I. M. Director_____
DIRECTOR

SAMPLE

ACCEPTANCE OF APPOINTMENT AS PRESIDENT

I, <u>IM Director</u>, having been appointed President of <u>YOUR COMPANY, INC.</u>, a Nevada corporation, do hereby accept said position effective as of the time of my appointment on <u>13 January, 2014</u>.

EFFECITVELY DATED the <u>13th day of January, 2014</u>.

I.M. Director
_____
IM Director, President

SAMPLE

ACCEPTANCE OF APPOINTMENT AS SECRETARY

I, <u>IM Director</u>, having been appointed Secretary of <u>YOUR COMPANY, INC.</u>, a Nevada corporation, do hereby accept said position effective as of the time of my appointment on <u>13 January, 2012</u>.

EFFECITVELY DATED the <u>13th day of January, 2012</u>.

I.M. Director

IM Director, Secretary

SAMPLE

ACCEPTANCE OF APPOINTMENT AS TREASURER

I, <u>IM Director</u>, having been appointed Treasurer of <u>YOUR COMPANY, INC.</u>, a Nevada corporation, do hereby accept said position effective as of the time of my appointment on <u>13 January, 2012</u>.

EFFECITVELY DATED the <u>13th day of January, 2012</u>.

T.M. Director
_____
IM Director, Treasurer

SAMPLE

ACCEPTANCE OF APPOINTMENT AS VICE PRESIDENT

I, <u>IM Director</u>, having been appointed Vice President of <u>YOUR COMPANY, INC.</u>, a Nevada corporation, do hereby accept said position effective as of the time of my appointment on <u>13 January, 2012</u>.

EFFECITVELY DATED the <u>13th day of January, 2012</u>.

I.M. Director
_____
IM Director, Vice President

SAMPLE
RESOLUTION

WRITTEN CONSENT OF DIRECTOR OF

YOUR COMPANY, INC.

We, the undersigned, being all Directors of YOUR COMPANY, INC., a Nevada Corporation, do hereby consent in writing to the adoption of the following resolution:

RESOLVED, that the authority of the Vice President, IM Director, extend to all matters whatsoever, such powers and authorization to include, but not be limited to, the following powers and attributes: To appear and represent the Corporation before all governmental departments, tribunals, and officials: to make and enter into agreements for the purchase, sale and transfer, and hypothecation of real and personal property, and to execute and accept conveyances and transfers thereof; to open bank accounts, to draw, sign, endorse accept, and negotiate checks, drafts, bills of exchange or other commercial documents (including promissory notes); to demand, collect, and receive any and all sums of money, securities, documents, and properties of every kind which may be due to the Corporation; to adjust, settle and compromise debts, accounts and claims pertaining to the business of the Corporation, and to give receipt and acquittance therefore, together with such other general and special powers as they may at the time deem necessary and expedient to and for the general welfare of the Corporation.

Dated this 13th day of January, 2012.

I.M. Director

SAMPLE

RESOLUTION OF THE BOARD OF DIRECTORS

OF

YOUR COMPANY, INC.

A Nevada Corporation

WE, the undersigned, being all of the Directors of YOUR COMPANY, INC., a Nevada corporation, having met and discussed the business herein set forth, have unanimously:

RESOLVED, that the common stock of the Corporation be issued to the named individuals in

the amount stated in exchange for cash, property, services performed, or other assets

received and indicated:

NAME	NO. OF SHARES	ISSUED FOR
Sylvia B. Director	510	Cash
IM Director	430	Cash
Rebecca Director (D.P.)	20	Cash
Ben Director (D.P.)	20	Cash
Matt Director (D.P.)	20	Cash

EFFECTIVELY DATED THIS 13th day of January, 2012.

I.M. Director
_____

SAMPLE

MINUTES OF FIRST MEETING OF BOARD OF DIRECTORS

OF

YOUR COMPANY, INC.

A Nevada Corporation

The first meeting of the Board of Directors of YOUR COMPANY, INC. convened on 13 January, 2012 pursuant to waiver of notice and consent to the holding thereof executed by each Director of the Corporation. Present were all the Directors:

Sylvia B. Director was elected temporary Chairman and IM Director was elected temporary Secretary, each to serve only until permanent officers are elected.

The Chairman reported that the Articles of Incorporation of the Corporation had been filed in the Office of the Nevada Secretary of State on December 23, 2011 to become effective on January 1, 2012 and that a copy thereof, certified by the Nevada Secretary of State, had been filed and given a document number of P96022453149, and that the Corporation is duly and validly existing and in good standing under the laws of the State of Nevada and qualified to proceed with the transactions of business. The Certificate of Incorporation of the Corporation then being exhibited, on motion duly made, seconded and carried, said Certificate of Incorporation was accepted and approved.

On motion duly made, seconded and carried, the Directors were recognized as the first Directors of the Corporation and it was further moved that they were to hold office until the first annual meeting of stockholders or until their respective successors shall be duly elected and qualified.

The temporary Chairman called for the nomination of Officers of the Corporation. Thereupon, the following persons were nominated for the Officers of the Corporation:

President: <u>Sylvia B. Director</u>

Vice President   <u>IM Director</u>

Secretary: <u>IM Director</u>

Treasurer: <u>Sylvia B. Director</u>

No further nominations being made, the nominations were closed and the Directors proceeded to vote on the nominees. All of the Directors present at the meeting having voted and the vote having been counted, the Chairman announced the aforesaid nominees had been duly elected to the offices set before their respective names. The permanent Officers of the Corporation then took charge of the meeting.

Upon motion duly made, seconded and carried, the following resolutions were adopted:

RESOLVED, that the Treasurer be and she hereby is authorized to pay all fees and expenses incident to and necessary for the organization of this Corporation.

RESOLVED, that the proper Officers of this Corporation be and they here authorized and directed on behalf of the Corporation, to make and file such certificates, reports, or other instruments as may be required by law to be filed in any State in which Officers shall find it necessary or expedient to file the same to register or authorize the Corporation to transact business in such State.

RESOLVED, that the Treasurer be and she hereby is ordered to open a bank account in the name of this Corporation with Nations Bank for deposit of funds belonging to the Corporation, such funds to be withdrawn only by check of the Corporation signed by its President and/or Vice President.

Chapter 8: Organization of the Corporation

RESOLVED, that the actions taken by <u>John Doe, Inc. and Sylvia B. Director</u> prior to the incorporation of the Corporation, on behalf of the Corporation, are hereby approved, ratified, and adopted as if done pursuant to corporate authorization.

RESOLVED, a form of Stock Certificate was presented, examined, approved, and duly adopted for use by the Corporation. Certificate No. 0 was directed to be inserted in the Corporate Record Book as evidence and sample thereof.

RESOLVED, that the Board of Directors of this Corporation deem it desirable and/or prudent to, from time to time, utilize an official corporate seal and, therefore, that the corporate seal presented to this Board, circular in form with the inscription of the corporate name, NEVADA, and the official date of incorporation, be, and the same hereby is, adopted as the official seal of the Corporation, and be it

FURTHER RESOLVED, that the impression of said seal be made upon Certificate No. 0 inserted in the Corporate Record Book as evidence and sample thereof.

RESOLVED, that the fiscal year of the Corporation shall commence on January 1, and end on December 31 of each year hereafter.

FURTHER RESOLVED, that <u>John Doe</u> be, and hereby is, appointed Resident Agent of this Corporation, in charge of the principal office and so authorized to discharge the duties of Resident Agent, and be it

FURTHER RESOLVED, that the Secretary forthwith supply a List of Officers and Directors to the Resident Agent for filing with the Secretary of State of the State of Nevada as required by law. (In the event the filing has not yet been accomplished), and be it

FURTHER RESOLVED, that the Secretary forthwith supply the Resident Agent with a certified copy of the Corporation Bylaws and a stock ledger statement to be kept on file at the principal office as required by Nevada law. (In the event this has not yet been done.)

There being no further business to come before the meeting, upon motion duly made, seconded, and (unanimously) carried, it was adjourned.

Effectively Dated the 13<u>th</u> day of January, 2012.

I.M. Director

IM Director, SECRETARY

_____

ATTEST:

Sylvia B. Director

Sylvia B. Director, DIRECTOR

SAMPLE

MINUTES OF FIRST MEETING OF STOCKHOLDERS

OF

<u>YOUR COMPANY, INC.</u>

A Nevada Corporation

The first meeting of stockholders of the above-captioned Corporation was held on the date and at the time and place set forth in the written waiver of notice signed by the stockholders, fixing such time and place, and prefixed to the minutes of this meeting.

The meeting was called to order by the Chairman of the Board of Directors, and the following stockholders, being all of the stockholders of the Corporation, were present:

<u>Sylvia B. Director</u>

<u>IM Director</u>

<u>Rebecca Director (D.P.)</u>

<u>Ben Director (D.P.)</u>

<u>Matt Director (D.P.)</u>

The Chairman noted that it was in order to consider electing a Board of Directors for the ensuing year. Upon nominations duly made, seconded and (unanimously) carried, the following persons were elected as Directors of the Corporation, to serve for a period of one year or until such time as their successors are elected and qualify:

<u>Sylvia B. Director</u>

<u>IM Director</u>

There was presented to the meeting the following:

1. Copy of Certificate of Incorporation;

2. Copy of bylaws of the Corporation;

3. Resolutions adopted by the Incorporators;

4. Corporate certificate book;

5. Corporate certificate ledger.

===   Upon motion duly made, seconded, and (unanimously) carried, it was

RESOLVED, that the items listed above have been examined by all stockholders, and are all approved and adopted, and that all acts taken and decisions reached as set forth in such documents be, and they hereby are, ratified and approved by the stockholders of the Corporation.

RESOLVED, that the Corporation elect, under the provisions of Section 1362 of the Internal Revenue Code, to be treated as a small business corporation for income tax purposes.

There being no further business to come before the meeting, upon motion duly made, seconded, and (unanimously) carried, it was adjourned.

EFFECTIVELY DATED THIS <u>13th day of January, 2012</u>.

I. M. Director
_____

IM Director, SECRETARY

ATTEST:

Sylvia B. Director
_____

STOCKHOLDER

SAMPLE

RESOLUTION OF THE BOARD OF DIRECTORS

OF

YOUR COMPANY, INC.

A Nevada Corporation

WE, the undersigned, being all of the Directors of YOUR COMPANY, INC., a Nevada corporation, having met and discussed the business herein set forth, have unanimously:

RESOLVED, that the Board of Directors be and are hereby authorized to issue the common stock of this corporation to the full amount or number of shares authorized by the Articles of Incorporation, in such amounts and proportions as from time to time shall be determined by the Board, and to accept in full or in part payment thereof such property or services as the Board may determine shall be good and sufficient consideration and necessary for the business of the corporation.

EFFECTIVELY DATED the 13<u>th</u> day of January, 2012.

Sylvia B. Director
Sylvia B. Director, Director

I.M. Director
IM Director, Director

SAMPLE
RESOLUTIONS ADOPTED BY INCORPORATOR

OF

<u>YOUR COMPANY, INC.</u>
A Nevada Corporation

The Undersigned, being the incorporator of this corporation hereby adopts the following resolutions:

RESOLVED, that the following persons be, and they hereby are appointed as the First Directors of the Corporation, to serve until the first annual meeting of shareholders, and until their successors are elected and qualify:

<u>Sylvia B. Director</u>

<u>IM Director</u>

EFFECTIVE AS OF the <u>1st day of January, 2012.</u>

_____

John L. Mann, Incorporator
200 South Orange St.
Reno, Nevada 89503

SAMPLE

WAIVER OF NOTICE OF FIRST MEETING

OF

BOARD OF DIRECTORS

OF

YOUR COMPANY, INC.

A Nevada Corporation

We, the undersigned, being all of the Directors, do hereby severally waive notice of the time, place, and purpose of the first meeting of Directors of YOUR COMPANY, INC., a Nevada corporation, and consent that the meeting be held on 13 January 2012, at 10:00am at 1425 Knoll Way, Reno, NV 89502, and we further consent to the transaction of any business required to complete the organization of this corporation and any and all such other business that may properly come before the meeting.

Effective the 13th day of January, 2012.

Sylvia B. Director

———————————————

Sylvia B. Director, DIRECTOR

I.M. Director

———————————————

IM Director, DIRECTOR

NOTES

9 Acts of the Company

- *Documenting With Resolutions*
- *When to Use a Resolution*
- *How to Draft Resolutions*
- *Acts of the Limited Liability Company*

Simply stated, a "corporate act" is an action taken by a duly authorized corporate authority of the corporation. Implicit in all of this is the notion that the corporate directors are the ones who are charged with doing the thinking of the corporation. Since they are charged with doing the corporation's thinking, the directors must then be the ones who can duly authorize an action to be taken. Thus, when the president or C.E.O. of the corporation takes a particular action, that action must have been authorized by the "brain" of the corporation, which of course is the directors.

This is not to say that the C.E.O. or president cannot make decisions. In fact, they will usually make a great number of decisions. Yet the president and C.E.O. cannot make unauthorized decisions. Normally, they are authorized to make day to day operational decisions by the corporation's Bylaws. This is a handy fact, because running a business in which the president must seek the approval of the directors before he or she could buy a box of paper clips, would hardly be an organization which would stand much of a chance of reacting to a rapidly changing marketplace, and highly competitive environment in which most businesses operate. Therefore, it becomes readily apparent that some sort of concession must be made so that the theoretical can operate in the face of practical situations. Such an accommodation can be found in the resolutions which the directors will adopt.

Documenting With Resolutions

Any action taken by the directors is documented by a resolution. Since actions of the directors are by majority vote, it follows logically that there must be some way of recording these actions. Thus, when the directors get together and take some action, that process will be documented with the minutes of a meeting. Yet, holding a formal meeting of the directors every time an issue arises which requires a decision is a terribly cumbersome way of doing business. Some sort of accommodation must be found. Such an accommodation is found in the "free standing resolution." A "free standing" resolution can be adopted without holding and noticing a formal meeting. In order for such a resolution to be effective, it must have the signatures of at least a majority of the board.

All other things being equal, a free standing resolution can be used for any decision or action appropriate for the directors to take. The question really should be, when would you want to bother with a formal meeting at all? There are really two times when meetings are necessary. First, the annual meeting should be held each year on the appropriate day called for by the Bylaws. Second, a meeting should be held when a particularly controversial subject is being considered which is likely to divide the directors. In such a case, it is often wise to hold a meeting, so that evidence can be given that nobody was misled, and that nothing was done behind someone's back. Not only will this lead to more harmony within the management of the company, but it will also cut down on the number of lawsuits resulting from someone who feels left out of things.

When to Use Resolutions

When to draft and adopt resolutions depends a great deal on the management style and preferences of the directors. These things will depend upon the

relationship of the directors with the president of the corporation.

For example, if there is only one director, and that person is also the president, fewer resolutions will be needed, because the director will be able to delegate most of the decision making process to the president. On the other hand, if there are several directors, and they aren't overly confident that the president will make decisions with which they will agree, then they will probably limit the actions which the president can take. This is done through a very carefully worded resolution which very closely limits the authority of the president, in setting out the policy of the corporation with regard to the regular and ordinary business of the corporation, and how the president is to handle things which normally come up.

Then, as things come up which are out of the ordinary, the directors will take a very close hand in directing the president to report on his actions, and which authorize very narrow and specific actions.

For example: *let's say that the regular business of the corporation is the retail sale of western wear, and that the directors do not wish the president to make too many moves which they don't personally approve first. They might adopt a policy resolution which states that the normal business activity of the corporation is "to purchase and sell to the public western apparel." Notice that the president doesn't have the ability to assume that he can wholesale the goods. Then, the resolution may go on to say that the president is authorized to conduct the day to day operation of the corporation's business "with the advice and consent of the Board of Directors." Such a statement would indicate that there is little the president could do without the directors' involvement.*

A situation in which the directors may prefer to give the president full latitude will look a little different. In the original policy resolution, the directors might grant the president the authority to transact all business, hire and fire all employees, make loans, borrow, and execute all documents necessary, and so on, without further approval.

As was stated previously, the manner in which you choose to proceed will depend largely on the circumstances in which you find yourself. One thing to keep in mind, though, is that if your directors are so lacking in confidence in the officers of your corporation, you should probably be asking why the people who are serving as officers are in those capacities in the first place.

Be careful before you confer "honorary titles" to the key positions within the corporation. Let's face it, usually this practice just brings problems. If you are the one who will be running the show, then be the president yourself. Use the other offices as "honorary titles" if you must, but not president (unless your Bylaws provide for a C.E.O. who

is senior to the president). It should go without saying that the position of director is not the place to put people who should not be making decisions!

How to Draft Resolutions

Resolutions can take on two forms; within the framework of minutes of a formal meeting, and freestanding resolutions.

As meetings will be discussed in a separate section, let's look at free standing resolutions. There are three parts to a resolution; the preamble, the body, and the authentication. After the heading of the resolution, the preamble should say something like this:

"We, the undersigned, being all or a majority in this, a (state) corporation, having met and considered the matters herein set forth, have unanimously..."

At this point, you are ready to insert the body of the resolution.

This is the important portion of the resolution, and needs to be specific to the action. Traditionally, you will skip a space, indent, and insert the word "RESOLVED". Resolved is always placed in all caps. After this comes your wording.

This wording is often the source of some confusion, because people feel the need to write in "legalize". Be careful about this. While it is true that resolutions are usually written in a very formal style, they must be very clear as to their meaning. If you are not comfortable using technical or legal expressions, don't despair. What you need is to be as clear as you possibly can in expressing exactly what is intended. If you are comfortable with "legalize" fine, but if not, then simply state clearly what you intend, and you will be fine.

The body of the corporate resolution also presents an opportunity. In many cases, you will have very specific reasons for what you are doing. State them in the resolution. This can be very important in certain circumstances, should the resolutions of your corporation come to be examined in court, or in a tax audit. Since these occasions usually result years after the fact, you may not always remember the reason (or business purpose) of a particular action. By placing reasons for actions in the resolution, you will not have to worry about this. In fact, the business purpose for an action becomes a specific and formally documented part of your records.

Example: *Let's consider an example: Suppose that you need to travel to Hawaii on business. Years later, the IRS is auditing your corporation's taxes, and questioning your travel deductions. It would be a rather juicy prize for the auditor to disallow all of your many business trips, and to assert that they were, instead, personal vacations, and thus income to you, subject not only to* *income tax, but to payroll tax. This could be quite dangerous if you did a lot of traveling. So here's this trip to Hawaii. The auditor wants to know why you went there.*

Since you can't demonstrate why you went on business, guess what? This trip, and all of your other business trips are disallowed, and then reallocated as income.

What if there was another scenario here? Suppose that the resolution authorizing the trip said:

WHEREAS, this corporation is in the business of selling sport clothing and accessories, and WHEREAS, the International Sportswear Association is holding its annual sportswear exposition in Honolulu, Hawaii in July of this year, and WHEREAS, this board considers attendance at this exposition by the President to be of prime importance to this Company, therefore be it RESOLVED, that the President be and is authorized and instructed to attend the International Sportswear Exposition, in Honolulu, Hawaii on July 10-14 of this year, and be it

FURTHER RESOLVED, that the President be and is hereby instructed to secure contacts of new manufacturers of sportswear which can be added to the product line of this Corporation so that the market share of this Corporation can be increased and maintained, and be it

FURTHER RESOLVED, that the

Treasurer be and is instructed to reimburse the President for all reasonable and ordinary expenses associated with this trip, including airfare, hotels, meals, and reasonable incidentals.

Assuming that there really was an exposition, he's barking up the wrong tree. Also, if all of your travel was documented the same way, you should come out of this part of the audit safely.

Naturally, there are numerous activities within your corporate operation, which could be benefited by drafting resolutions in this fashion. Also note one other thing: the president in this resolution was not only authorized to go, but instructed to go. By adding this dimension, the directors are not making the trip a nice little option, but a condition of continued employment. Since the president has been required to attend, there should be no question as to the deduction of reasonable expenses.

Notice also that the business reasons for the trip were set off by the word "whereas". This is an indicator that what follows is a reason. What follows the word "resolved" is an action, instruction, or authorization.

Finally, what follows the body of the resolution is the authentication. This consists usually of a date, and then the signatures of at least a majority of the directors. Should you have three directors, for instance, then the

signatures of at least two must appear on the resolution.

Specific Areas Where Resolutions are Appropriate Policy

As has been discussed above, policy resolutions tend to set the tone for all which comes later. Usually, the directors will call upon the president to handle the day-to-day activities of running the company. Policy resolutions set forth what the regular business of the corporation is. Further, they should reflect what actions the president may take within this sphere. We often refer to such a policy resolution as a "catch all" resolution. Such a resolution would look something like the sample of the next page.

As you can quickly see, the president in this case can do pretty much anything, as far as the regular day-to-day business is concerned.

Another case where a policy resolution would be advisable is the case of listing corporate goals, objectives and plans. This area, too, can be handled a couple of ways. First, the president (or other officer) may be directed to make recommendations in one of these areas. When these recommendations are reported to the directors, then they could either adopt them, amend them or reject them. If they are adopted, then the report of the president would be ratified and attached to the resolution, making it official policy. The same would be done with an amended version of the president's report.

Alternatively, the directors could draft their own goals, objectives or plans within a resolution. Either way, the officers would have a clear cut guideline, within which they could act without further action from the board. This is an excellent way to handle marketing plans, financial plans and business plans. When this type of approach is taken, it becomes quite difficult for an adversary to claim that a corporation is a sham later, because all of the policies and business of the corporation is duly and properly adopted and formalized. The actions of the officers on behalf of the corporation become rather obvious, and apart from their own personal actions.

Acts of the LLC

The premise of using and documenting company decisions for an LLC are the same as a corporation. Because LLC's are still being defined as far as their requirements for corporate formalities you may find that certain states have enacted different regulations when it comes to documenting business decisions made by the LLC. The corporation follows the guidelines set forth under the Model Business Corporation Act and they are currently working on developing an LLC Act that will govern the workings of an LLC. Until this is finalized it is recommended you take the additional step and document your

major business decisions. You can never go wrong by "over" documenting.

It's important to document any decisions that affect the members financially, employee benefits, tax benefits, or holds the LLC to a long term financial obligation.

Holding a Meeting

Your operating agreement should outline when you need to hold a formal meeting. The LLC may also need to hold a special meeting.

For Example: *It's the end of the year and Collins LLC, which is owned by 4 members, all family relations, gets notice that two of the members want to sell out their ownership interest in the company. The LLC decides to hold a special meeting to discuss the changes and decide if they want to take on more members. Each member is located in a different part of the country so the Secretary of the LLC sends out notices of the meeting at least 10 days in advance. Since they haven't had their annual meeting they decide to meet at a convenient location and discuss the possibility of new members and their plan for the coming year. While the meeting is taking place the secretary takes notes which will be the minutes of the meeting. The members decide to buy out the interest of the other two, which means now they will need to ratify the articles of organization at the Secretary of States' office and change the operating agreement.*

Maintaining accurate minutes is very important. Once a meeting takes place the minutes should be approved. Once they are approved a copy of the minutes need to be placed in the corporate record book. These records could be your saving grace during an IRS audit, during litigation proceedings or possible disputes between the members.

If you can't all get together but you still need to hold a meeting you can do what is called a "paper meeting". A paper meeting is a little less formal than a real meeting. It allows the members to hold a meeting without getting together in the same location. When you hold a paper meeting you still document the meeting with minutes and have the members sign and approve the decisions made at the meeting.

Authorizing a Decision

The "brain" of the LLC is the members. Many times when important business decisions need to be made concerning the financial obligations of the LLC, the members will pass a resolution. Resolutions are passed based on a majority vote of the members or in some states a unanimous vote of the members.

A resolution is a formal record showing a decision was made based on a majority of the members. When the LLC has a meeting, the resolution is the documentation that shows what decisions were finalized and approved at the meeting.

Resolutions are also used to set the level of decision making authority for members and/or the manager of the LLC. If you have members who want to be active in the decision making process of the LLC but can't be involved with the day-to-day operations they might pass a resolution restricting the authority of the manager. This would require the members to come together at formal meetings to pass written resolutions before the manager can make certain business decisions.

The documentation can also be a great tool to use when disputes arise between members. If all important business decisions were presented to the members and a vote was received then documented it would be hard for a member to come back later and say that a decision was not disclosed to them.

If you are using a manager and you have members who have a financial interest in the company you would be better off to document all major business decisions.

You would use resolutions to open a bank account, purchase property, sign a long term lease, or make a financial obligation for the LLC. Some business transactions that take place require a resolution showing that the decision makers of the company knew and approved the decision. For instance some banks, leasing companies, loan companies or if you are signing a contract with a 3rd party require this kind of documentation.

On the next page you can see a sample LLC resolution.

Summary

Documenting key business decisions with formal resolutions will keep you and your business out of hot water. It's important to weigh the time it takes to keep up the documentation and the time you need to spend running your business. If you are unsure of what documents need to be kept or you don't think you'll ever have the time to keep up with the documentation you can hire an outside service that will monitor, inform and complete any corporate formalities you will need to keep your company in compliance.

Resolutions offer the documentation to show that company decisions were approved by the board of directors and or shareholders. Resolutions are used to document employee benefits, company loans, equipment purchases, bank accounts, accumulated earnings, employee contracts, approval of leases and contracts and many other important business decisions.

When in doubt, write it out. If you are unsure when to complete a resolution, do a resolution. All completed resolutions should be signed and held in the company's record book.

Resolutions are the basis for establishing your company's corporate formalities, the documentation that establishes the separation between you and the company.

SAMPLE

RESOLUTION OF THE BOARD OF DIRECTORS

OF

_____(state)_____

A _____(state)_____ Corporation

I, the undersigned, being all of the Directors of

_____ _____, a

_____ corporation, having met and discussed the business

herein set forth, have unanimously:

RESOLVED, that the President be and is hereby authorized to borrow money for the corporation and/or make loans of any size, type or kind whatsoever, at his/her discretion, on behalf of the corporation, and be it

FURTHER RESOLVED, that the President be and is hereby authorized to negotiate, consummate and/or enter into any type of financing, purchases, conditional sales contracts, leases, lease purchase agreements, co-sign for or make loans to employees or enter into and execute any documents representing debt or encumbrances or obligations of any nature, for and on behalf of the corporation, at his/her discretion and in his/her best judgment, and be it

FURTHER RESOLVED, that the President be and is hereby authorized to enter into any type of contractual agreement at his/her discretion, and be it

FURTHER RESOLVED, that the President be and is hereby authorized to handle all employment of corporate employees which in his/her discretion is in the best interest of this corporation, and be it

FURTHER RESOLVED, that the President be and is hereby authorized to make any decisions, take any actions, issue any directives, and/or consummate any business

transactions whatsoever in the pursuit of the corporation's business.

DATED THIS _____ day of _____, _____.

_____

DIRECTOR IN TOTO

SAMPLE

RESOLUTION OF THE MANAGER

OF

YOUR COMPANY, LLC

A Nevada Limited Liability Company

Re: Contract negotiations

I, the undersigned, being the Manager of Your Company, LLC, after review of the circumstances do hereby give my written consent to the following resolutions:

RESOLVED, that the Manager will negotiate with Your Company, LLC to develop prototypes and production specs for the Fat Buster product line, and be it

FURTHER RESOLVED, that as he deems to be in the best interests of the Company, the Manager may enter into contracts and agreements allowing for the development, production and marketing of the product lines of the Company with manufacturers and service providers of his choosing. Such agreements will be considered to be binding upon the Company and are in compliance with the authority and powers granted the Manager under the Operating Agreement of the Company.

DATED THIS _____ day of _____, _____.

_____

10 The Importance of Corporate Formalities

- *Piercing The Corporate Veil*
- *Case Studies*
- *Corporate Formalities Checklist*

As we have seen in the previous chapter, corporate formalities are the means by which you document the actions of your corporation and maintain the separation between you and your corporation. Some examples of corporate formalities include; keeping the corporation in good standing in the state of incorporation, maintaining the stock ledgers properly, keeping your minutes and resolutions up to date, and the issuance of stock is considered the foremost of corporate formalities.

Yet, it may seem that all of the things listed above are merely technicalities and that nothing of any real substance is included. After all, you may not have issued stock certificates, and made entries into your stock ledgers, but the corporation received capital from somewhere. You may not have written up formal minutes and resolutions, but obviously, if the company is operating, decisions were made and carried out. How you sign a contract isn't such a big deal; the fact that the contract was negotiated and executed is what really counts.

Next to whether or not you make the payroll, pay your bills and earn a profit, these little details seem to be nothing more than a nuisance. After all, it is a fact that many small and medium corporations operate successfully year after year, with dozens or hundreds of happy employees, and thousands paid in taxes and dividends, with little or no attention paid to the formalities.

I must admit that as long as things go along just fine, formalities are hardly an issue that seems worth the time they take to observe... and then, something happens.

Example: *Years of operation go by. Everything seems great. One day, a customer slips on a just mopped floor. This isn't great, but it's really no big thing. After all, there was a yellow caution sign on the floor and nobody was hurt. You fill out an accident report and give it to your insurance company. Then, you comp the unfortunate customer's meal; he is happy, if a little embarrassed, and goes on his way. This has happened before* over the years, not often, but it has happened, and nothing ever came of it before, so why worry about it?

Six month go by, still nothing. You forget about the incident. No insurance claims, no phone calls; it's over. Then, one day, while you are in the store room counting cases of napkins, one of your employees says that someone is asking for you up front. It's probably somebody who wants to fill out an employment application.

You go up front. The person waiting for you has something in his hand, probably a resume. He looks kind of old to be applying for a position as a dishwasher!
"Hi, can I help you?" you ask.
"Are you John Smith?"
"Yes, I am."
"This is for you," says the process server. You've just been served with a lawsuit.

It seems that the customer who slipped six months ago, and went away unhurt, has been seeing his chiropractor quite regularly for the problem he now has with his back and is seeking to recover his damages. You go back to the office, a little chagrined. Why didn't he just file an insurance claim? You look at the document. It says something about gross negligence and punitive damages. Better call the insurance company.

A few days later, your insurance company informs you that the other party is seeking punitive damages in excess of a million dollars. No problem, you have an umbrella policy that will cover this. The lady from the insurance company tells you that they will be settling the actual damages and the doctor's bills, but that the policy doesn't cover punitive damages and she suggests that you might wish to speak to an attorney.

You do. Your attorney looks into the case and finds out that the plaintiff is requesting a mountain of documents and the first one on the list is your corporate record book. It's empty! A chill goes down your spine. "What do they want that for?"

"It's customary in these cases for a plaintiff to examine your corporate records," says your attorney, "because they will often try to pierce through the corporation to get at your personal assets so that they will be available in case the assets of the corporation are insufficient to satisfy a potential judgment. Don't worry though, because I'm sure that you've kept them up to date. After all, I remember telling you how important they were when we incorporated the business."

You can just picture that empty book sitting on the shelf where it has been for the last five years. "Well, they aren't exactly in order," you reply squeamishly.

Your attorney informs you that you might just be in real trouble. You could lose your house, your boat and your kids' college fund.

Are corporate formalities important? You say, "Ha! Restaurants are a high liability business, my business isn't like that. Nobody slips and falls here! I'm a consultant."

Example: *Okay, let's try something different. Let's say that you are an Internet consultant. Nobody will sue you (famous last words, these days).*

Your Internet consulting firm goes along great for three years. No problems. You notice that business is a little flat, so you increase your advertising. Still though, it stays flat and gets flatter still. Why did you have to go and move to larger offices? What's going on, anyway?

Your bank balance gets smaller and smaller. Where have the customers gone? You miss a rent payment, and then another. Your landlord is getting upset. The only thing left to do is to move to a smaller location on the other side of town to cut your losses.

Your landlord doesn't seem to get it. If you couldn't pay a couple of months' rent, how can that idiot expect you to pay four and a half years of rent in one lump sum? A couple of months go by and you are served with a lawsuit from the landlord. He knew you were a corporation, why did he sue you and not the corporation? Your attorney looks over the rental agreement and wonders aloud, "Why did you sign this?" It's in your name; you signed as an individual!

The fact is that, even if you're in a "safe" business, if you don't watch out for the little things, the little things will kill you. It won't be anything dramatic. No eerie music in the background when you mess up, like in the movies. Everything will be normal and fine, until there's a problem and then jumping off a cliff will look good.

This is the importance of corporate formalities. When you incorporated, you expected to limit your liability. After all, limiting liability is one of the reasons people incorporate these days. But failing to do business in the corporate format can undo all of that if you don't do things right. That is why corporate formalities are important. The tragedy is that, doing things right really isn't very difficult and doesn't take much time, once you learn how.

Piercing the Corporate Veil

This is a concept which lurks in the backs of the minds of untold numbers of business people in every corner of America. It is sort of like the IRS for some; a dangerous, somewhat mysterious peril lurking in the dark, ready to pounce at the worst possible moment. Like the IRS, this concept becomes much less threatening when seen under the bright light of day. Also like the IRS, this concept must be given a healthy respect. For no matter how confident we may be, no matter how invincible we may think we are, there can be devastating consequences for those who don't do things right.

The whole idea of piercing the corporate veil is based on the alter ego theory. Under this theory, a corporation can be set aside by a court if it is just another self for its owners. In other words, if a court can't tell the difference between you and your corporation, then the court can disregard the corporation. Most text books on the subject will say something like this:

Alter Ego Doctrine

The requirements under the alter ego theory are: 1) The corporation must be influenced and governed by the person asserted to be its alter ego. 2) There must be a unity of interest and ownership such that one is inseparable from the other. 3) The facts must be such that adherence to the fiction of a separate entity would, under the circumstances, sanction fraud or promote injustice. The person or persons running and owning the corporation will be deemed its alter ego if their interest, and that of the corporation cannot be separated, and if maintaining the corporate entity would be unjust or create fraud.

Once again, separation is a major issue. What can you do to make the corporation look different than you? There are many possibilities and, of course, keeping proper and appropriate corporate formalities is a big factor. This is not the only factor, though. Keeping very careful and specific documents relating to transactions between yourself and the corporation is another.

In fact, as hard as it may seem to imagine, one of the most troubling areas for many business people is the area of commingling cash and assets. A sole proprietor can grab some cash from the till and use it to buy groceries on the way home, because the business and the proprietor are the same. Not so with a corporation. A sole proprietor can also grab his business inventory and convert it for personal use. Again, not so with a corporation.

Everybody is familiar with the concept of the home business. Actually, this sort of business is becoming more and more popular with the advent of home computers, faxes and all of the other electronics of recent years. A proprietor can easily do business at home. There may be an IRS red flag there, if you aren't careful, but that's about the extent of the problem. A corporation can't just live in your house without some sort of documentation creating a reasonable explanation for it, such as a lease. Without it, you are commingling assets. If you have a lease, or some other form of documentation, then everything is okay.

Another criterion in piercing the corporate veil is under capitalization.

A corporation must be capitalized with enough capital to give it a fair and reasonable chance of success. If not, then it doesn't appear to be real. Unhappily, there is no benchmark figure for how much is enough. Obviously, different businesses require differing amounts of capital to give them a reasonable chance of success. A manufacturer of aircraft engines will require considerably more capitalization than will an Internet consultant, for instance. In your planning, you must give this issue careful consideration.

Failure to keep the corporation in good standing

This one is so obvious that it's almost embarrassing to mention it, and yet, it is alarmingly common. Imagine that you are on the witness stand in a court case in which piercing your corporate veil is at issue, and you are maintaining what a great and viable corporation you own, when the plaintiff's attorney tells you that your corporation has been revoked by your state for failing to pay its annual fees, what are you going to say? You can avoid this disaster by simply making the required filings in your state and paying the required fees.

Failure to sign documents in the corporate fashion

As we have discussed earlier, this can be a major error. It can be avoided by signing in the manner indicated below:

AJAX CORPORATION

By: _____
President

In this instance, the person signing the document is clearly and obviously signing on behalf of the corporation, and not on his or her own behalf. No opponent can expect to assert that they thought the contract was with the individual, or that the individual misrepresented the nature of his or her involvement. It is clearly a corporate signature.

Failure to identify the business as a corporation

This error falls closely behind the last one. It is important that people you do business with know that they are doing business with a corporation, and not with an individual; especially if they are going to be extending credit. It may well be that they would not have extended the credit to the corporation and actually relied on the fact that they were dealing with you individually. It is much better to clear this up right from the beginning. If you wait until you are involved in litigation with this party, they are likely to devour you in court. If you want to provide a personal guarantee, that's fine, but do it from the beginning to avoid more problems than you ever imagined.

Failure to operate related corporations autonomously

If you have more than one corporation, be sure to operate them one at a time. Each one should have its own meetings, its own records, its own bank accounts, and so on. It's fine if you are a player in all of them, as long as they are operated separately.

In short, most of these things are things that you have heard about over the years. There really is nothing new or earth shattering, and none of these are really that tough, but they can add up to trouble if you aren't careful.

Finally, there is another issue when protection of your corporate veil is considered, and that is at the initial set up of your entity. If you want it to look different than you do, ask yourself these questions:

1. Is your corporation sharing the same physical address as you?

2. Since you are not commingling funds, does your corporation have its own bank account?

3. Does your corporation have its own phone line?

4. Since your corporation is a distinct entity, does it have a business license?

5. Since your corporation is not simply your "other self," does it ever do business with anybody but you?

Obviously, these are five test questions that you need to be able to answer "yes" to. Look over your situation carefully to ensure that you haven't made any mistakes, or overlooked anything. If you can answer, truthfully and verifiably, with the correct responses and, if you keep proper corporate records, then your corporation should be able to withstand most attacks and, any future adversaries

who travel down this road will do so for naught.

Piercing The Corporate Veil- Case Studies

In looking at the issue of piercing the corporate veil, several cases stand out as benchmarks for understanding how the courts view the issue. Please understand that what follows is a brief summary intended for explanation purposes only, and in no way should be considered a legal opinion. For such an opinion, we suggest that you consult your attorney.

The Stone v. Frederick Hobby Associates II, LLC, 2001 Conn. Super Docket #CV00181620S

The court found that the "instrumentality and identity rules" could be applied, under the facts of the case, to "pierce the corporate veil" of an LLC and hold the individual members personally liable.

Decision: Yes

Opinion: Turning to the facts of the case, the court found that Hobby and Leiendecker were the sole members of Hobby II, and that Hobby II's office located was located in Hobby's private home (although Hobby II did not pay any rental for such space). The court found that the evidence also demonstrated probable cause for the court to apply the identity rule. This was so, the court ruled because "Frederick L. Hobby, III and Sally M Leiendecker use Hobby II interchangeably with their own personal identities and with identities of other entities under their control, and failed to observe formalities for the limited liability company. The court reasoned that because of a lack of observance of formalities between the entities the court reasoned that because there was such unity of ownership and interest, Hobby II's existence as a separate entity had never really existed or had been terminated, and the existence of Hobby II as an LLC with a separate identity: would serve to defeat justice and equity by permitting the individual defendants to escape liability arising out of a "shell" operation conducted for their benefit.

DeWitt Truck Brokers, Inc., Appellee W. Ray Flemming Fruit Company and No.75-1653, United States Court of Appeals, Fourth Circuit May 13, 1976

In this action on debt, the plaintiff seeks, by piercing the corporate veil under the law of South Carolina, to impose individual liability on the president of the indebted corporation individually.

Question: Can the debt of the corporation fall directly onto its officers and/or shareholders?

Decision: Yes

Opinion: The district court found, and there was evidence to sustain the findings, that there was here a complete disregard of "corporate formalities" in the operation of the corporation, which functioned, not for the benefit of the stockholders, but only for the financial advantage of Flemming, who was the sole stockholder to receive one penny of profit from the corporation in the decade or more that it operated, and who made during that period all the corporate decisions and dominated the corporation's operations.

One fact which all authorities consider significant in the inequity, and particularly so in the case of the one-man or closely held corporation, is whether the corporation was grossly undercapitalized for the purposes of the corporate undertaking. There have been numerous cases lost for undercapitalization.

John C. CULPEPPER, Jr. and Culpepper Properties, Inc., Respondents Supreme Court of Texas Dec 12, 1990.

Mancorp, Inc. sued John C. Culpepper, Jr. and Culpepper Properties, Inc. for breach of a construction contract. Mancorp alleged that it had performed the contract by completing work on the First Bank of Galleria building in Bryan, Texas, and was owed

$510,650, the unpaid balance under the contract.

Question: Was Culpepper Properties simply an alter ego of John C. Culpepper, Jr.

Decision: Yes

Opinion: The jury found....that Culpepper Properties, Inc. was the alter ego of John C. Culpepper , Jr... Culpepper and Culpepper Properties, Inc. moved for judgment non obstante veredicto on the jury's alter ego finding. The trial court rendered judgment for Mancorp in the amount of $221,273.10.

Rowland v. Lapire
308, 662 P.2nd 1332 Nevada (1983)

Glen and Martin Rowland, officers, directors, and shareholders of the Rowland Corporation, which was the holder of a general contractor's license had been sued by Eugene and Judy Lapire, who had obtained a judgment. This action had, among other things, resulted in the piercing of the Rowland Corporation's corporate veil, and the judgment being entered against Glen and Martin Rowland individually. Among the several points which were contested by the Rowlands when they appealed the case to the Nevada Supreme Court was

that insufficient grounds existed for piercing of their corporation.

Question: Is under capitalization sufficient grounds for asserting the Alter Ego Doctrine?

Decision: No

Opinion: The opinion of the Court held that "in order to apply the alter ego doctrine, the following requirements must be met: 1) the corporation must be influenced and governed by the person asserted to be its alter ego; 2) there must be such unity of interest and ownership that one is inseparable from the other; 3) the facts must be such that adherence to the fiction of a separate entity would, under the circumstances, sanction a fraud or promote injustice."

The corporation was undercapitalized, and at the time of trial it had a negative net worth. The Court's opinion goes on to make several interesting observations: "Although no formal directors or shareholders meetings were ever held, Martin testified that in lieu thereof he personally phoned the directors and shareholders regarding corporate business. No dividends were paid to shareholders, nor did the officers or directors receive salaries. The corporation did not have a minute book, nor is there evidence that any minutes were kept. The corporation did obtain a general contractor's license and a framing contractor's license, both in its name. It also obtained a surety bond in the amount of $5,000. The corporation also obtained Workman's Compensation insurance and transacted business with the Employment Security Department. In addition, there was a corporate checking account."

Finally, the Court held: "Although the evidence does show that the corporation was undercapitalized and that there was little existence separate and apart from Martin and Glen Rowland, we conclude that the evidence is insufficient to support a finding that appellants.

Wyatt v. Bowers,
747 P.2d 881 (Nev. 1987)

John Bowers and Frederick Boulware, Jr. sued Ancillary Services Corporation over an equipment lease which had gone bad. They persuaded the District Court to pierce the corporate veil of Ancillary Services Corporation and enter a judgment against Oscar Wyatt, individually, for damages. In taking the case to the Supreme Court, Wyatt asserted that, while he was an investor in Ancillary Services Corporation, he was not its alter-ego.

Question: Does merely influencing and governing a corporation mean that the unity and interest is such that the corporation becomes the alter-ego of the person influencing and governing it?

Decision: No.

Opinion: In answering the question the court said, "Ancillary was formed as an investment for Wyatt. Adequate funds were injected into the company for capitalization purposes. Wyatt was neither a director nor an officer of the company. Wyatt's personal funds and assets were never co-mingled with those possessed by Ancillary. There was no diversion of corporate funds into or out of Ancillary and into the pockets of Wyatt. No evidence can be found in the record which would indicate that Wyatt treated the corporate assets as his own individual holdings. These factors weigh heavily against the application of the alter-ego doctrine."

"Although it is possible that Wyatt influenced Ancillary operations, it cannot be said that he governed the business."

"The mere fact that officers and directors of Ancillary were confidantes of Wyatt, while relevant, is insufficient without more to show that Ancillary was Wyatt's alter-ego. Moreover, merely influencing and governing a corporation does not necessarily demonstrate the unity of interest and ownership resulting in the requisite inseparability of a corporation and shareholder."

Polaris Industrial Corporation v.
Kaplan 747 P.2d 884 (Nev. 1987)

Polaris was owed money by two

different Nevada corporations, both of which had gone out of business. In their suit they asserted that Michael Kaplan and Jerome Kaplan were alter-egos of the two corporations. Polaris then presented evidence which indicated that the Kaplans had systematically used bank counter checks to withdraw funds from the corporate accounts, leaving the corporations unable to pay the note.

Question: Does the siphoning off of corporate funds for personal use constitute a unity of interest and ownership sufficient to pierce the corporate veil?

Decision: Yes.

Opinion: The court held that there are three general requirements for application of the alter-ego doctrine. "(1) The corporation must be influenced and governed by the person asserted to be the alter-ego; (2) there must be such unity of interest and ownership that one is inseparable from the other; and (3) the facts must be such that adherence to the corporate fiction of a separate entity would, under the circumstances, sanction fraud or promote injustice."

The court went on to explain how it arrived at its decision. "In determining whether a unity of interest exists between the individual and corporation,

courts have looked to factors like co-mingling of funds, under capitalization, unauthorized diversion of funds, treatment of corporate assets as the individual's own, and failure to observe corporate formalities. These facts may indicate the existence of an alter-ego relationship, but are not conclusive. There is no litmus test to determine when the corporate fiction should be disregarded. The result depends on circumstances of the case."

The court noted that Kaplan and his partner Davis had diverted a significant amount of funds from their corporation which could have been used to pay their debts. These funds were used for Kaplan's and Davis' personal benefit. In addition, the corporation was found to have paid directly the personal bills of Kaplan and Davis. An auditor, hired by Polaris to audit the corporation's books, determined that, "CRI would have had the funds to pay its debts if the withdrawals had not further limited the capitalization of the corporation."

The court concluded, "We are compelled to recognize that the district court clearly reached a wrong conclusion in determining that Michael Kaplan had not been shown to be an alter-ego of IMS and CRI.

"Accordingly, we... reverse the judgment as to Michael Kaplan."

Chapter 10: The Importance of Corporate Formalities

Summary

The conclusion to disregard the corporate entity may not, however, rest on a single factor, whether undercapitalization or disregard of corporate formalities, but must involve a number of factors.

What you do after you incorporate is more important than the steps you take to incorporate. Many people incorporate and are excited to get on the road to success but they fail to follow corporate formalities and document important business decision.

In fact the greatest risk is placed on small closely held company's because they often over look corporate formalities and make decisions that only benefit themselves. All company actions should be looked at as if you had 300 shareholders and whether the decision you are making now benefits the whole or just an individual.

At the back of this chapter we have included a Corporate Health Checklist. If you are already incorporated or you are thinking about incorporating, take a few minutes to go through the checklist and make sure you are starting your company on the right path.

Your Corporate Health Checklist - Are You Meeting The Legal and Critical Requirements That Keep Your Company Strong?

If we asked you how healthy your business is *right now*, what would you say? Unfortunately, many business owners can't answer that question because they don't have a clear picture of what is required to maintain the legal validity of their companies.

This simple to use checklist is designed for corporations or limited liability companies, from brand new start-ups to existing businesses, you must meet the minimal requirements to stay in compliance.

Score your company's health. Simply click Yes or No, if the question doesn't apply you can skip it.

Establishing A Solid Foundation

1. Have You Completed A Business Plan? ❏Yes ❏No

2. Have You Issued Ownership For Your Company-Shares Or Membership Interest? ❏Yes ❏No

3. Have Your Bylaws Or Operating Agreement Been Certified? ❏Yes ❏No

4. Have You Filed All Your Business Licenses/State/Country/Federal? ❏Yes ❏No

5. Have You Filed For Your Employer Identification Number (EIN)? ❏Yes ❏No

6. Have You Set Up A System For Bookkeeping/Accounting? ❏Yes ❏No

7. Have You Opened A Separate Bank Account For Your Business? ❏Yes ❏No

8. If You Are Using A DBA (Doing Business As) Has It Been Filed? ❏Yes ❏No

9. Have The Shareholders Voted For The Directors? ❏Yes ❏No

10. Have The Directors Officially Accepted Their Positions? ❏Yes ❏No

11. Have You Held Your First Board Of Directors Meeting? ❏Yes ❏No

12. Do You Have The Articles Of Incorporation Or Articles Of Organization For An LLC? ❏Yes ❏No

13. Is Your Company Doing Business In Another State? ❏Yes ❏No

14. Has It Qualified To Do Business In Those States? ❏Yes ❏No

15. Have You Notified Your Vendors You Are Doing Business As A Corporation/LLC? ❏Yes ❏No

Complete If Your Corporation Or LLC Is Over A Year Old

1. Have You Checked With The Secretary Of State In Which You Incorporated To Make Sure Your Company Is Current? ❑Yes ❑No

2. Have You Filed Your Business Tax Return? ❑Yes ❑No

3. Do You Have An Emergency Action Plan In Place For You Business? ❑Yes ❑No

4. Do You Have An Exit Plan? ❑Yes ❑No

5. Have You Taken Out Personally Guaranteed Loans For The Business? ❑Yes ❑No

6. Was Your Company Properly Capitalized? ❑Yes ❑No

7. Are You Strict About Keeping Your Personal And Business Finances Separate? ❑Yes ❑No

8. Did You Formally Document Your Annual Meeting With Minutes? ❑Yes ❑No

9. Are Meetings Of The Board Of Directors Regularly Scheduled And Conducted? ❑Yes ❑No

10. Are Shareholder/Member Meetings Regularly Scheduled And Conducted? ❑Yes ❑No

11. Have Resolutions Been Completed For The Following Acts?

    Compensation To Officers ❑Yes ❑No

    Authorization To Sign Contracts ❑Yes ❑No

    Sale Of Assets ❑Yes ❑No

    Acceptance Of Loans ❑Yes ❑No

    Employee Benefit Plan ❑Yes ❑No

    Opening A Bank Account ❑Yes ❑No

Corporate Health Score: _____

This checklist is a general guideline on items you should have done already. If you feel you need help please call 1.800.648.0966 and we would be happy to provide you with a complimentary review of your Corporate Health Checklist.

NOTES

11 Taking the Steps to Protect Your Assets

- *Putting Yourself at Risk*
- *A Right and Wrong Way to Obtain*
- *Asset Protection*
- *Summary*
- *Frivolous Lawsuits*

As you can see at the end of this chapter, there is an epidemic in this country that is spiraling out of control: frivolous lawsuits. No company regardless of size, is immune from the tidal wave of lawsuits in America. In 2003 there were 24 million lawsuits filed by 1 million attorneys.

Americans are sue happy. Pick up the paper, listen to the news or your favorite talk show; everybody is suing everybody. Why? We are the only country in the world that doesn't have a loser pays system. You can sue somebody and not pay the attorney a dime if they think the person you are suing has assets they can take. Most attorneys will work on a contingency basis.

In a loser pays system, if you want to sue somebody you have to put up a bond, you have to pay an attorney and if you lose you pay all the legal fees for the defendant. Can you imagine how many frivolous lawsuits would be stopped today if we had this system? Unfortunately, until we do have a better system in place it is up to you to make sure you've done everything you can to protect your assets.

"But, it won't happen to me!" If you are a doctor, lawyer, CPA, contractor, landlord, daycare provider, you are in a high risk profession. But, it doesn't stop there. Just owning your own business makes you a target because you are perceived as being wealthy.

Those people who don't think they are at risk are usually the ones being targeted because they haven't taken the steps necessary to protect themselves.

It's no wonder that more and more business people are taking steps to protect their assets, yet what can they really do? What exactly is asset protection? Is it legal? Is it moral?

First, let's look at what asset protection

actually is. Asset protection is the lawful process by which a person or entity makes its assets difficult for a creditor to attach. Often, this involves setting up roadblocks to discourage people from wanting to attack. The idea here is to take steps to make you less of a target. Let's face it, many people in the general public feel that business people are all rich, ruthless individuals who gain obscene profits by cheating ordinary people. Simply by being in business, you become a target.

It's one thing to be a perceived target, but quite another to be a target in actuality. This is often the case. Consider what happens when someone goes into an attorney's office to discuss a typical suit.

Take Jill, who was involved in an auto accident. Her car was damaged, she was a little shaken up, and sore the next day. At the urging of her boyfriend, she called an attorney they had seen advertised on TV, and soon had an appointment. What had caught her boyfriend's attention was that the ad said that there was no charge for the initial consultation, and that if a case had merit, you would never pay anything.

When Jill went to see the attorney three days after the accident, he asked her some questions about what had happened, and made a copy of the accident report. Then he told Jill that he would look into the merits of the case, and get back with her in a week.

At her next appointment, Jill was thrilled to hear the attorney thought that she really had a great case. The other motorist had seriously erred, and Jill's chances of recovery were very promising. In fact, Jill was told that she should go see a specialist. The attorney was so nice, he even suggested that she see a Chiropractor to make sure everything was all right. The Chiropractor found that she had sustained a potentially serious neck injury that would have to be treated immediately to prevent lasting complications. Jill's boyfriend was delighted that he had suggested this attorney, because he had earned major points.

Jill was thrilled, because she certainly didn't need a lasting injury, and she didn't need to come up with any money for either the attorney or the doctor, and could expect to receive a tidy little sum for herself, after all was said and done.

On the other side of this case, Claire realized that she shouldn't have changed lanes when she did. She hadn't seen Jill's car, she really hadn't. That night, she and her husband had talked it all over, and she felt much better. This, after all, is what insurance is for, right? They would take care of everything. Her agent had said so. The damage to both cars, the headaches, everything. Claire had almost forgotten the whole thing when one day her assistant told her that there was someone in the outer office who had something for her. It was Jill's lawsuit. Jill was suing for a quarter of a million dollars! How could this be? That was even more than her insurance limit. She could lose her house and her business. What had happened? Jill's car didn't have more than a couple of thousand dollars in damage, and Jill wasn't hurt…

Here's the part that neither Claire nor Jill knew about. After Jill had left the attorney's office, the attorney contacted an asset search company. The asset search people ran a routine check on Claire, and found out that she had a home, a business, and signed on several bank accounts, and that she was worth about a quarter million dollars. When Jill's attorney received the report, he realized that the case had "merit" and was ready to take it on a contingency fee basis, meaning that Jill didn't need to put up any money, and the attorney would keep a substantial percentage of the collected amounts from the judgment after court. Of course, he would also deduct the costs incurred, including those of the Chiropractor. Jill would receive the rest. Even though Claire's insurance only covered fifty thousand dollars, Jill and her attorney could proceed with a larger suit, because there was money to collect from Claire.

Let's take another look at this case. Suppose Jill's attorney had found out the asset search indicated that Claire had nothing to take. She had no home, no business, no bank accounts, and nothing else, except for her insurance. How much "merit" would the case have had then? Enough for the attorney to take it on a contingency? In that case, perhaps an insurance settlement would have looked better! In the first instance, Claire was a target. In the second scenario, Claire was not an attractive target because she had nothing to lose.

Asset Protection is Not

Before we continue, let's take a moment to discuss what asset protection is not. Asset protection is not about defrauding people. It is not about skipping out on your bills or other obligations, it is not about cheating and it is also not about taxes. If it were, it would not be legal, moral or proper. Any ethical businessperson must realize that he or she must pay their bills, their other obligations, and their taxes. If an ethical person or business damages someone, then they will not only need to compensate the damaged party, but they should also want to do so. If you are someone who takes pride in your accomplishments and doing your best, you will have no problem with this concept. This is precisely what insurance policies are all about, compensating people who are damaged and making them whole again. But insurance policies don't cover punitive damages, and in many cases, if they do have to pay out, you'll have trouble getting coverage again.

Sadly, however, there are not only people in this world who wish to get away without taking care of their obligations, there are also people who desire to profit inappropriately from a claim. They see opportunity in filing claims, in claiming damage that was not incurred, and telling lies in court. They file frivolous lawsuits because they realize that someone will settle, because it's less expensive than fighting the case. They prey on the unsuspecting, or on those who have something to lose. Such people have plenty of help, too. Attorneys sometimes wonder why their profession is held in such low regard, yet those who have been the victims of unscrupulous lawyers who make fortunes abusing the legal system know full well why they are held in low esteem.

Of course, politics enters the scene, as it always does when money is involved. Trial lawyers make millions in encouraging such claims. They are huge contributors to political campaigns, and have influence well in excess of their numbers in the legislative halls of this nation. Tort reform never seems to get out of committee time and again, and for those of us who are targets, there is no relief in sight. So who is immoral, the person who seeks to protect what he has worked for, or the one who seeks to take it away with a frivolous claim? You be the judge. Who is unethical, the one who seeks to limit his liability, or the one who adds millions in punitive damage

claims to a small injury? Again, you be the judge. Who is in the wrong, the one who seeks to protect his livelihood, or the unscrupulous attorney who seeks to enrich himself by inflicting ruin on other people?

The whole concept of asset protection is to level the playing field when liability claims arise. The playing field needs to be leveled, because there are no contingency fees for defendants. There is also no "loser pays" system in the United States, like there is in all of the other industrialized nations. Why, you ask? Because trial lawyers would lose money! That's why they are so aggressive in the political arena.

What happens if you are sued, anyway? Here's a quick sketch. First you contact defense counsel, who must file an answer to the complaint, usually within thirty days. Never mind the fact that the plaintiff may have taken a year to file, you must respond in a month. Your attorney isn't going to work on a contingency, because there isn't going to be a collection. Your attorney needs a retainer to get started, $5,000, $10,000, $20,000? That of course is money you must pay right now, then, each month you'll need to pay more.

What if you don't have the money? You'll lose the case. What if you don't respond? You'll lose the case. After you initially respond, then you have what are usually several years to defend the case, paying out more and more money each and every month to keep your attorney on the job. What if you decide to quit paying? You lose.

Then, the trial comes, and more money, more agony, more worry. Then let's say you win, and you don't lose everything to the plaintiff, you're out tens of thousands of dollars, perhaps hundreds of thousands. How much can you recover from the plaintiff? Nothing. What about your mental anguish? Can you sue? Of course not.

What has the plaintiff lost? Not one cent, is the answer. Who was the winner? Your lawyer. Is this justice? Yes, in America, this is justice!

It would be difficult to imagine that anyone who reads this will not see why the playing field needs to be leveled, but how? The answer is simple; don't be a target. The way to not be a target is also simple; be poor! This may seem silly, but when was the last time you picked up the paper and read about a multi-million dollar judgment against a homeless person? Yet every day you can pick up a paper and read about such judgments against millionaires. The reason is that a homeless person doesn't have anything to take. They don't have enough in the way of assets to start the wheels of justice turning against them!

The obvious problem here is that you don't want to be poor. In fact, that is precisely why you went into business in the first place.

Consider this story: In the early 1990's it was widely reported that Donald Trump was experiencing financial difficulties. Apparently he had made a killing in real estate in the 80's, but with the recession that had hit in the early 90's, the tide had turned. A reporter asked him at that time how much he was worth, and to the amazement of the reporter, Trump pointed to a homeless man across the street, and said that he was worth a hundred million less than the homeless man. Looking back on things, which one would you rather be; the homeless person, or Donald Trump? Trump lived pretty well during that time, as everyone knows. He was worth less than the homeless man because Trump was in debt. Judging from the newspaper accounts, Trump still had plenty of walking around money, though!

Think back to Jill and Claire. In the second scenario, an asset search revealed that Claire had no assets. What would happen if she had both assets and secured debt? Let's revisit the first scenario, where Claire had a house, a business and bank accounts. Suppose that an asset search revealed a house mortgaged to the hilt, and business mortgaged to the hilt, and bank accounts mortgaged to the hilt. Jill's attorney would have looked at the report, and found no "merit" to the case because there was nothing to collect, because the

Chapter 11: Taking the Steps to Protect Your Assets

existing creditors would have to be paid from Claire's assets before Jill and her attorney could see a dime, and if Claire was mortgaged to hilt, there would be nothing left. Yet Claire would still have the house, business and accounts. In fact, Claire would be just like Donald Trump, only with smaller numbers. This is an example of leveling the playing field. Poor Jill would have to "settle" for being compensated for the damages she really had incurred, and wouldn't have had the opportunity to make a profit from an accident. That is one form of asset protection.

Incorporating a business is another form of asset protection, because by incorporating, you place a non-person in the line of fire. Remember Jack? He had a very serious problem because someone sued his business and obtained a life ruining judgment against him. Could his situation have been different? Consider what may have happened had Jack been incorporated. The plaintiff's suit would most likely have been against the business, and not against Jack personally, as a sole proprietor. The judgment would not have reached Jack's personal assets in that case, and although the situation would still have been very bad, at least Jack would not have lost his home and all of his personal assets.

Corporations can provide additional benefits and protection as well. To see this more completely, you need to understand that a corporation is not only an artificial person; a corporation is also a citizen. In fact, it is a citizen of the state in which it is incorporated. Thus, a corporation that is incorporated in the state of Wisconsin is a citizen of the state of Wisconsin. If it travels to Minnesota, it is a visitor there, and if it decides to conduct its business in Minnesota, it must follow the laws of Minnesota while it is there, but it can return to Wisconsin at any time, and deal with Minnesota no further.

If you think about it, this is really no different than you as a natural person, being a citizen of the nation in which you were born. If you were born in the United States, then you are a citizen of the United States. If you travel to Morocco, you must follow the laws of Morocco while you are there, yet when you return to America, your connection with Morocco is over. During the time you are in Morocco, you still retain your US citizenship, and have all of the rights and privileges of US citizenship, and the same is true of a corporation.

A Right & Wrong Way To Obtain Asset Protection

Let's take a look at what we define as the interpretation of asset protection. It is often bandied about, and I think a lot of people just assume they know what it means. It's actually an area of the practice of law relating to how one arranges their assets. I think the definition we have put together is probably the most concise and powerful definition available.

Asset protection is a collection of tax and legal strategies that arrange the control of assets so as to preserve value in the face of taxation, lawsuits, claims and future creditors without resorting to what is known as fraudulent transfer.

Fraudulent transfer is the movement of value-whether it's property, money, stocks or what have you from your name, if you're the defendant, to someone else.

Good example: You get the receiving end of a lawsuit and you run out and transfer your home to your sister for a dollar. You transfer your stock account worth three hundred thousand to your kids. You take rental property that you might own and transfer it to your mom.

If you're in the middle of a lawsuit, what's likely to happen is that plaintiff is going to march into court and say, "Your Honor, the defendant is engaging in fraudulent transfer to avoid paying me and to avoid having these assets available to me when I win my claim." Now in the United States, there is a presumption that, that is true. Unlike a criminal case where the plaintiff, the prosecutor, has to prove their case beyond a reasonable doubt, in the case of a fraudulent transfer claim against you, you're presumed guilty until proven innocent. In fraudulent transfer claims, you're presumed to have done it, and it's up to the defendant to prove that they didn't. Moreover, anybody who's found to be involved in an act of fraudulent transfer can receive severe sanctions by the court.

So what we want to do is structure your assets, structure ownership and control to avoid the issue of fraudulent conveyance ever coming up. If, in fact, the assets are controlled by entities which are arranged in such a fashion to avoid these problems, then, of course, you will not be engaging in fraudulent conveyance, because you will have already put into place structures that protect you long before they are ever needed.

What lawsuit protection is not: It is not a tax evasion or a tax scam. The doers of dastardly deeds open up bank accounts, they don't tell the government that they have income there and profits growing there, etc. That's tax evasion. But setting up lawsuit protection structures is not a tax evasion scam.

Summary

Unfortunately, at the time this book is written we lived in a litigious society and perception is everything. If you are a small business owner you are perceived as being wealthy by your neighbors, family and employees, which makes you a target.

Running your own business is risky but, you shouldn't have to risk it all to live the American dream. By forming a corporate structure you are establishing a barrier between your personal and business assets. Achieving asset protection should be the number one item on your agenda.

Without a sure and solid asset protection plan there is no need to worry about tax saving strategies.

You have a choice. You cannot take risk which eliminates possibility of reward or you can take the right steps to protect yourself from frivolous litigation.

Frivolous Lawsuits

A jury awarded a woman $178,000 in damages because her former fiancé broke off their seven week engagement. She was awarded $93,000 for pain and suffering, $60,000 for loss of income, and $25,000 in psychiatric expenses.

• •

A man asked a woman to dance. While doing a spin, the woman fell and broke her finger. She sued her dance partner, and a jury awarded her $220,000.

• •

A drunk driver, who was speeding, went through several detour signs and crashed. He sued the engineering company that designed the road, the contractor, the subcontractors and the state highway department. Five years later, all the defendants agreed to make the case go away and settled it for $35,000. However, the engineering firm had to pay $200,000 in legal costs.

• •

A California lawyer is suing a phone company because in the company's yellow pages, her legal practice was accidentally listed under the heading of "Reptiles". The listing was in between "Prehistoric Pets" and "Radical Reptiles". Since the phone number mix-up, the attorney claims she has been subjected to many jokes and hostile phone calls, hissing sounds as she walks by, and other forms of ridicule. She is seeking $100,000 in damages.

• •

A multi-millionaire trial lawyer filed class actions against several cell phone companies and service providers. The suits do not claim anyone has suffered injury, but seek money for headsets to reduce radiation exposure, plus punitive damages.

• •

A nationwide class action was filed against major toothbrush manufacturers arguing that the product was actually dangerous when used improperly, possibly causing tooth abrasion and other problems.

• •

In a class action suit against Cheerios over a food additive-with no evidence of injury to any consumers-lawyers were paid nearly $2 million in fees, which works out to approximately $2,000 per hour. Consumers in the class received coupons for a free box of cereal.

• •

In a class action involving 6 million customers of Southwestern Bell in Oklahoma, Missouri, Texas, Kansas and Arkansas, the company was sued for allegedly misrepresenting a service plan to consumers, despite any conclusive evidence. As reported in *The Austin American Statesman*, the trial lawyer who filed the suit even admitted that he had uncovered little, if any, evidence of misconduct, and that the case was settled simply to avoid the high cost of litigation. The result? Consumers got a $15 credit. The lawyer got $4 million.

• •

A man drove into his fiancée while riding bumper cars at Disney World. The injured woman sued both her fiancée and the company. A jury found the woman 14 percent at fault, her fiancée 85 percent at fault and Disney, one percent liable. At trial, Florida's spousal tort immunity law prevented the woman from seeking any award from her-now-husband. Thus, although Disney was deemed one percent at fault, it had to pay 86 percent of the judgment.

• •

A class action results in a $349 million award to flight attendants due to second-hand smoke. The flight attendants receive nothing while attorney fees are set at $49 million. The rest goes to a foundation established to research second-hand smoke.

• •

Out of control asbestos litigation and non-meritorious claims force 28 companies into bankruptcy, jeopardizing future payments to the truly sick and paying victims as little as 10¢ on the dollar.

• •

A woman suing Universal Studios contends the theme park operator's annual Halloween Horror Nights haunted house attraction is too scary and caused her emotional distress.

• •

A couple questions their bank about $91.33 deduction. They learn the charge is for the legal fees in a successful class action against the bank. The couple's award in the lawsuit is $2.19. So, they actually lose $89.14. Meanwhile, the trial lawyers split $8.5 million in fees.

A Florida man sues six bars and liquor stores and the local electric company after he sustains injuries from his drunken climb up an electrical tower. The "victim" climbed over a fence and a locked gate to reach the power lines.

NOTES

12 Lawsuit Protection Using Multi-state Strategies

- *Warbucks/Red, Inc. Strategy*
- *What Happens If You Are Sued Personally*

As we briefly saw in the case of Jill and Claire, "poverty" can be quite an asset protection technique, at least on the surface. If Claire had no assets to take away, Jill had little incentive to proceed with a lawsuit. If Jill were to proceed anyway, she could make Claire's life somewhat miserable, but she would not be able to recover anything if Claire didn't have it to take. But how is this helpful, after all, isn't the whole point of being in business to accumulate assets and net worth?

Let's look at another example. *Sean wanted to go into business, so he did some research and discovered that he could open a small retail store in his hometown. He got all of his cash together, formed a corporation, and rented some space in a small strip mall. He realized that he was running low on cash, so he went to the bank to get a loan. His banker agreed to make a loan of $50,000 to Sean's corporation, if Sean would personally guarantee the note. Of course, Sean was only too happy to do so, so everything*

was fine. Sean got his money, and bought display shelves and inventory, and opened for business. The bank took all of Sean's fixtures and inventory for collateral to secure the loan, and filed a UCC-1 Financing Statement against the assets. So far, so good.

Everything went along just fine for about six months. Sean's store was reasonably successful, and Sean was very pleased. One day, a client named Chris came into the store, but slipped and fell. As would be expected, Chris sought an attorney to file a lawsuit. The attorney discovered that there wasn't much "merit" to the case, because the bank was first in line for Sean's assets, because of the loan, and the UCC filing. With the bank already in line as a secured creditor against all of the assets of the store, what could Chris take? What could Chris' attorney use to ensure payment of a contingency fee? Nothing, because the bank would have to be paid in full before anybody else could receive a cent from Sean's assets, and there just weren't enough assets to go around.

Business people refer to this situation as being "judgment proof". Sean was judgment proof from any creditor other than the bank. The bank was still in a good position to be paid as long as

Sean made his payments to the bank. In a situation such as this, Chris would probably need to seek relief from Sean's insurance. Chris is compensated for the injury sustained in the fall, Sean stays in business, and everyone is as happy as can be. The only flaw in the situation has already been identified, and that is the need for Sean to make the monthly payments. If Sean doesn't, the bank takes everything, and the ballgame is over for Sean's business.

What makes this concept work, is not just the fact that the bank made a loan to Sean, and it's not just that the bank has collateral. What makes this work is that the bank filed a UCC-1 Financing Statement. By doing so, the bank has "priority of lien" over any subsequent claims. Priority of lien means that the bank must be paid in full before any other creditors can come along after the bank's UCC-1. Priority is not a new concept. It is what happens whenever you finance a house and the finance company requires a mortgage or deed of trust on the property. By recording this instrument, the bank or finance company puts the world on notice that they have a collateral interest in the property. The result is that anyone can find out about the interest, and if anyone wants to loan you money against that house, they will know that they are in line after the bank or finance company. The same holds true for a judgment. The judgment creditor would be in second position behind your lender, and can't be paid until the lender is paid in full.

There can be any number of people in line, but the rule is that the first one to file, is the first one paid, the second to file is the second paid, and so on. It is for this reason that interest rates are typically higher for second and third mortgages than they are for first mortgages. If the property were ever auctioned off to pay debts, it will be more and more difficult for lenders to recover their money the farther down the list they are. A potential plaintiff would be well advised to know where they might find themselves in line before they get a judgment, if they are really sure that they want to be paid.

Notice that in our example, Sean's bank filed a UCC-1 financing statement, rather than a mortgage or deed of trust. This is because Sean's business had "personal property" and not real estate. Please understand here that there are two types of property, real property (real estate) and personal property. Personal property is everything that is not real estate. This would include inventory, furniture, art, jewelry, cash, accounts receivable and so on. When dealing with real estate, a lender will file either a mortgage or a deed of trust, depending on the state where the property is located. When dealing with personal property, you file a UCC-1 financing statement. If this is new to you, you can think of a UCC-1 as a mortgage for personal property.

When the mortgage, deed of trust, and/or UCC-1 is filed, we would say that the creditor has "perfected" his security interest in the assets of the debtor. Perfecting a security interest is what establishes priority of lien, and is a critical step to take if someone wants to have that place in line secure. Even though a lender may have a valid promissory note, and a security agreement which describes the collateral for the repayment of the note, if his security interest is not perfected, by filing the necessary document on the public record, they don't have a place in line if subsequent debts come along. This is a very crucial fact to remember as we continue our discussion!

Now, what would happen if, instead of the bank having made the loan to Sean's business, Sean had a preferred state corporation such as a corporation in Nevada make the loan? Here's what Sean would have had to do:

First Sean's preferred state corporation negotiates with Sean's home state corporation about the loan amount and repayment terms. Next, when they agree, Sean signs a promissory note for the loan. Third, Sean's preferred state corporation wants collateral for repayment of the note, just like a bank would. Sean must sign a security agreement which sets forth the description of the collateral, and the provisions in case of a default. Then, the preferred state corporation insists that Sean sign a UCC-1 on behalf of his home state corporation. Then and only then does the lending corporation write Sean's home state corporation a check, and it files the UCC-1 in Sean's home state.

At this point, reenter Chris. When Chris is looking to sue Sean's business, the outcome would be the same as if Sean had borrowed from the bank, because the preferred state corporation did exactly the same things that the bank did, and has the same rights that the bank had. The difference in the second situation is that if Sean had difficulty making his monthly payments, he would probably have had a much easier time dealing with his corporation than he would have in dealing with the bank!

At this point, let's take names out of the picture, and look at it in conceptual terms. You have a business in your home state. You incorporate that business for all of the reasons we have already covered. Let's call the home state corporation Red, Inc. Then, you establish a corporation in a preferred state; let's say in tax-free Nevada, called Warbucks Nevada, Inc. Warbucks and Red, Inc. get together and agree that Warbucks will loan money to Red, Inc. in the amount of $100,000. Red, Inc. signs a note, a security agreement and a UCC-1, which Warbucks files in Red, Inc.'s home state. Let's say that the interest on the note is 24%, because this is a difficult loan to get, and because it is at 100% loan to value. Since Nevada has no usury laws, the interest rate can be at whatever rate the parties agree to but it should be reasonable.

Now that this has been accomplished,

what happens if someone wants to file a suit against Red, Inc.? They find out that Red, Inc. is heavily indebted to Warbucks, and there are no assets from which to recover a judgment. The attorney isn't particularly interested in a contingency fee, and the plaintiff has to lay out real cash to get the suit moving. Once again, it is quite likely that the plaintiff decides to settle for what his real damages are. But let's say that he doesn't, and goes on with a suit, and is awarded a judgment. He calls you at Red, Inc. and demands to be paid. You tell him that he can just have the whole corporation, because it is hopelessly in debt to this company in Nevada, who just called its note. Probably the next thing you will hear is a dial tone!

What if you had this structure, but there was never a lawsuit? Red, Inc. must pay interest to Warbucks on the loan it received, 24% interest on $100,000 would be $24,000 per year (simple interest). If your home state has an income tax that is based on net income, the interest paid by Red, Inc. to Warbucks would be deductible in your home state, and taxable in Nevada. Since Nevada has no income tax, the interest you pay to Warbucks would reduce your state income tax, and be earned state income tax free in Nevada, allowing you to significantly reduce the income taxes you pay to your home state, as an added benefit to protecting your business assets.

This strategy, called the Warbucks/Red, Inc. strategy cannot only save your assets, but in most cases can reduce your state income taxes if structured correctly.

This strategy is one of the most powerful business tools that exist for asset protection purposes. Yet, it must be used carefully. If you wait until a lawsuit is filed to get started, you have waited too long. This is something to establish while your legal seas are calm, when there are no creditors, no lawsuits, and no one who is ready to file one.

The law does not allow you to set up any structure which has as its purpose the obstruction, delay or hindrance of a legitimate creditor. Thus, if someone is owed by Red, Inc., they need to be paid. However, if there is no creditor, no claim, and potential claim, then Red, Inc. can do whatever it wants. If someone comes along years later, then they may proceed against Red, Inc. with their eyes wide open, and take their chances. In such a case, you have effectively evened the playing field, and moved to encourage your claimant to accept compensation for real and reasonable damages, and not astronomical ridiculous and devastating judgments.

Up to this point, we have only considered the strategy dealing with protecting the assets of Red, Inc. as a corporation. However, there are situations where you may not wish to incorporate. Even though incorporating your home state business is a very important step in protecting your assets, if you are in a circumstance where this is inappropriate, you can still have protection from Warbucks. To do so, simply insert yourself in the place of Red, Inc., and do everything else, and you will have personal protection. What is more often the case, however, would be a business person who wanted not only to protect their business assets, but also their personal assets. In a case such as this, and this is probably more common than not, there are a number of things you can do.

First, suppose you were concerned that not only your home state corporation could be sued, but that such an event would also include you personally. As you know, in most situations where a corporation borrows money, a lender will require a personal guarantee from the corporation's owner or principal. Very often, the lender will also require that the guarantor put up additional collateral for such a loan, very often the person's home. Warbucks in your situation may do the same thing. By requiring you to sign a personal guarantee and add additional collateral, and then filing a UCC-1 against you personally, as well as recording a deed of trust or mortgage against your real estate, you would find yourself in the same position as Red, Inc., judgment proof.

Alternative Consideration

The strategy we have looked at thus far assumes that Warbucks has the cash available to fund a loan to Red, Inc. A transaction of this nature needs to be funded, because if it is not, the encumbrances against Red, Inc. are not likely to withstand scrutiny. What happens, then, if Warbucks doesn't have the cash necessary to make this situation work? Debt can be created by more than just a cash loan. Anything of value can be used to provide consideration for a note. Some possibilities are, advertising services, marketing services, mental property, purchasing, contract rights, real or personal property, or lines of credit, to name a few.

Can Warbucks perform a service for Red, Inc.? Does Warbucks have something to sell? These are a couple of the questions that you would need to explore to find alternatives to cash consideration.

Let's look at a couple of examples to get things rolling. First, suppose that Red, Inc. is accustomed to doing a considerable amount of advertising. What would happen if Red, Inc. were to contract with Warbucks to handle its advertising for the next five years. Suppose that Red, Inc. spends $25,000 on advertising now, and plans on expanding its efforts. It hires Warbucks to handle the future advertising. Warbucks agrees to take care of everything for $50,000 per year, inclusive of hard costs and Warbucks' fees. A five-year contract at $50,000 per year would total $250,000 for the contract. Warbucks wants to be paid up front, but Red, Inc. lacks the cash right now, so Warbucks agrees to accept a down payment and a note for the rest at 18% interest. The result is that you are now ready to begin the strategy. Of course, Warbucks will be the one that actually contracts the advertising for Red, Inc., Red, Inc. pays the money to Warbucks to cover the hard cost, Warbucks pays the vendor, and there is consideration for the note. Warbucks earns a profit in tax-free Nevada, and Red, Inc. generates deductible expenses back home.

Second, what about mental property? Mental property can consist of many things, copyrights, patents, recipes, formulas and so on. If Warbucks has this sort of mental property, and Red, Inc. needs it, there is no reason that Warbucks couldn't sell it to Red, Inc. Let's say that Red, Inc. is in the business of producing resins and epoxies, and it needs a formula that Warbucks owns. Red, Inc. offers to purchase the formula, or the rights to use the formula from Warbucks. They agree on a price of $100,000, but Red, Inc. doesn't have that kind of cash. Warbucks agrees to take a note at 21% interest. You probably get the idea!

The same thing can work for almost anything of value. In the section on case studies, we will look at many different possibilities in greater detail. What you need to understand at this juncture is that the Warbucks/Red, Inc. strategy can be put into effect even if Warbucks

doesn't have the cash to make a loan.

Is Warbucks a Real Corporation?

Before we continue further, we need to examine whether or not Warbucks is a real company. The potential weak link in all of this is Warbucks itself. Warbucks as a validly existing Nevada or Wyoming corporation needs to have certain things in place to be a legitimate business. The easiest way to figure out what Warbucks needs is to look at what any other legitimate business has; telephone number, address, bank account, third party transactions and a business license. Suppose that you were investigating Warbucks to determine if it is a force to be reckoned with in a possible lawsuit against Red, Inc. You have discovered that Red, Inc. is encumbered to Warbucks, and if you can't get past the encumbrance, then you see no reason to proceed with a suit. If you were in this position, what would you look for?

The most elementary thing you would probably look at would be its address. Does it have one? You find an address listed on the UCC-1 that it filed against Red, Inc.'s assets. Is it a real address, or is it a post office box? If it's not a real, physical address, you may be quite curious to check further. Next, you wonder what would happen if you called its offices, so you call information for the city listed in the address to get a phone number. If there is no phone number, wouldn't you be a little suspicious? If it is an answering machine, things won't look too good for Warbucks. Then you call the city offices to see if Warbucks has a business license, after all, how could a legal operation not have a business license? The city gives you a license number.

At this point, we need to take a quick break from our investigating and consider what we have found. First of all, if we laymen could figure these simple steps out, it would seem to be rational to assume that a professional investigator would figure it out. Does Warbucks have these bases covered? If so, then it has passed several tests. If not, it has a problem. A professional investigator may also be able to find out whether or not it has a bank account, as well. It needs to have a bank account if it is really an operating business entity, actively doing business. Over the years, courts have looked at many things when trying to figure out if a corporation is "real". From these many cases, the following five tests have emerged as critical ones that your corporation must not fail:

1. **An actual business address, and the documentation to prove it.**

2. **A telephone listed in the corporation's name.**

3. **A business license.**

4. **A corporate bank account.**

5. **Transactions with unrelated parties.**

These are the same five things that we thought of checking out right off the bat. If a corporation has these things, then it can usually be considered to be operating legitimately. If Warbucks is supposed to be doing business in Nevada or Wyoming, then it needs to meet these tests in the correct state, and not in your home state.

In the event that someone checks further into the corporation, there are certain operational questions that need to be addressed as well. Most of these are covered in the section on piercing the corporate veil, and eight others are listed below:

1. **Commingling Assets**

   - Keep all personal and corporate funds separate
   - Document all transactions with the corporation

2. **Commingling Assets**

   - Never commingle assets such as inventory or property between yourself and your corporation, or between related corporations

3. **Failure to Sign Documents in the Corporate Name**

4. **Failure to Operate Each Corporation Autonomously**

- Keep separate corporate record books if you have more than one corporation
- Keep separate accounts if you have more than one corporation
- Hold separate corporate meetings if you have more than one corporation

5. **Failure to Keep Adequate c Corporate Records**

6. **Failure to Identify Your Business as a Corporation**

- Make sure that creditors know they are dealing with a corporation
- Use the corporate name whereever you use the business name

7. **Failure to Keep the Corporation in Good Standing**

- Pay all corporation annual filings on time
- Never dissolve a corporation if it has debt

8. **Under Capitalization**

- Ensure that your corporation is properly capitalized, with enough capitalization to give it a reasonable chance to succeed

At this juncture, there are some additional questions that need to be considered, and they are who should be the officers and directors, and who should own the stock of Warbucks.

First, officers and directors. You have several choices here, beginning with you, your spouse, an adult son or daughter, a relative, friend or business associate. Each of these possibilities has its advantages and disadvantages. There is also another factor to consider, and that is privacy. How much privacy do you want or need to achieve is a question that you will need to consider before making a decision.

Financial privacy is something that most Americans assumed they had in the past, but as has been discussed already, it is not necessarily a fact of modern life. Whether or not you should care about it is another question. Who needs to know your business? Where Warbucks is concerned, would it be more to your advantage to have another person show on the public record as the officer and director? In most cases the answer is yes. This is because a quick search on the Internet will show anybody who is looking to see if you are the officer of Warbucks, and that is likely to lead to questions from a potential opponent who would like to sweep Warbucks out of the picture to take your assets.

Having another person, unrelated to you will often take this sort of attack away. In such a case, privacy can be an important consideration. When you file a UCC-1, do you want to have to sign it for both corporations? Again, the answer is probably not. Thus, you would be well advised to have different people listed as officers and directors of Warbucks. Another possibility for the officers and directors for Warbucks would be your attorney, or a professional nominee. Professional nominees are people who will serve in these capacities for you, with a binding contract that sets forth what they will and will not do, and who can direct their actions. They enable you to retain control of the corporation, without serving in the offices yourself. The next matter for your consideration will be who should own Warbucks. Once again, you can own the stock yourself. However, in most cases this is not the best way to proceed, because if you are sued yourself, you could lose the stock of Warbucks, and end up losing everything. You also need to be aware that by owning two companies you could be putting yourself into a control issue. Some other possibilities would be to have a relative own the stock, a friend, a business associate, or use another entity, such as a limited partnership or LLC. Again, each has its advantages and disadvantages, but you need to consider how you will maintain control of Warbucks. Can you control your relatives, and do you want them knowing your business? How about friends and associates? For most situations, the use of a limited partnership makes a tremendous amount of sense, because they are easy to control, you can be protected against losing

your interest, and they can also be used for estate planning. In the section on case studies, you will learn how others have successfully used them to own Warbucks.

Bearer shares and encrypted shares, on the other hand, usually create more problems than they are worth. Bearer shares are available to Nevada corporations, and are stocks that are issued to the bearer, not to a specific individual or entity. In effect, they are cash. Whoever holds them physically owns them. If you lose a bearer certificate and someone else finds it, they own your stock, and there is nothing that you can do about it. This should be enough to avoid their use. However, some persist, because they believe that they can put the certificate away somewhere, like in a safe deposit box, and say under oath that they don't own them. Bearer Shares are not a very good solution if you plan on using them to enable you to lie. If the opponent pushes the matter far enough, you will usually be found out, and find yourself in more trouble than you ever could have imagined or wanted.

Encrypted shares are share certificates which are electronically encrypted so that no one can view them without the correct software and key. They are usually regular, registered shares issued to an individual or entity. Like bearer shares, they are often used by people who believe that they will have the ability to lie about stock ownership without getting caught. Such people are nothing more than future felons, and this practice is not recommended. There are simply too many legitimate methods of holding stock to even consider such things.

In the next section, we will discuss several special situations, which will assist you in understanding how the Warbucks – Red, Inc. strategy can be modified to fit special circumstances. As you read this section, be thinking about which of these things may apply to your situation, and how you might apply them.

Special Circumstances

How to use an asset as a capital Contribution to Warbucks, without owning its stock is a common situation which can be easily overcome by anyone who wants to follow these simple steps. A capital contribution is made when something of value is transferred to a corporation in exchange for its stock. It is a tax neutral transaction, and provides the basis of ownership, allowing you to retain control of the corporation. Such an asset can be anything of value, including cash, mental property, real estate, equipment, motor vehicles, or whatever. Here is how to accomplish the transfer, without owning stock in Warbucks.

First, incorporate a Nevada corporation. Second, form a limited partnership. This in most cases will be a family limited partnership, with you and potentially your spouse as general partners, and your adult children or a family security trust as limited partners. By using a family security trust, you can maintain the estate planning benefits of the partnership without directly involving your children in the partnership, creating gift tax implications, or confusion regarding a controlled group.

Next, contribute the asset to the partnership in exchange for your interest as a general partner. Now, you have "paid" for your control position in the partnership. Then, have the partnership contribute the asset to the Nevada corporation in exchange for the corporation's stock. The partnership ends up as the stockholder of the corporation, you are the general partner of the partnership, with full management authority over the partnership, and as a result, you are also the one who, on behalf of the partnership, will vote the corporation's stock, and controlling the corporation without owning it. Finally, you also have an estate plan set up for the benefit of your heirs.

What Happens If You Are Sued Personally?

How do you get personal protection? What if somebody sues you personally or tries to pierce the corporate veil? Well, what do you do? First of all remember that you personally guaranteed the loan or line of credit from Warbucks. But what about the stock you hold in Warbucks? You can be personally sued and lose ownership of that stock.

Your solution... Have somebody else own the stock of Warbucks Nevada, Inc. If the somebody else that owns this stock gives you control, or the somebody else is an entity that you control, you would retain full rights to control and use these assets but you would not own them and therefore the assets cannot be taken away from you.

You could just take the stock of Warbucks Nevada, Inc., contribute it to what is known as a Family Limited Partnership, and make you the general partner and owner of 1% of that partnership. You could then make your family members limited partners who own the remaining 99%.

This would give you complete control while someone else has 99% equity ownership. Remember that the partnership merely holds the stock to Warbucks. As the General Partner of the limited partnership – you call all the shots!

Warbucks just never pays out dividends to the partnership, (so that it can build the business with it's retained earnings). And the partnership never transacts any other business. This keeps the stock safe and the earnings of Warbucks under your entire control.

Now if you get sued personally, your judgment creditor can get what? Well you do own 1% of the partnership that owns Warbucks. But because there are other limited partners who are not party to the actions against you, what remedy does the individual have that sued you and won a judgement. They can only obtain what is known as a charging order. This would be a charging order against your limited partnership interest of 1%. This means if you distribute income out of the partnership, (which isn't recommended) they would get 1% of that.

Providing Asset Protection for Licensed Professionals

Licensed professionals have a more difficult time separating their business liabilities from their personal liabilities than non-licensed business people, because they cannot simply incorporate out from under their business liability that derives from their licensed profession. However, they can still have asset protection using Warbucks/Red, Inc. In their case, they can encumber their personal assets through a personal guaranty of Red, Inc.'s loan and providing additional assets for collateral. By doing so, while they may still face liability, they are less attractive targets because their assets are not available to judgment creditors who come along later.

Using a Line of Credit

A line of credit can be useful in the implementation of the Warbucks strategy when no other option is available. It has one drawback that will need to be understood in advance, and that is that it will not completely stand up in the collection phase of a lawsuit. It will, however provide your first line of defense, which is making you an unattractive target.

It is also important that Warbucks lends money to unrelated third parties, another business, friend or whatever in addition to Red, Inc. In using this tool, first realize that a line of credit is an agreement to loan money up to a certain amount, usually in regular installments called advances. If the line of credit is $100,000 the lender will loan up to that amount in advances that can be requested by the borrower. As an advance is made, it begins to accrue interest. The unadvanced portion, of course does not accrue interest. In some cases, the line of credit will contain provisions that require up front fees, often set at a percentage of the credit limit. These fees may be paid in cash, or be allowed to become advances on the credit line and subject to interest. If you had a million dollar credit line containing a set up fee and annual facilities fee of 2% each, you could pay Warbucks $40,000 at the inception of the note, giving Warbucks cash to advance back to Red, Inc., or simply allow the fees to become advances on the credit line. Either way, you will begin to pay interest to Warbucks, providing Warbucks a pool of cash to advance to Red, Inc. later on, which in turn will increase the amount of interest to be paid.

Over a period of time, you can extend the entire amount of the credit line, which will work to your benefit, should the worst come. It is important to cause as much use of the credit line as possible, because the portion of the credit line that is not advanced is the portion that will not stand if someone is trying to take your assets. If you have 30% of your credit line advanced, a judgment creditor could take equity in your assets amounting to the other 70% of the credit line.

The saving grace of the structure is that the encumbrances that would be found in an asset search would cover the entire line of credit, whether advanced or not. This fact may be quite familiar to you if you have a home equity line from a bank. They file a deed of trust or mortgage against your home for the entire amount of the home equity line at the time of the note, before any advances are taken, and Warbucks would do no less. The opposition is not entitled to know about the details of the credit line and how much had been advanced until after a judgment is rendered, and a debtor's exam is under way, usually a process requiring several years.

That's all there is to it. To summarize:

1. Red, Inc. owes Warbucks Nevada, Inc. money.

2. The money Red, Inc. owes to Warbucks Nevada, Inc. is evidenced by a promissory note due when Warbucks Nevada, Inc. says it's due.

3. As security or collateral on that note, Warbucks Nevada, Inc. and Red, Inc. have agreed that the assets of Red, Inc. will be collateral and security for the note.

4. As notice to the world and evidence that these assets are collateral on the loan, a UCC-1 filing is done in Nevada and in your home state, and a trust deed is filed

The pieces are now in place to lawsuit-proof your business assets and reduce a good portion of your current state taxes. Your home state company, Red, Inc., will have little or no profit until it pays back the loan to Warbucks Nevada, Inc. The good news is that Warbucks Nevada, Inc., your Nevada company, has had a fantastic year and the profits from interest are in tax-free Nevada.

Well, what are you going to do? Are you going to distribute? No, because we're going to word this limited partnership so that it has been set up for asset accumulation and preservation of the wealth within it. The partnership is not for immediate distribution, and therefore it's not customary for you to make distributions and it's in your complete and total discretion as to whether or not you want to make a distribution. So the judgment creditor gets zip, except, of course, if there is any income that is distributed from the limited partnership, they now have the right to receive it.

Let's just say that Warbucks has distributed money to the limited partnership but the partnership still doesn't intend to actually disburse the profit as it has been set aside for asset accumulation. Since limited partnerships don't pay taxes because of their pass through attribute, the person that has the right to receive the income is still liable for the taxes even though they don't actually receive the money.

So along with your thank you card, you send your judgment creditor a K-1 explaining the judgment creditor's share of the tax liability for the partnership for the year. This would really have a way of waking someone up. They didn't get a dime but they have received a tax bill. I tell you at this point they are, more than likely, highly motivated to settle for an amount that you feel is fair.

What do you own? You own a partnership interest and that's it. Does the percentage matter? Not necessarily, but the reason we set you up with the 1% whenever possible is because let's say that you've got a tenacious judgment creditor, and they keep renewing that judgment against you forever. And one day you die. And someday your heirs want to dissolve this partnership. Well, if that happens, then they could get the 1%. But if you died with 80%, then they could have that 80%. In this case your heirs could wipe it out with salaries and management fees and all sorts of things.

Developing Your Base Of Operation In Nevada

Meeting the five tests of a legitimate operating business is your first step in this powerful strategy. This is the underlying truth that shows the world you are really doing business in Nevada and not just taking advantage of some tax benefit.

Regulatory and predatory lawyers have become increasingly aggressive in their attempt to discount the legal viability of Nevada companys that do not pass the litmus test of a legitimate base of operation.

But, how do you do it? Well you can rent office space, hire employees, install a phone, open a bank account and pay for utilities. Not, really a practical solution unless you plan to move to Nevada.

Average Cost of Doing Business

Small Office Rent	$	775
One Person Staff		1,500
Utilities		85
Phone		60
Maintenance & Janitorial		100
FICA		115
Employment Security		41
Worker's Compensation		11
Local Tax		35
Office Equipment/Supplies		160
Insurance		166
TOTAL		$3,048

Another way is sometimes people have friends that have businesses in Nevada, and they'll rent a portion of their office and use their people as their contract employees and enter into an agreement with their friends. But there goes some of your privacy and how much do you trust your friend to be open everyday; to answer the phone every time it rings; to make sure your licensing and everything is kept up to date, etc.

Of course we recommend using the Nevada Headquarters Program. Pioneered by Laughlin Associates over 38 years ago. A legitimate operating presence for your Nevada Corporation without all the headaches and expense. It's a real office with real people, with your company's name on the building directory. It's your companies phone number answered by a live operator in your companies name.

Summary

You've got to implement these asset protection strategies while your legal seas are calm, and before you have a creditor out or   a potential creditor or you know of a claim being filed against you. Once your head is on the chopping block It's too late to implement asset protection plans at that point.

The Headquarters Program and the Nevada corporation is the required fundamental foundation for any of the asset protection plans that you're going to learn in this book. This is the starting point. This is the first step. It's the first necessary action to take, and from there you can add limited partnerships.

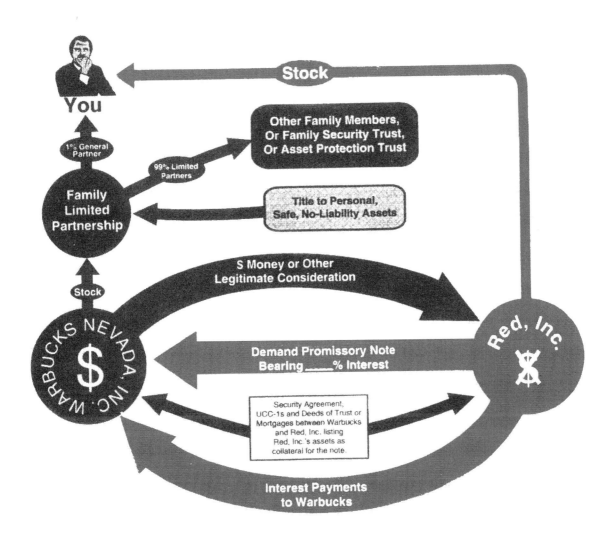

NOTES

13 Understanding FLPs and Asset Protection

By Kevin L. Day, Esq.
© Copyright 2012 Kevin L. Day

Asset Protection and Estate Planning Uses of Family Limited Partnerships

Now you have formed a Nevada corporation, hopefully with a Headquarters Program to do the paper work and act as a nominee service to lower your profile. This corporation is your first line of defense. Properly implemented, it protects your assets from the most customary threats created by your various business liabilities and places major roadblocks before your personal liability adversaries.

What is the next step of protection? You do not want your lawsuit adversaries coming in through the back door and taking the stock of your Warbucks Inc. You must protect your assets from your *personal* liabilities. So, the next building block is a legally recognized "third-party owner" as part of your estate plan to hold the stock of your Warbucks company.

Of course, you *can* actually give your asset away to someone else which is an effective asset protection strategy.

However, that does not benefit you or your family. Surprisingly enough, though many people say – "I'll give the stock in Warbucks to my brother; he doesn't have any liability. He can give it back to me later when I'm ready to retire." There are many defects with such thinking.

(1) If there is an enforceable way for you to get the assets back, the Court may deem the transfer a sham and thus the asset will still be subject to your creditors.

(2) The other person may have unforeseen liabilities (i.e. car accident resulting in judgment, their own breach of some contract).

(3) The other person pre-deceases you and their estate lawyer does not think the estate should give that asset to you.

(4) the worst, there are negative tax consequences to all involved when the asset is transferred back.

If you are successful in your business endeavors, these assets grow, and the assets are in fact "given back" (actually gifted back), there will be serious tax consequences to both, the person you gave it to and to you when receiving the assets back. All the while the assets were subject to that person's potential lawsuits.

So, with the understanding that, that type of "third party owner" is not advisable, what *will* the Courts recognize as a legal third party owner that is *not* you but still protects the asset and keeps them in your family? There are two excellent entities that fulfill this need:

(1) a Family Limited Partnership (FLP) and

(2) an Irrevocable Trust. We'll discuss both so that you can understand the differences and determine how they apply to your needs. At least, you should be able to ask intelligent questions of your advisors.

There is a great deal of history to Family Limited Partnerships, but they really got their steam in 1993 when the Internal Revenue Service acknowledged in Revenue Ruling 93-12,1 that fractional interests would not be denied a minority discount for gift and estate tax purposes merely due to family members holding the controlling interest in the aggregate. This ruling propelled the Family Limited Partnership (FLP) into a premiere device for reducing gift and estate taxes on lifetime and testamentary gifts from parents to children. [We will be using the term 'children' throughout

to represent whomever your heirs may be]. As a result of the ruling, the value of the underlying assets within the FLP could be given a "Tax Value Discount" (undervalued for tax purposes) on gifts of fractions interests, primarily due to lack of marketability of the interests and lack of control over the assets that the limited partners have, even if it was all in the family. Therefore, more could be gifted incurring less tax.

In a *Forbes Magazine* article regarding Family Limited Partnerships, the headline claimed "Cut Your Estate Taxes in Half". In typical media fashion, such a position is exaggerated, but the CPAs that I have worked with usually find a 20% to 30% discount to be appropriate and reasonable for most clients' circumstances.

Of course, once the gift is made, the gain in value over time is growing in the name of the donee, (children) and out of the estate of the donor (parents) who originally owned the interest and gifted it away. The limited partnership interests gifted away avoid probate since they will not be in your estate on your death.

The classic example is Sam Walton with Wal-Mart. You too can grow the value of your Nevada company; have it growing for your children, yet retain control over the assets, all by using an FLP. The FLP is a great estate planning tool. But with its increased use it became evident that it is also a great asset protection tool.

FLP for Asset Protection

The basic premise at the heart of all asset protection -type estate planning is the concept of OWNERSHIP. The Court will only take away things that you legally and technically own. The issue of control should not be part of the analysis.

As Rockefeller suggested, and as is certainly true for effective asset protection: control your world, but do not own it.

Partnerships are Partnerships right?

General Partnerships

First, we should say a word about the different types of Partnerships. There is a little confusion on this point and for good reason. General Partnerships and Limited Partnerships are two distinct entity types. As distinguished from a General Partner who is the 'manager' of a Limited Partnership. A "General Partnership" is very different from a "General Partner" and the first is very dangerous from a liability point of view.

In our opinion, General Partnerships should be avoided at all costs. Under the law, a general partnership is formed when two of more persons agree to conduct business together. Such agreement may be written or oral. Even without an express agreement, an adversary may be able to prove up the existence of a General Partnership

relationship by looking at behavior that shows you had an intent to carry out a business with another person or to assist in that business.

Whether the agreement is written or oral, there is no requirement to file or register the general partnership. This makes it very dangerous. This is very different from any other business entity. Corporations, Limited Partnerships and Limited Liability Companies must comply with specific registration requirements to be valid and to be provided the various levels of protections they each afford.

A general partnership is different from the other entities in another critical way. In a General Partnership each of the partners has unlimited liability. Each partner is bound by the acts of the other partners and each is responsible for all the debts related to the partnership. This liability attaches whether or not the other partner knows of the activity of the other partner(s). This means if Partner Able enters into a contract, Partner Baker is responsible for the full amount of that contract. This is the case even if Partner Baker and Partner Able had an overt argument about proceeding with the specific contract where Partner Baker condemned going forward. Partner Baker is responsible for the full amount of the contract that Partner Able entered and unlimited liability means unlimited liability. That means that you are also responsible for the negligent actions of your partner(s). Again you are responsible for the full amount even if you are merely a small fractional partner. Partner Able negligently drives his car into a café. If Partner Baker's other partners are unable to pay their respective shares, Baker will be required to pay the entire amount.

Another classic example of people entering into a General Partnership where they do not realize it is where one Partner has an existing business (sole proprietor) and has another person come in to do a special project or limited duration event, where the two will share in the proceeds of that project.

For example, Dr. Adam, a physician who also knows a specific treatment asks Dr. Baxter whether he can come into his practice one day a month to offer these additional services to patients. Dr. Adam and Dr. Baxter have entered into a General partnership. Something goes wrong with Dr. Adam's treatments. Dr. Baxter's business and personal assets are available to the full extent of the damage. The example applies to any sort of business endeavor; not merely professionals.

Able and Baker are both W-2 wage earners. They decide to make some extra money on the weekend making Snerbs at the park. Able and Baker alternate the weekend that they each work. Someday with success, they hope to quit their jobs "enter into the business" and form a corporation. Whether they intended it

or not, Able and Baker are partners in a General Partnership. This was Adam's weekend and he had a wheelbarrow full of Snerbs proceeding to their favorite sales spot. Some picnickers had gotten there early that day and despite Partner Adam's continued vigilance, a mishap occurred. Due to the unlimited liability of partners, Partner Baker's wealth is subject to the four creditors for the entire amount to the full extent of the damages. Partner Baker is responsible for pursuing his own action against Partner Able to obtain a reimbursement for his outlays.

Corporations, Limited Partnerships, and LLCs (in one way a form of Limited Partnership) all provide limited liability to the shareholders, limited partners or members. The very nature of a corporation, the reason for their first being legislated was for asset protection. Protecting the shareholders from personal liability of malfeasance of the corporation. Additionally, the individual shareholders are not personally liable for the performance of a contract when entered into on behalf of a corporation.

Limited Partnerships

Legislatures in every state have enacted law allowing the formation of a different type of partnership known as a *Limited Partnership*. This was clearly in response to the very harsh treatment befalling partners in General Partnerships. Again, these were created by lawmakers to provide limited liability, that is, asset protection. For a Limited Partnership, there must be at least two parties: one or more *General Partners* and one or more *Limited Partners*. [There also are certain formalities of registration with the Secretary of State] The same person may hold both general and limited interests, as long as there are at least two legal persons who are partners in the Limited Partnership. Mr. Baker may hold 5% as General Partner and 45% in Limited Partnership interest, as long as at least one other holds some interest (i.e. Mr. Able holds 50% limited partnership).

In a Limited Partnership the General Partner is responsible for the management and control of the affairs of the partnership. The Limited Partner has no right to management- decision making, but the Limited Partners liability for any debts and obligations of the partnership is limited to the value of their interest in the assets held within the partnership. They have no personal liability whatsoever.

Limited Partnerships are commonly used for large projects or investments where a large amount of cash is required. Those making an investment into the project will not be able to participate in managing the project, but they will not have any personal liability for the debt of the endeavor. Limited Partnerships are also very convenient due to the minimal amount of paperwork required in maintaining them in good standing.

A common mistake is placing the same legal person on both sides of the partnership. Although a husband and wife are technically two legal persons, so that the Limited Partnership is technically in compliance, depending on how the partnership is configured, there may be no asset protection at all.

Estate Planning Attorneys, unfamiliar with asset protection (and perhaps FLPs for that matter) form an FLP at the client's request and place a client's limited partnership interest in their Living Trust and make the clients the General Partners. Since Living Trusts are for probate avoidance and are revocable, they provide no asset protection. They are considered the client, thus making all parties in the FLP one person under the law, the client. This structure may be the appropriate first step to a gifting campaign, but does not protect assets until partnership interests have been gifted to another person.

Unfortunately, we have seen hundreds of Family Limited Partnerships in this configuration: the Client and their Living Trust as the only two partners in the FLP with no gifting plan in place and that was the end result of the planning. This is bad planning for asset protection planning, as well as for estate planning. We will discuss Charging Order protection later where you will see in more detail how having an "innocent party" as one of the partners is essential to the legislative history.

Though not appropriate for basic asset protection, it should be noted that Living Trusts are very important for a complete estate plan. Often a Client will ask, since we are gifting to our children the majority interest FLP and that interest is now out side our estate and will avoid probate, can we shut down our Living Trust. The answer is usually not. For two primary reasons:

(1) Rarely would you want to place your primary residence into *any* entity other a Living Trust, or your personal name. Doing so forces you to give up your $250,000 ($500,000 married couple) exclusion on capital gains tax when selling your personal residence.

(2) Your Living Trust should also be the owner of the two percent (2%) General Partner interest held in the FLP, along with other assets that you would never place within your "safe harbor" wealth preservation side of Warbucks Inc. (Automobiles, Red Inc., both of which are valuable, but are also high liability). If Mr. And Mrs. Baker have successfully gifted the 98% limited partnership interest to an irrevocable trust for their children, and are holding their two percent general partnership interest in their own name, the value of that two percent (2%) could be sufficient to trigger a probate.

Although California probate has the highest probate trigger in the country with $100,000 in total value real and personal property, it will also be triggered based solely on real estate valuing greater than $20,000. This is an extremely high anomaly. Most state probate are triggered with only $7,000 - 25,000 in total value. Thus, it is easy to see that there are very few people that would not want a Living Trust to own

(1) their residence,
(2) their two percent General Partners interest and
(3) the stock of their home state company (Red Inc.).

A Word of Caution

Certain activity of a limited partner may subject the partner to liability. Court precedent has shown that limited partners who behave like General Partners will be treated as such by the Court. Thus, if Mr. Able, a Limited Partner, negotiates a lease for the partnership, he has just caused himself to become a General Partner, despite the documents stating he only has a Limited Partnership interest. Therefore, the activities of a Limited Partner in furtherance of any Partnership interest should be avoided.

Taxation of Partnerships

Partnerships are tax neutral entities, meaning the tax responsibilities are passed through to the partners. The partnership itself is not a tax paying entity. Corporations and most irrevocable trusts are responsible for paying taxes.

(As you learned earlier, the benefit of your Nevada corporation being its own taxpayer is convenient in "stopping" the tax burden from passing through either to your children or to an irrevocable trust benefiting them.) Although the Partnership does not pay taxes on its net income, partnerships are required to file an annual informational return showing income and expenses. "K-1" forms are issued to each of the partners documenting, in pro-rata proportion to their ownership, the income or loss of the partnership that is being passed through to them. Each of the partners then claims their share of the income or losses on their own tax returns. This avoids double taxation issues.

Limited Partnerships are very convenient entities for projects where there is an expectation of a net loss if the partners can use such losses on their personal tax returns. Limited partnerships have been used for real estate investments and tax shelter investments well before the estate planning zeal for them arose, due to limited liability, low maintenance requirements and the tax pass through uses by the client's CPA. Taxation rules are generally complex and it is certainly the case with partnership activities. It is generally held that transfers of property into and out of a partnership, if retaining the percentages of the various partners, will not ordinarily cause a tax consequence. If this is one of the objectives, you usually will want to use an irrevocable trust as the Limited

Partner, so that you will only be dealing with the Trustee (which you appointed) representing the class of beneficiaries and not each of the individual children that you had made Limited Partner.

[Note: We are not CPAs or tax advisors. However, we wanted to provide you a rounded overview of Limited Partnerships including the generally known tax aspects and common usage. These can be very useful tools for tax issues as well as asset protection. You must discuss any and all tax objectives with your CPA]

Lawsuit Protection Aspects of Limited Partnerships

Family Limited Partnerships are phenomenal tools for providing lawsuit protection for the wealth of the family. Although everyone's circumstances are different the best use of the FLP for lawsuit protection is usually in conjunction with other business and estate planning entities.

A typical structure would have the FLP formed with Husband and Wife owning 1% each of General Partnership interest. The remaining ninety 98% interest would be limited partnership interest, which would be held by other family members, usually through an irrevocable trust for a variety of reasons that will be discussed below. The percentage gifted might be the full 98% if the underlying assets were embryonic and going to be grown over time. If mature (and ascertainably valuable) assets are being transferred to the FLP, then the amount able to be gifted, without gift tax, would depend on the value of the initial assets held, the remaining gift exemption available to the donors and the overall estate transfer strategy available to the client and suggested by their CPA.

After these transfers, Husband and Wife no longer directly own any of the assets transferred to the FLP. Rather, they own the controlling interest in the FLP. It is the FLP that owns the assets. This is an incredibly significant distinction from an asset protection point of view. As stated above, your judgment creditor can only take assets that you own. The amount of control, over the asset is not the issue. It is in this way that FLPs as estate planning and asset protection tools can allow you to "have your cake and eat it too". You do not own it, but you legally control everything. As the General Partner you have complete management and control over the affairs of the partnership. You can buy and sell any assets you wish. You have the right to transmute assets from one asset to another, without the consent of the Limited Partners. You of course may be paid from it. You choose whether it is best to make distributions to the partners or to continue to invest in additional assets. A Limited Partnership as a business tool is great, and if profits are made, they are either distributed or reinvested. The slight variation labeled Family Limited Partnership, merely

gives more rights to the G.P. As the name implies, the FLP is for estate planning purposes. As such, it is being used for wealth transfer and estate wealth accumulation. Therefore it is more likely than not that distributions are not being made during the lifetime of the General Partners.

FLPs' Unique Protection: Personal Creditors Cannot Take Assets

Limited Partnerships are unique from other entities in that underlying assets cannot be attached (taken) to satisfy a partner's personal liability. This is not to say assets cannot be taken to satisfy a judgment creditor of the Limited Partnership itself. However, assets cannot be attached to satisfy the personal judgments against a partner, be it you or your newly licensed teenager. Therefore, if Dr. Baker, one of two GPs in an FLP set up five years ago, has just received a judgment against him for a mishap with a patient's health, which he caused. The judgment is for $1,000,000. Once the plaintiff becomes a "judgment creditor," he will now try to collect the $1,000,000 on that judgment. He will have the Marshal seize bank accounts, investments, and foreclose on real estate owned by Dr. Baker. However, any of these assets that were successfully transferred to the FLP or to it underlying corporations will be safe from seizure, because they are not owned by Dr. Baker. Therefore, the judgment creditor will not be able to take these assets to satisfy the judgment.

Contrast this to a scenario <u>without</u> the FLP. The judgment creditor can have the Marshal take things owned by Dr. Baker. Allowing that any senior lien holders are satisfied, the Marshal can take the stocks held in his investment account, the cash in his saving account foreclose on any real estate held in his name. He has the option of coming in a unbolting the machine that is responsible for making revenue and they can take stock in any privately owned companies (Warbucks Inc.).

Under the Uniform Limited Partnership Act, *a creditor of a partner cannot reach into the partnership and take specific partnership assets*. The creditor of an individual partner does not have the legal right to any property held by the partnership. Since title to the assets (including stock of Warbucks Inc.) is in the name of the partnership and not in Dr. Baker's personal name, they are out of luck. It is Dr. Baker personally who is liable for the debt, not the partnership.

 This is why it is important to have the Warbucks stock owned by an FLP. Properly implemented Warbucks Inc. ends up being your families private "nest egg". As such you do not want personal creditors of any individual partners coming in through the back door and take Warbucks' stock or its underlying assets. The FLP will prevent that attachment.

Charging Orders v. Attachment Orders

A judgment creditor can take assets of a corporation to satisfy the judgment, but not those held by a Limited Partnership. What can the judgment creditor do in relation to a partner's interest in the FLP? Where an Attachment Order will allow seizure of almost all other types of assets, when a Limited Partnership (or its equivalent) is involved, the judgment creditor would have to ask the Court for a *Charging Order.* A "charge" in this instance is a "directive" or "instruction" from the Court. It is an instruction to pay the creditor instead of the debtor partner. Thus, once the Partnership has received a Charging Order from the Court, when and if distributions are made, the portion that was to go to the debtor partner should be sent to the judgment creditor and continue so until the judgment is satisfied. Thus, if cash distributions were going to be made this year, the creditor will take that portion going out of the FLP to Dr. Baker. The Charging Order does not give the creditor the right to "step into the shoes" of the partner. He on us has the right to divert distributions as they may come. The creditor does not "become" a partner. The creditor does not have a right to interfere with the operation or management of the partnership. (Whereas a creditor of a shareholder does become a shareholder with all the rights that entails). If the partnership does not make a distribution, the judgment creditor will not receive a payment. As mentioned previously the FLP, unlike its business counterpart, tends not to make distributions as a regular course of operation. It is attempting to preserve estate wealth and ultimately give over the control at the death of the second parent. Therefore, if assets are merely accrued and reinvested, then the judgment creditor is not receiving any income.

Nevada and FLPs

You have learned that the Uniform Limited Partnership Act states, *a creditor of a partner cannot reach into the partnership and take specific partnership assets.* Courts in all states of the Union have recognized this and, through Court precedent, a long established history has developed. There have been some anomaly cases (in California) where the Charging Order was not applied. These cases were in the early 1990s and related to very unique circumstances. However, there are two states, Nevada & Colorado) with statutory certainty in the law that the Charging Order is the *only* remedy available to a judgment creditor against Limited Partnerships. Nevada's legislature enacted law that will give you that certainty so that you do not need to rely on the Court following precedent. Nevada is also superior to Colorado for most client due to the privacy law there that are not available in Colorado.

"K-1s"

As we learned earlier, partnerships are tax neutral and the tax obligation passes through to the partners. This is documented with a K-1 form sent to each partner outlining his or her portion of the tax responsibility. Under the Charging Order, the judgment creditor who is entitled to receive any distributions also becomes responsible for paying any taxes under the K-1 of that debtor partner. This is true whether distributions are made or not.

In the configuration, which most people adopt, the FLP is the 100% owner of Warbucks, Inc, a "C" corporation. If no dividends are sent up to the owner no tax consequences befall the children as Limited Partners or an irrevocable trust as the Limited Partner. In this configuration the FLP, is acting as a mechanism by which the original owners have a legal right to maintain complete control as General Partner, but have a safeguard of the third-party ownership of Warbucks, Inc. If a corporation in this structure starts declaring dividends, but the partnership reinvests its profits rather than make distributions, the judgment creditor will now be paying taxes on phantom income. This usually promotes quick and favorable settlement.

It is clear that the use of a Family Limited Partnership will preserve assets that could otherwise be taken under an Attachment Order. A successfully implemented Warbucks company, as the ultimate protector of "nest-egg" assets of your estate should always have the additional armor of this very versatile and powerful estate planning and asset protection tool. In conjunction with your Nevada "C" corporation, the FLP strategy not only protects your estate's wealth from your business liabilities, but it prevents personal liability creditors from being able to take the stock of Warbucks, Inc.

Who Should Hold the Limited Partnership Interest?

The Charging Order protection of the Limited Partnership is extraordinary. Next to that a classic motivator for clients using the FLP is the fact that they can gift assets away to their children, yet have a legally recognized right to control. Still most clients do not wish to gift the Limited Partnership interest *directly* to their children.

There are essentially three typical options for the Limited Partner:
(1) your children (directly);
(2) an irrevocable Domestic Security Trust (DST); or
(3) an offshore Asset Protection Trust (APT).

Making your children the limited partners of your partnership is certainly the least expensive way to go. Unfortunately this approach is very inflexible, and the partnerships will have an annual obligation to send a K-1 to each limited partner detailing their interest. Other than in some advanced tax strategies, the K-1 will be zero each year, so there usually is no tax effect. However, some families desire privacy and the annual K-1 to their children (and their spouses) may give them more information that the parents wish to divulge. So, instead either type of irrevocable trust is the better answer.

A Domestic Security Trust (DST) is particularly important if your children are minors. Although they have no control, when children directly own the limited interest, the value of their interest is on their personal balance sheets. This may prevent them from applying for certain grants or scholarships when entering college. Despite their lack of control and with no access to these funds, they are seen as owning that wealth. The DST is the perfect answer. The K-1 now goes to the trust, not to the beneficiaries. Your CPA usually handles these affairs, so they remain private. And since the children do not directly own the interest, but are beneficiaries of the trust, the value does not fall on their balance sheet, thus leaving them open for potential grants and scholarships. DSTs will also customarily contain divorce-proofing provisions along with your other conditions to inheritance.

Offshore Asset Protection Trusts (APT) are the ultimate in asset protection. They remove U.S. Court jurisdiction – under

U.S. law. APTs move the jurisdiction to countries that do not have contingency fee lawyers and do have, like the rest of the world, a "loser pays" system. They have to put up funds for your costs and fees in the advent that they do not win the case. In addition to the great history of U.S. law that supports the use of APTs by U.S. citizens, there are IRS declaratory filings required, giving incredible force to these entities if challenged in the courtroom. If you are not married yet, an APT as an irrevocable trusts with you as the primary beneficiary, will provide powerful divorce-proofing - well beyond what the courts typically afford pre-nuptial or post-nuptial Agreements. There are a great many other benefits to APTs that are covered later in this manual, but in this FLP section, it should be mentioned that for those that do not have a family yet, an APT is very convenient because, unlike domestic irrevocable trust, you are allowed to name yourself as the primary beneficiary. You are also allowed to add or remove secondary beneficiaries in some jurisdictions. The structure remains somewhat flexible. If you do not have a family yet it is sometimes hard to feel comfortable with the establishment of a domestic irrevocable trust, which is *very* inflexible.

Dangerous Assets

In the construction of your FLP, make sure that the FLP does not hold dangerous assets, even if the assets are valuable. Either encumber the dangerous asset's equity, thus having a senior lien holder or place that asset in an entity (Corporation, FLP or LLC) that the FLP can own. Airplanes and rental properties, for example, are very valuable assets; yet have more than their share of liability. Holding this type of asset in a separate LP whose 98% limited partnership interest is held by your primary FLP. As we have seen with many of our clients, CPAs favor this since you gain your asset protection, yet still have pass though for tax right-offs and depreciation.

Summary

The Family Limited Partnership offers a wide range of benefits, providing answers to a great variety of planning concerns. Such breadth is offered in no other entity.

- Assets held in the FLP are effectively protected under the law from potential future claims. The Charging Order protection is unique and unprecedented.

- Income taxes can be shifted beneficially to lower tax bracket corporations and trusts or lower tax bracket family members, under the counsel of your CPA.

- Estate taxes can be minimized or eliminated on the

interest effectively gifted to your children or domestic irrevocable trusts for <u>their</u> benefit.

- Tax Value Discounts are usually available on the interest in the FLP that you gift to your children or trusts for their benefit.

- The FLP is the perfect owner for Warbucks, Inc. The FLP is a legally recognized third-party owner. It is "not you" under the law, yet the FLP gives you a mechanism for legal control.

NOTES

14

Case Studies

The Warbucks/Red, Inc. strategy we discussed is a potent and powerful strategy that can actually protect your assets and save a smart business person a lot of money in taxes. But to help you really understand the beauty of this strategy we have put together a few case studies.

Case #1

The Situation: An East Coast consultant named John, living in a high tax location, desired to limit his liability exposure and reduce his state income taxes. John's clients were large corporations who hired him to train their management employees in employee relations. Because of the nature of the business, John needed to update his presentation materials regularly to reflect changes in regulations and laws. His training consisted of in-house training presentations, including workbooks and videotapes. John's main concern was that he and his firm could be held liable in the event one of his trainees took an action that resulted in litigation against one of his clients. John's objective: Protect his business and personal assets and lower his home

state taxes.

The Strategy: Since John needed to regularly update his materials, John established a Nevada corporation to research and develop his training materials. Since he had four different training programs, John would contract with the Nevada corporation to produce those materials, one program at a time. First, his home state firm contracted for one of the training programs for the following year. The price for the production of the program was $125,000. Of this, $25,000 was paid up front, and the balance was carried on a one year, interest only note, secured by the assets of the firm. Included in the contract was a set number of workbooks and tapes. Orders for those training materials would involve an extra charge. Next, John's firm entered into similar agreements for the production of the other three training programs, at the same price and terms for each one.

Because there would be significant additional purchases of training materials from the Nevada corporation, the Nevada corporation extended a line of credit to John's firm in the amount of

$100,000. Because the assets of John's firm were not sufficient to cover an additional hundred thousand dollars, John signed a personal guarantee, and offered his residence as additional collateral for the note.

In the next year, John's firm was pleased with the work of the Nevada corporation, and once again contracted with the Nevada corporation to produce its materials. At the end of each one year contract, John's firm paid the respective notes in full, and entered into the new arrangement for the following year.

The Result: First, John's business and personal assets were encumbered to his Nevada corporation, resulting in John's firm, as well as John himself being an unattractive lawsuit target. Second, John was able to reduce his home state income taxes significantly be deducting in excess of $500,000 per year in his home state, and earning it in tax free Nevada. Third, when a potential lawsuit did arise, John's opponent decided against a suit, and settled for a small amount, because there were no assets from which to finance unnecessary litigation.

Case #2

The Situation: Maria, a software developer, had a new software product which was destined to make her a great deal of money. Before she even had the final version finished, she had orders from several large companies that she knew would only be the tip of the

iceberg. Concerned that she could be at risk in the event of litigation, Maria wanted to protect her fledgling software business, while also ensuring that her children would be provided for in the event she passed away unexpectedly.

The Strategy: In order to make her new software firm as unattractive for lawsuits as possible, Maria needed its assets, meager now, but very shortly to be quite significant, encumbered. Yet her Nevada Warbucks corporation was new, and lacked the capital necessary to make a loan. The newly copyrighted software which would be the basis of her software firm was copyrighted by Maria, who developed it. Since Maria was also concerned about providing for her heirs, she formed a family limited partnership, and a family security trust for the benefit of her heirs. She contributed the software copyright to the family limited partnership in exchange for a general partnership interest. The family limited partnership contributed the software copyright to Warbucks, which in turn sold the copyright to her home state firm for $500,000. Obviously the home state firm didn't have that kind of cash, so it executed a note in favor of Warbucks, and put its assets, both those it had at the time, and those it would acquire later, up as collateral to secure the note to Warbucks.

The Result: Maria retained control of both Warbucks and the family limited partnership. She also succeeded in encumbering the assets of her home state software company, which soon became very successful. She also succeeded in reducing state income taxes, because the home state company was able to deduct the interest payments it made to Warbucks. Because this was an installment sale, Warbucks paid taxes on the interest, and on the principal paid by the home state company for the purchase amount as it was paid, and the principal was paid very slowly. In short, Maria was able to accomplish all of her objectives.

Case #3

The Situation: Hank is a used car dealer in Texas. His used car dealership, incorporated in Texas, offers financing to anyone, no questions asked. His corporation buys low priced used cars from new car dealerships who take them in as trade-ins at low wholesale prices, and then sells them to first time buyers. These first time buyers pay a third to a half down, and then Hank's dealership finances the balance for twelve months at high interest rates. This type of used car dealership, called a "buy here – pay here lot" can be very profitable, with fairly low risk of default, because in the event of a default, the dealership repossesses the car, and repeats the process. In addition, interest rates are often in excess of 30%. Hank was concerned about two things. First, used car dealers find themselves in lawsuits frequently, and second, his taxes were becoming quite hefty and he was looking for ways to

reduce them.

The Strategy: Hank took all of the extra cash he could lay his hands on, including proceeds from the sale of some real estate, as well a second mortgage on his home, and decided to set up a finance company and an estate plan. The finance company (Warbucks) was incorporated in Nevada, with nominee officers. Hank took his cash, and contributed it to his family limited partnership in exchange for his general partnership interest. The family limited partnership then used the cash to buy the stock of the finance company.

Then, the finance company entered into an agreement with Hank's car lot to provide financing for new inventory. They agreed that the lot would use this money to buy used cars, and when they were sold with financing, the lot would keep the down payment, and then assign the notes to the finance company, who would then release the car which had been collateral, and agree to loan more money for new purchases.

The Result: Because of the lending relationship, Hank's inventory was encumbered by the Nevada finance company, making the used car dealership an unattractive target. Next, with the dealership keeping the down payments from sales, but assigning the notes to the finance company to obtain new financing, the profit of the dealership dropped significantly, which the Nevada finance company was in a position to make the main portion of the profits in tax free Nevada. Hank saved on both state and Federal taxes because of the income splitting from one to two taxpayers, and he later began doing financing under similar terms for two start up used car lots owned by friends. Hank was successful in accomplishing his goals.

Case #4

The Situation: Paula and Janet are attorneys in California. They have a unique business, at least for a couple of lawyers. They are in the business of establishing, managing and operating medical clinics. The way they do it, is to find a doctor who wants a job, and incorporate a professional medical corporation for the doctor. The doctor works regular hours in the clinic, gets a paycheck every Friday and spends the weekends at home. The doctor also owns the stock of the clinic, because only a doctor can own stock in a professional medical corporation. Paula and Janet, however make all of the investment, run the offices and are forced to trust that the doctor will not "go south" on them. Their dilemma was how to open more clinics, and maintain control of the doctors?

The Strategy: Paula and Janet had some rather difficult problems. Not only controlling the doctors, but liability protection and tax planning were issues to tackle. They formed a new California

corporation to perform management services for medical clinics. This management corporation would hire all non-professional staff, provide all equipment, manage all office functions and lease all office premises. Paula was the owner and officer of this corporation.

The management corporation needed money to do this, so Janet formed a Nevada corporation to act as finance company for the management company. The Nevada corporation loaned money to the California management company, taking all of its assets as collateral. The management company entered into agreements with the current, and all future medical clinics to provide the services mentioned earlier. To ensure that it received timely payment, the management company required the medical clinics to provide their assets as collateral. The only assets that the clinics would have were their receivables, which had to remain in the ownership of the professional corporation under medical licensing regulations in California.

The Result: The fees that the management company charged the clinics left little if any profit in those companies after the doctor's salary was covered, leaving little income in the PSC rate. The doctor, if he or she decided to cheat the attorneys who had set them up in business, would have nothing to take, because the only asset of the clinics was their receivables, which were liened by the management company. The management company held real assets, and was certainly in a potentially difficult liability position, but all if its assets were encumbered by the Nevada corporation. Much of the management company's income also had to be paid to the Nevada corporation in the form of interest on its loans, where the income would be earned state tax-free. As this structure unfolded, it became so successful that Paula and Janet opened twelve more clinics, and left the practice of law to operate their business full time. All of their objective had been accomplished.

Summary

The case studies used are general examples to try and get you to understand how you can use multiple corporations to your advantage. The door is open to extraordinary possibilities if the pieces are put together legally. In most cases you are only limited to your imagination. One strategy does not fit all so it is always important to consultant with a professional.

NOTES

15 Tax Planning Considerations of Multiple Corporations

• Controlled Groups

If the ownership of multiple corporations can be structured so separate corporations are not considered part of a "Controlled Group" there are significant tax advantages to using multiple corporations.

1. **Accumulated Earnings Tax Credit (AETC):** Multiple corporations that are not members of a "Controlled Group" each have their own $250,000 accumulated earnings tax credit as opposed to only one $250,000 credit per controlled group. The AETC applies to a regular C-corporation's accumulated earnings, not needed for business expansion purposes, that may be maintained in the corporation without being distributed to the Shareholders as dividends.

2. **Alternative Multiple Tax Credit:** Multiple corporations that are not members of a "Controlled Group" are each allowed their own $40,000 exemption in calculating a minimum corporate tax.

3. **Election to Expense Certain Depreciable Assets Section 179:** Multiple corporations that are not members of a "Controlled Group" are each allowed their own $18,500 limitation amount for purposes of expending personal depreciable property in the year of acquisition.

4. **Other tax advantages of using multiple corporations are:**

   a. The ability to use different year ends and different accounting methods (cash or accrual), whereas, one corporation with different business divisions must use the same method for all divisions;

   b. The ability to more easily dispose of a business segment operated as a separate corporation, and, in certain cases, be able to effect a tax free disposition of a business segment operated as a separate corporation in a tax free reorganization;

c. The ability to separate foreign from domestic source income and, in some cases, avoid double taxation;

d. To allow Section 1244 ordinary loss treatment, as opposed to restricted capital loss treatment, on up to $100,000 of stock invested in a segment of a business separately incorporated, that required less than $1,000,000 in total stock investment; and

e. The ability to set up a separate Subchapter S "Brother" corporation to make start-up losses from a new enterprise a current tax benefit to the individual Shareholders on their personal tax returns, instead of being required to carry the corporation losses forward until future profit exists so that the tax benefit can be utilized.

Tax Planning Considerations Of Multiple Corporations

Obviously, having a group of corporations that isn't a 'controlled' group is great! You can save big tax dollars and just because a group of corporations is not a controlled

group, it doesn't always mean you cannot control them.

What Is A Controlled Group?

There are basically two types of controlled groups. One is a parent subsidiary controlled group. The other is a brother sister controlled group.

Parent-subsidiary Controlled Group

A parent subsidiary controlled group exists where one or more corporations, through a chain of ownership, own at least 80% of the stock and value of another corporation.

Brother-sister Controlled Group

A brother-sister controlled group consists of two or more corporations in which:

1. Five or fewer persons (individuals, estates, or trusts) own at least 80% of the voting stock or value of shares of each corporation; and

2. These five or fewer persons own more than 50% of the voting stock or value of shares of each corporation, considering a particular person's stock only to the extent that it is owned with regard to each corporation.

Stock Attribution Rules For Brother-sister Controlled Group

In applying the above two tests for a brother-sister controlled group you are considered to own:

1. Stock owned by your spouse, in a corporation in which you also own stock or take part in management.

2. Stock owned by your children under age 21.

3. Stock owned by your children over age 21 and grandchildren, if you own more than 50% of the value and voting power of the stock in the corporation.

4. Stock owned by your parents, if you are under 21 years of age.

5. Stock owned by your parents or grandparents, if you own more than 50% of the value and voting power of the corporation's stock.

6. Stock held by a trust, estate, partnership or corporation in which you own a 5% or more interest.

7. Stock on which you hold an option.

Note that stock owned by a brother, sister, or in-law is not considered owned by a Shareholder through attribution, nor is stock owned by children over 21, or parents of children who are over 21, if the person in question does not own more than 50% of the stock of the second corporation.

What Are The Disadvantages Of Being A Controlled Group?

The main disadvantage is you don't get "seconds" on the tax breaks. You only get one helping of tax breaks no matter how many corporations you own if they are part of a controlled group.

Multiple corporations that are members of a controlled group must allocate the lower tax brackets, accumulated earnings tax credit, etc. so that the controlled group members, in total receive only one each of the above listed tax benefits.

Likewise, members of a controlled group receive only one $250,000 Accumulated Earnings Tax Credit to be allocated among the controlled group corporate members, one Alternative Minimum Tax Credit, one Environmental Tax Credit, and one Section 179 election.

Example Of A Brother-sister Controlled Group

The following example assumes Shareholders "A," "B," "C" and "D" are unrelated taxpayers in regard to the above listed stock ownership attribution rules.

Remember that "B," "C" and "D" can be brothers, sisters, adult children, parents of adult children, or in-laws and not be related per the stock ownership attribution rules, because neither "B" "C" or "D" owns at least 80% of either corporation, and more than 50% of the other.

However, since "A" owns at least 80% of Corporation 1 and more than 50% of Corporation 2, "A" would be deemed by attribution to also own the stock of his adult children and his parents.

Example 1

PERCENT OF STOCK OWNERSHIP

Shareholders	C1	C	% of Identical Ownership
A	80%	60%	60%
B	20%	20%	20%
C	0%	10%	0%
D	0%	10%	0%
TOTAL	100%	100%	80%

Because the identical ownership column is greater than 50%, and Shareholders "A" and "B" own at least 80% of both entities, Corporations 1 and 2 are a Brother-sister controlled group, subject to the limited tax benefits of a controlled group.

Example 2

However, if the stock ownership is adjusted as follows:

PERCENT OF STOCK OWNERSHIP

Shareholders	C1	C 2	% of Identical Ownership
A	80%	29%	29%
B	20%	20%	20%
C	0%	26%	0%
D	0%	25%	0%
TOTAL	100%	100%	49%

Then corporations 1 and 2 are not part of a Brother-sister controlled group. Even though the greater than 50% identical ownership test is met, the same Shareholders that meet the 50% test must also meet the 80% test. Since Shareholders "A" and "B" do not control at least 80% of corporation 2 (Vogel Fertilizer vs. U.S., a Supreme Court tax case) the 80% test is not met. Therefore, Corporations 1 and 2 are not a controlled group, and both corporations are entitled to their own and separate surtax exemptions, accumulated earnings tax credit, alternative minimum tax credit, environmental tax credit, and section 179 election.

What Is Not A Controlled Group?

As you'll see when you read about what one is, it's easier to understand what one isn't. The following are examples of what would not constitute a controlled group:

1. You own 100% of one corporation and your spouse owns 100% of another corporation. You and your wife manage your respective corporations separately. These two corporations are not a controlled group. It's important to remember that there can be no cross over activities between the two companies. This is usually hard to maintain so using a husband and wife to avoid a controlled group is usually not recommended.

2. You own 49% of one corporation and your child over 21 years of age owns the balance. You own 100% of another corporation. The two corporations are not part of a controlled group.

3. You own 79% of one corporation and a totally unrelated third party owns 21%. You own 100% of another corporation. The two corporations are not part of a controlled group, yet, you do have control over both.

Avoid Perils Of Section 482 By Doing Business At "Arms Length"

It is essential that owners of multiple corporations doing business with each other transact business at arm's length,

on normal commercial terms. Otherwise the IRS may invoke the dreaded Section 482 and treat all members of a controlled group as one corporation, with all the ensuing tax consequences.

Section 482 applies to "controlled groups," which for the purposes of this section is loosely defined and can mean "any type of control, direct or indirect. It is the reality of the control which is decisive, not its form or mode of exercise." Even worse, there is a "presumption of control if income and deductions are arbitrarily shifted." In other words, if two or more companies act like a controlled group, they are a controlled group.

What the section says is that if a controlled group manipulates its component companies (not just corporations but any business form) in such a way that either "the (federal) taxable income is understated" or "the true income is obscured," the district Director may intervene "and determine the true taxable income." The Director can consolidate the results of the controlled group and assess tax based on that consolidation (even if the different companies have different fiscal years).

The fundamental basis for judging whether Section 482 applies and in what manner it should be invoked is "arm's length" transactions — transactions that would occur between unrelated third parties. The more members of a controlled group interact like unrelated third parties, the less likely that Section 482 applies.

Section 482 is usually invoked under two circumstances:

1.   When there is a significant element of tax avoidance or evasion.

2.   When there is a sharp separation of the expenses of producing gain from the gain itself. (For example, if profit is shifted from one company to another to take advantage of accumulated losses of the second company.)

If Section 482 is invoked, the district Director may reallocate income from interest on loans based on an arm's-length rate of interest, taking into account "amount, duration, security, credit standing of borrower, and prevailing interest rates."

The Safe Haven interest rate is not less than the Federal Rate and not greater than 130% of the Federal Rate. (There are different Federal Rates for loans: short, up to 5 years; medium, 5 to 10 years; long-term, 10 years or more. The rate is based on the Treasury bill rate and is adjusted quarterly.)

Section 482 Vs. Warbucks/Red, Inc.

Section 482 should not affect the Warbucks/Red, Inc. strategy (in which a corporation in Nevada lends money to a corporation in another state with corporation tax) as long as the net effect on the Federal tax liability is the same. However, if a corporation owner tries to get too clever and uses that strategy, with a few added wrinkles, to avoid Federal taxes, and charge an unrealistic rate of interest, then Section 482 may be invoked.

Summary

The complications and necessary planning considerations of multiple corporations, and controlled groups can be complex and dependent on the facts of each situation. So remember, when setting up your corporate empire, professional tax advice is recommended.

16 S-Corporations

An S-corporation is a regular corporation whose shareholders elect to qualify it under Section 1361 to Section 1379 of the Internal Revenue Code. A common misconception is that there is something special or extra to be done in "forming" an S-corporation. That is not true. An S-corporation is just like any other corporation at the outset. It is a regular corporation, and later files an election with the IRS to become an S-corporation.

For example, a newly-formed corporation shell may remain a regular corporation, or you, the shareholder(s), may convert it or elect to qualify it as an S-corporation under the IRS Code.

It is exempt from paying income tax by virtue of its S-corporation status. Instead of the corporation paying tax, the profit or loss of the corporation flows through to the individual shareholders' personal tax returns in the pro rata amount of their stock ownership in the corporation.

Those who have not had experience working with S-corporations usually believe that there is some horrendous procedure to go through or some mysterious red tape that must be coped with to become or qualify as an S-corporation. That is not true.

The election must be timely and proper. The corporation must file IRS Form 2553. The election can be made at any time during the preceding taxable year or at any time during the first 75 days of the taxable year for which the election is intended. If not filed within 75 days, it will be effective for the following year. The shareholders, who are all required to consent, are those who hold stock on any day during the period the corporation was eligible to make the election.

Those qualifications for S-corporation status are as follows:

1. For tax years beginning after 1996, an S-corporation may have up to 100 shareholders, with a husband and wife being counted as one, regardless of the manner in which their shares are owned. The estate of a deceased spouse and the surviving spouse are to be treated as one shareholder.

2. The shareholders must be

individuals, estates, or certain types of trusts, not corporations or partnerships. However, a partnership can hold S-corporation stock as a nominee for an eligible shareholder. The Small Business Protection Act of 1996 [hereinafter 1996 Act] has added a number of eligible trusts to aid estate planning for S-corporations, as well as tax exempt organizations which may participate with S-corporations (e.g., QSST, ESBT, 401(a) qualified retirement plan trust, 501(c) (3) charitable organizations). The requirements for creating these shareholders are quite technical and if you have a need to operate with one, you should contact a tax planning expert to assist you.

3. There can be only one class of stock. Dividend and liquidation rights must be equal. Also, voting rights in the one class of stock may be different.

4. There must be no nonresident alien shareholders.

5. The corporation must be a domestic corporation.

6. If an S-corporation has no C-corporation earnings and profits left over from its C-corporation years, its entire income can come from passive income — dividends, interest, rents, royalties, annuities, or securities gains. A corporation with C-corporation earnings and profits will lose its qualification if it has earnings and profits at the end of each of three years, and its passive income comes to more than 25% of its gross receipts in each of those years.

An S-corporation election does have to be filed within certain time frames and according to certain time limitations if you want S-corporation treatment for the current tax year. If your corporation is newly formed, you should file Form 2553 within 75 days of your date of incorporation. Actually, the rule says that you must file for your election within 75 days from the beginning of your tax year.

If you want to get technical then your S-corporation election must be made before the 15th day of the third month in the first tax year of the corporation (in English, that is 75 days). Now that we have firmly established that you must file within 75 days from the beginning of the corporation's tax year, you can probably see that it is very important to know when, according to the law, the first taxable year of the corporation begins. So when does the taxable year begin? Well, the first month of the corporation's initial taxable year begins at the time that the corporation issues stock, acquires assets, or begins doing business, whichever comes first.

Therefore, you can wait longer than 75 days after the date of incorporation if you have done absolutely nothing with your corporation. In other words, if you have purchased a newly-formed corporation shell, you really have 75 days from the date that you issue the stock to the shareholders, commence doing business, or from the date the corporation acquires assets. Prior to that time, you cannot have done any business as a corporation. You cannot have transferred any assets to your corporation. If you even so much as open a corporate bank account with $10, this avenue is not available to you. Note that this does not mean that your corporation cannot elect "S" status—it simply means that your corporation cannot elect S-corporation status for that current tax year—it can be treated as an S-corporation for the next tax year. If you have an existing corporation, as opposed to a new one, you can elect S-corporation status within 75 days after the beginning of each corporate tax year.

The sub-chapter "S" Revision Act of 1982 totally changed the regulations applicable to sub-chapter "S". It changed the name of these corporations to "S-corporations," and named heretofore non-electing corporations "C-corporations." The 1986 tax reform act made some changes to S-corporations and the tax years. They must use and to the conversion of regular C-corporations to S-corporations. The 1986 tax act also excepted S-corporations from certain restrictions placed upon the use of the cash accounting method for

regular corporations with gross receipts of over $5,000,000. It also made certain changes as to how income is classified when it is passed to shareholders, as to whether it is passive or active.

The new regulations closely resemble the rules that apply to partnerships. The shareholders put into their own income the current taxable income of the corporation. This income, in the hands of the shareholders, is classified in one of three ways: Active, passive or portfolio.

If the shareholder "materially participates" in the business, that shareholder's income is active income. If the shareholder doesn't "materially participate" in the business, then his income is considered to be passive income. (A brief word as to what "materially participate" means. A taxpayer is said to be materially participating if he or she is involved in the business activity on a regular, continuous and substantial basis.) Now, any rental income is considered to be passive income regardless of whether the owner materially participates in the activity or not, and it retains its character when passed through the conduit from the corporation to the shareholder. Income such as interest, dividends, etc., is classified as portfolio income (S-corporation dividends excepted) and it retains its character when passed through the conduit from the S-corporation to the shareholder.

Except for S-corporations that were

formerly C-corporations, and may have earnings and profits in the corporate till, the treatment of distributions from S-corporations, whether cash or property, is precisely the same as the distribution from partnerships. Distributions first reduce basis to zero; if in excess of basis, they are taxed as income. There are specific changeover regulations for corporations that were S-corporations in prior years.

There are also specific regulations for corporations that have earnings and profits for any reason. Also, a regular "C" corporation with assets or earnings that wishes to elect "S" status after 1986 may be subject to a so-called "built-in gains" tax placed upon the "recognized gain" on the disposition of certain assets within a defined "recognition period." If you need more information regarding this, you should contact a qualified tax professional.

It seems everybody hears a lot about S-corporations being the tax deduction of today. Of course, no business exists solely for the purpose of being a tax deduction. But any business trying to make a profit can lose money.

So, are you ready for this? We are actually going to tell you how to enjoy that tax deduction very simply and concisely!

1. First, of course, you obtain your complete corporation package.

2. Then the corporation acquires for your business use, by purchases or whatever, various and sundry assets such as a company car or an airplane, for example.

3. Now, this expense is necessary to the conduct and pursuit of the corporation's business, in the judgment of the corporation, as reflected in the corporate record book in the form of resolutions or minutes. That judgment may be good or bad and it may be successful or unsuccessful. It may be profitable or unprofitable, and it may go on for up to five years or so. The corporation continues trying to make a profit. If it is unprofitable, and the corporation loses money, that loss under S-corporation status is a direct deduction from your personal 1040 federal income tax return up to what you have invested in the corporation!

4. There are many other expenses the corporation will obviously have which may in turn result in a bigger loss to the corporation and a bigger personal tax deduction for you. Some examples are: Office rent, telephone bills, travel expense, and on and on.

5.   By now you are probably thinking, "Very good, that's all great, but where does, or where did, this newly-formed corporation shell we started out with get the money to spend for these expenses and assets in the first place?" That is very simple, too.

You use the money that you normally would have spent for those items to purchase stock in the corporation. That money is not taxable to the corporation and it is money you have invested in the corporation that the corporation can use to purchase the assets we talked about in Step one.

So, you buy the stock in the corporation, which gives the corporation money to spend, and the corporation spends the money for the expenses that we have discussed. If the corporation loses money, then that loss is a deduction for you, instead of just money out the window.

6.   Under tax regulations, the loss deduction you take from the S-corporation cannot exceed the investment (basis) you have in the ownership (stock) of the S-corporation. So, we suggest you stick to putting money in or investing money in the corporation stock through equity investment instead of loaning money to the corporation.

7.   In many instances, a Nevada S-corporation is not even required to qualify or register in any state so long as it is simply trying to get in business as above described. That can also solve a lot of headaches for you.

For example, under this S-corporation procedure, your corporation can move you across the nation. The moving expense can become a tax deduction for you instead of a total loss.

By the same plan, lawyer and legal expense can often be handled through the corporation as a corporate expense instead of a personal expense and, therefore, become a tax deduction for you.

Until recently, fringe benefits paid to shareholders of an S-corporation were treated specially. For example, if these benefits were paid to owners of more than 2% of the shares, the cost of the benefits was to be included in the W-2 income of the shareholder. The benefits were treated as taxable compensation. The IRS has changed that position. The health insurance premiums that have been paid by the corporation for coverage of an employee/shareholder are now not subject to either Medicare or Social Security taxes if the amounts paid are made on the basis of a benefits plan that gives medical coverage to either a whole class of employees or to all employees.

If this is the case, the block on the W-2 which shows the income subject to Social Security taxes should not include the amounts paid for these premiums but it is still deductible to the corporation.

This is a clear benefit for the small S-corporation. It allows the shareholder/employee to enjoy health coverage without being taxed on it. The safe way to be certain that your S-corporation has this advantage is to make sure your insurance benefits apply to all employees. More than likely any drawbacks you incur by having to cover more employees would be outweighed by the tax-free purchase of medical coverage for the owners of the S-corporation.

Here is the case history of Mr. and Mrs. John Doe, who tried and failed and still ended up with a profit. (We are trying to illustrate to you some of the merits and advantages that could result from conducting your activities within the framework of your own Nevada S-corporation). You will constantly discover and develop new advantages from the myriad of possible variations and ramifications as you manage and run your own corporation, be it large or small. You will find it usually gets better as you go along. The point is, you have to start, and the time to do that is NOW!

For example: *Mr. and Mrs. John Doe got smart. They decided to form a Nevada S-Corporation with the idea in mind of selling pictures painted at home by Mrs. Doe,*

who at the time was a homemaker. Keep in mind that she was already at home. Mr. Doe was a good, hard-working, ambitious man. Inflation had driven up their cost of living, the price of food, clothing, gas — everything has gone up faster than he could increase his paycheck.

Mr. Doe was a bit of an entrepreneur at heart. He was determined to better provide for his family. Mrs. Doe was not working and had difficulty, under the circumstances, obtaining work. So to them, their little picture painting business seemed like a good idea. They became entrepreneurs and started their small business. They kept books and properly paid her Federal Social Security (FICA), state unemployment insurance, state workman's accident compensation insurance, etc.

Mr. Doe claimed enough dependents in this particular case so that no income tax withholding was necessary. They had no money to start with (permissible under Nevada law). Now, the 64-dollar question! How did the corporation get enough money to pay Mrs. Doe?

Mr. Doe took all of his paycheck each week and bought stock in the corporation. The money that Mr. Doe put into the corporation is to the corporation paid-in capital. The total contributions made by shareholders to a corporation, whether in exchange for stock or otherwise, is paid-in capital. These contributions are not taxable income to the corporation. The corporation took the same money that Mr. Doe purchased stock with and paid Mrs. Doe and, of course, the various employer/employee insurance contributions required. Mrs. Doe, in turn, used her earnings (the same money that Mr. Doe earned and invested) to support the Doe family.

NOTE: Mrs. Doe could have been paid all or in part by an accrual method, stock, promissory notes or other instruments from the corporation so long as the employer/employee requirements were paid in cash. The effect of this can be to: 1) decrease the investment capital required; 2) conserve cash flow; and 3) increase her protection and the amount of benefits payable to her under the various coverages in the event she should become eligible for any benefits. (Consider the protection and cash benefits Mrs. Doe could have from State Industrial Insurance or Workman's Compensation if she were temporarily or permanently disabled on the job.)

Their intentions were good and they valiantly tried. Mrs. Doe painted pictures for the corporation and the corporation tried to market and sell the pictures.

At the end of the year of trying diligently to succeed, the corporation had sold only a few pictures to relatives and friends and certainly had no profit. In fact, as a result of this failure and other bad judgments and circumstances, the corporation had lost all the money Mr. Doe had invested. The corporate loss predominately amounted to all of the

money the corporation had spent in wages paid to Mrs. Doe. Therefore, the corporation finally made a good decision and put Mrs. Doe on lay-off status due to the lack of sales.

It also happened that Mr. and Mrs. Doe were able to deduct the corporate loss (to the extent of their investment) from their other individual earnings and they legally saved a considerable amount of income taxes. In fact, Mr. Doe got a nice, fat refund check from the friendly IRS for the federal income taxes withheld by his employer.

The corporation then became dormant for a year or so.

After the dormant year or so, the corporation decided to try again. (They were already incorporated and did not have to incorporate again.) Try again they did! The corporation decided to rehire Mrs. Doe. Regretfully, the same failure resulted, but once again the Does came out many thousands of dollars ahead, by the same set of circumstances. In fact, as a result the Doe family prospered.

Again after a period of dormancy and inactivity, the corporation decided to try again. The third time's a charm! This time the corporation finally found a market for its pictures. Like all good entrepreneurs, they finally made it, and made it big! The Does now have paid executives to run their company and they are paid Directors of the corporation.

They live happily and comfortably on the dividends and earnings paid to them from the corporation, plus many other outstanding fringe benefits they enjoy from the corporation.

Note that even in apparent failure, the Doe family as individuals profited substantially and materially in good, old-fashioned money. Take a lesson from someone else's mistakes: Winners never quit and quitters never win. You, too, can be as smart and innovative as the Does. This should be a case in point that it pays to try—that when you try, you can lose and still win—that it pays to incorporate!

Summary

These are all ideas and the list could go on and on, but we hope these concepts will stimulate your thinking and show you how to operate an S-corporation. Keep in mind that under S-corporation status, the corporation is NOT taxed. In the event that the corporation has a profit, that profit is passed through to your 1040 personal tax return just like the loss discussed above. This eliminates double taxation. Otherwise, the profit would be taxed first on the corporate level, and second when the individual received it from the corporation.

NOTES

17

Corporate Stock

- *All About Corporate Stock*
- *Who Should Own Stock*
- *Reading a Stock Certificate*
- *Selling Stock & Going Public*

CORPORATE STOCK: WHAT DOES IT ALL MEAN?

If following proper corporate formalities is your intention, and it must be for the sake of your corporate health, the issuance of stock, as the principal corporate formality, deserves your careful attention.

Do I Have To Issue Stock?

Most corporations are vulnerable to attack because they don't follow proper corporate procedure (formalities); they have sloppy records, few resolutions, and little documentation of corporate activities. Plaintiffs' attorneys lick their chops at the prospect of ripping through these corporations to get at the shareholders' personal assets. Since proper corporate formalities are a major factor in piercing the corporate veil, and the issuance of stock is the major

formality that any corporation will deal with, not issuing stock is a serious mistake.

How can someone pierce the corporate veil and get "my assets" if "I" don't own the stock? The answer, of course, is that the plaintiff's attorney asserts that you are the effective owner of the stock, because your fingerprints are all over the corporation.

Types of Consideration

Stock is issued for cash, property, or services. Cash is fairly obvious as a form of consideration, but property and services will vary in form and substance. Property can take many forms, stocks can be issued for tangible assets, such as office equipment, and real estate, or it can include such items as mental property, formulas, copyrights, trademarks, and so on. Services can be such things as actual work for the corporation, longevity, consulting, and service contracts. You may have a special circumstance, which isn't mentioned, and yet could be a valid consideration for the stock.

Issuance of the Stock

The actual issuance of the stock is rather simple. You issue stock by corporate resolution. First you will need a resolution to authorize issuance, and then you will need to draft a resolution issuing a specific number of shares to a specific individual or individuals for a type of consideration, cash, property or services. The resolution need not state how much money is involved, just the particular type of consideration. As an accounting function, you will have an equity account, usually called "paid in capital" on your books which indicates the total amount of cash, or the cash value of the property or services performed in exchange for the stock.

When stock is issued, one of those three words should be inserted into the resolution authorizing its issuance by the Board of Directors. All items for which stock may be issued will fall under one of those three headings. The actual accounting as to dollars and cents is documented in the accounting records or books of the corporations and is not necessary in the resolution to issue the stock. It is better not to clutter resolutions with accounting matters.

All states require that corporations maintain a stock ledger as a record of share ownership. Stock ledgers usually are in two steps. First is the Register of Original Certificate Issue (See page 174), which performs much the same duty as a check register. It allows the secretary of the corporation to keep track of your numbered certificates, so that at anytime, he or she can determine where they are. The register will indicate to whom and when each certificate was issued, and when combined with the remaining blank or unused certificates in the record book, will indicate if any certificates are missing.

The second ledger that you will need to keep is called the shareholder ledger (See sample located at the end of the chapter). The shareholder ledger is a separate ledger for each shareholder that indicates each stock transaction the shareholder has been involved in, and shows a running total of the shares each person owns. It also has the address of the shareholder. The shareholder ledger is what is used in determining who is entitled to vote in shareholder meetings, and how many shares each shareholder is entitled to. The address on the ledger is used for providing notices of meetings to each shareholder.

States will vary on whether or not a copy of the shareholder ledger must be kept by the Resident Agent. In some states, such as Nevada, only a statement stating who is the custodian of the ledger is provided to the Resident Agent. You should contact your Secretary of State office to find out what is required in this area.

As you have seen, stock represents shares of ownership in a corporation. A corporation may be owned by or have anywhere from one Stockholder, in the case of a private, one-man corporation, to thousands of Stockholders, in the case of a public corporation.

Under Nevada statutes, there is no law that any of the authorized shares have to be issued. Under Nevada law, there is no time period in which you have to issue shares. State laws differ, and the various requirements are different. You will want to learn what these laws are in the state in which you incorporate. This is an example of the point that we have tried to make: You have certain rights, powers and privileges as a result of the state in which you incorporate. This is one of them. If you incorporate, for example, in Nevada and qualify to do business in some other state, the stock issuance regulations of your statutory domicile will be accepted in the state in which you qualify to do business.

Therefore, the number of shares reflected on the stock certificate is the percentage or portion of ownership represented by the certificate that the owner owns. When the articles of incorporation are filed with the Secretary of State, they contain the number of shares that the corporation will be authorized to issue. When the articles are accepted for filing by the Secretary of State, the number of shares as set forth in the articles are authorized to be issued by the corporation.

That really does not tell you a great

deal. Probably what you want to know is what percentage of ownership of the corporation the number of shares of the stock certificate represents. To know that, you have to inquire of the secretary of the corporation as to how many shares of the corporation's stock are issued and outstanding. If it is a small private corporation, you undoubtedly know that. If it is a larger corporation, one you are not intimately familiar with, you should make that inquiry to the secretary of the corporation in writing and request an answer in writing.

It's the percentage of ownership that counts. For example, if the corporation has only issued one share and you own that share, you own 100% of that corporation. If, for example, the corporation has issued 100 shares and you own 50 shares, you own 50% of that corporation.

Profits from the corporation will be prorated and distributed according to the percentage of ownership the shares in the corporation reflect that you own. If, for example, you own 50% of the corporation, you receive 50% of the profits.

In private corporations, the question of control is always a matter of paramount importance and usually of considerable negotiation and maneuvering. Control of the corporation is achieved by owning more than 50% of the issued and outstanding stock of the corporation.

If only 100 shares of the corporation's stock are issued and outstanding, 51 shares control that corporation. If 2,500 shares have been issued and are outstanding, 1,251 shares of ownership control that corporation. In a privately-held corporation, we do not recommend issuing all the shares that are authorized to be issued. You may, for example, issue only 100 shares divided or prorated as you wish among the Stockholders, and so long as you keep 51 of those shares (51%), you control the corporation.

When you are dividing up a corporation, simply figure out the percentage that goes to each party, and then issue shares of the total amount to be issued in that percent to the recipient. That will leave you a healthy amount of authorized but unissued stock. That means the corporation is authorized to issue more stock or can issue more stock when and if its Board of Directors wants it to. The situation may arise where you wish to take in others and issue stock to them. Just be sure when you issue more stock that you increase the stock issued to yourself as required to maintain that majority of stock issued in order to maintain control (if that is your wish).

Remember, there is nothing irrevocable about a corporation. In the event that you have issued all of the shares authorized by your articles of incorporation, and you at some point in time wish to issue more, or possibly split them into different classes and kinds of stock, you may do that by majority vote of your Directors, by amending your articles of incorporation, and by paying the additional fee required for the increased capitalization to your secretary of state.

We have said that stock is a negotiable instrument, it is like a check. When the stock certificate is properly endorsed and witnessed on the back, it can be cashed or transferred on the books and records of the corporation. It is very similar to a check. When a check is endorsed, it can be cashed or transferred. That makes both of them negotiable instruments.

Types of Stock

The most common type of stock is called "common stock". Common stock usually comes with the right to vote, which, of course, is where control comes from. However, common stock can also be non- voting, which retains the right to receive dividends, but has no right to vote. Thus it comes without the ability to control. In most small corporations, there is one class of stock, which is common, and all shares retain the right to vote. There is also the possibility of having another class of stock, which is called "preferred stock".

Preferred stock carries that name, because it has two characteristics which give it an advantage over common stock. First, preferred stock has first position in the event that a corporation is dissolved. After all of the corporation's creditors have been paid, holders of preferred stock are first in line to be paid for the par value of the stock, from the remaining assets of the corporation. Second, in the event that dividends are to be paid, holders of preferred stock are always paid first.

Preferred stock is usually issued because it has features that give it a more attractive and saleable position than common stock would have to a potential investor. Often, preferred non-voting stock is used for this purpose, allowing for an attractive investment to an investor, without giving up control of the business.

Another way to accomplish this, is to fix the dividend right of preferred shares to a dollar amount or a percentage of par value. For example, the stock can be 5% preferred or $5 preferred, meaning that the particular amount specified is guaranteed as a dividend, if dividends are to be paid. Such stock can also be cumulative, meaning that if no money is available for the payment of dividends in a given period or year, the dividend for that period is carried forward, to be paid in the next dividend period in which dividends are to be paid. As you can see, this would be more attractive to a potential stock purchaser than it would be if only common stock were available for sale. If you have a key person, or a brother-in-law preferred non-voting stock is often a better way to go, than surrendering voting power.

In looking at these matters, you need to be conscious of how many shares your corporation is authorized to issue. Authorized stock represents the number of shares that your state has authorized you to issue. As you can imagine, you may not lawfully issue more shares than are authorized, without amending your articles of incorporation to expand the number of authorized shares. You do not have to issue all of the shares that are authorized, however. I always recommend to business people that they keep a significant percentage of their authorized shares in reserve, so that they will be available in the future, should they need to be issued.

Pre-Emptive Rights

Other considerations in the area of stock, which must be noted here, are pre-emptive rights, and assessable stock. Pre-emptive rights give shareholders the right to avoid having their ownership and voting power diluted by the subsequent issuance of stock to others. Dilution occurs when the Board of Directors of a corporation issues stock to a new shareholder. Figure that you have 30% of the issued shares of a corporation. In connection with your brother-in-law who has 21%, you control the corporation. You show up at the annual shareholders meeting expecting that the two of you will control the corporation, just like you always have. Surprise! Last month the Board of Directors sold stock to a new shareholder. Your mother-in-law has purchased, unbeknownst to you, 1,000 shares in the corporation, doubling the number of issued shares. Now your voting power is 15%, she has 50%, and when combined with the 200 shares your brother-in-law has, which is now 10% of the vote, your in-laws have 60% of the voting power. They now control the company, and your brother-in-law announces that he has just filed for divorce from your sister! Your position in the corporation has been diluted!

Pre-emptive rights would make this nightmare scenario much more difficult. With pre-emptive rights, each shareholder must be offered the opportunity to buy stock, in any new issuance by the Board of Directors, in a proportion equal to their current ownership percentage, thus preserving their current position. Naturally, whether or not your corporation has pre-emptive rights really depends on which side of the fence you find yourself on.

If you wish to maintain the maximum of flexibility in the day to day management of your corporation, and you will have investors as shareholders; you will want to avoid giving them pre-emptive rights if you can help it. On the other hand, if you are an investor, pre-emptive rights may well be a must. In making your decision, especially if you are the investor, remember that pre-emptive rights do have one limitation. In order to exercise them, you must be in a position to buy the stock that would preserve your position. The Board of Directors will set the price in most cases. They set this price at their sole discretion, so this may not be possible for you.

Assessable Stock

Also of great importance in getting started, is assessable stock. Assessable stock is stock, which can be held liable for the corporation's debts, in the same proportion as the ownership that the stock represents. In other words, if you owned 100% of the stock in a corporation, and the corporation is bankrupt; you are now responsible personally for 100% of the debts of the corporation. If you owned 50% of the stock, you would be responsible for 50% of the corporation's debt. If you have purchased an ongoing corporation from someone else, you need to find out about this little feature! Few corporations that your attorney would form for you and few corporation shells that you would purchase from an incorporating company will have assessable stock, but you should still check it out.

We had a call from an elderly lady who had a little business problem. She and her husband, a retired dentist from Texas, had, at their son's urging, purchased an ongoing business for him. The business was a corporation, so they purchased the stock in the corporation for their son, who ran the company, and was supposed to pay them back with dividends over a period of time. Unfortunately, the business failed, having debts in the area of $600,000. Suddenly, the corporation's creditors were at their door, demanding payment. They had never even heard of assessable stock, but guess what they had... As luck would have it, they were living off of investments that they had made before retirement, which currently amounted to about $600,000. Faced with the loss of their life's work, after they had retired, they had literally gone into hiding. They had left their home, and moved into a motor home, and were cruising the west, trying to buy time while they figured out what to do. The lady thought that they might have a way to quickly start over, because they had the opportunity of a lifetime, if they quickly bought stock in a new, up and coming business. Could they do that?

We asked her to fax a copy of the Articles of this fantastic new business, for a quick look. Guess what? They would be buying more assessable stock!

I am often asked at this point, "Why would anyone have assessable stock?" There are really two occasions when someone would have assessable stock. First, some types of lenders will require that you make your stock assessable, so that they can collect from you individually in the event of default, without a personal guarantee. Be wary of such lenders! The second case when assessable stock is used, is when the person forming the corporation is certifiably insane. Assuming that you

are not borrowing from Uncle Guido, and that you are sane, I would shy away from assessable stock.

Who Should Own the Stock in Your Corporation?

Who the shareholders should be in your corporation, depends largely on the purpose for your corporation. If the corporation in question is your own operating business, with which you are identified, then you should probably own it.

Should you give stock to other key players in your organization in exchange for sweat equity, or their position in the family? Only you can answer that one, but keep in mind how you are going to handle things when trouble arises.

How To Read A Stock Certificate

A stock certificate is simply a piece of paper that represents the ownership of stock. It is like a deed to property or title to a vehicle. It is evidence of ownership. Therefore, the stock certificate should reflect the following information (except in the case of bearer stock, which carries no identification of the owner):

1. The name of the corporation of which the stock represents ownership.

2. The state in which the corporation is incorporated.

3. The number of the stock certificate. (They are progressively numbered in

sequence.)

4. How many shares of stock ownership the certificate represents.

5. What the authorized capitalization of the corporation is as of date of issue.

6. What kind and class of stock it is.

7. Whether it is a stated value or no-par value stock.

8. Whether it is fully paid and non-assessable, or if it may be assessable and is not fully paid.

9. Who the owner of the stock certificate is as recorded on books and records of the corporation. (The exception here is for bearer stock, which is issued without identification of the owner.)

10. The date that the certificate was issued to the recorded owner.

11. When you are dealing with an established resident or statutory agent of long standing and character, that information will also usually be reflected on the stock certificate.

12. Finally, the stock certificate is signed by duly authorized representatives of the corporation. In a private corporation, that is the secretary and president. There can be exceptions where it is signed by a duly authorized agent, usually known as a transfer agent. Public stock is usually countersigned by a transfer agent.

Look carefully at the sample stock certificate on the next page. You will note that there is a blank space provided for the number of shares at the upper right-hand corner of the certificate. In the space you type or print in ink the number of shares of ownership that the stock certificate represents.

We often get inquiries from people who think that they need one stock certificate for each share of stock issued. That is not true. You do not need 2,500 stock certificates to issue 2,500 shares. You simply note on the stock certificate the number of shares that the certificate is for, in the same way as you note on a check the number of dollars it is for. You do not issue a check for each dollar of a larger sum. You put the total amount on a single check, and the same is true with a stock certificate.

Be sure to check with the rules of the state in which you are incorporating before you place a value on your stock. Some states will charge additional fees if you place a large value on your stock.

You also enter in the name of the owner (except in bearer shares), and enter the number of shares the certificate represents. You date the stock certificate.

The Officers (secretary and president) sign or execute the stock certificate.

If one person is both the secretary and president, then that person signs the stock certificate in both places provided.

You do nothing to the back of the stock certificate at the time it is issued. The owner later transfers or cashes in the stock if desired.

You also fill in the stub, noting the number of shares and the name of the person to whom it is issued (except for bearer stock).

You date it, and then you have the recipient of the stock sign for the stock certificate at the very bottom of the stub (again, except for bearer stock).

You fill in the stock certificate number, the number of shares, and the date and have the recipient sign that receipt for the corporation as evidence that he received it (except for bearer stock).
Then the secretary records that information in the stock ledger section of your corporate record book

Voting Agreements & Voting Trusts

Now, let's say you are a minority Shareholder and want to have a continued power base to retain your directorship on the corporate board. Not having the financial resources to purchase enough stock to become a majority owner, what options do you have? One way to keep your power base is through a voting agreement, something called a "pooling agreement" This is a contract made between shareholders of a corporation that they will vote their stock in a particular way or in accordance with a

particular procedure. Typically, these agreements must be in writing. For the protection of the involved shareholders they certainly should be, even though your state of incorporation or corporate activity may not require them to be.

Another type of arrangement to maintain voting power for a minority Shareholder is a "voting trust." This is a more formal, more involved procedure than the voting agreement. Under the voting trust, the actual ownership of the shares is typically transferred to a third person, the "trustee." The trustee is granted the right and authority to vote the stock, in accordance with the terms of the trust agreement.

The laws regulating voting trusts are usually more stringent than those regulating voting agreements. A formal agreement must be drawn up, meeting the laws of the incorporation state. The duties of the trustee must be spelled out in detail. The agreement typically must be filed with the corporation. And while the voting agreement is between the shareholders, the voting trust agreement usually must be filed with the corporation. It may be necessary to file it with the corporation's registered agent and it must be open for inspection by Shareholders or their representatives during the term of the agreement.

Usually, the duration of voting trusts and agreements are limited by the laws of the states. Nevada limits them to 15 years,

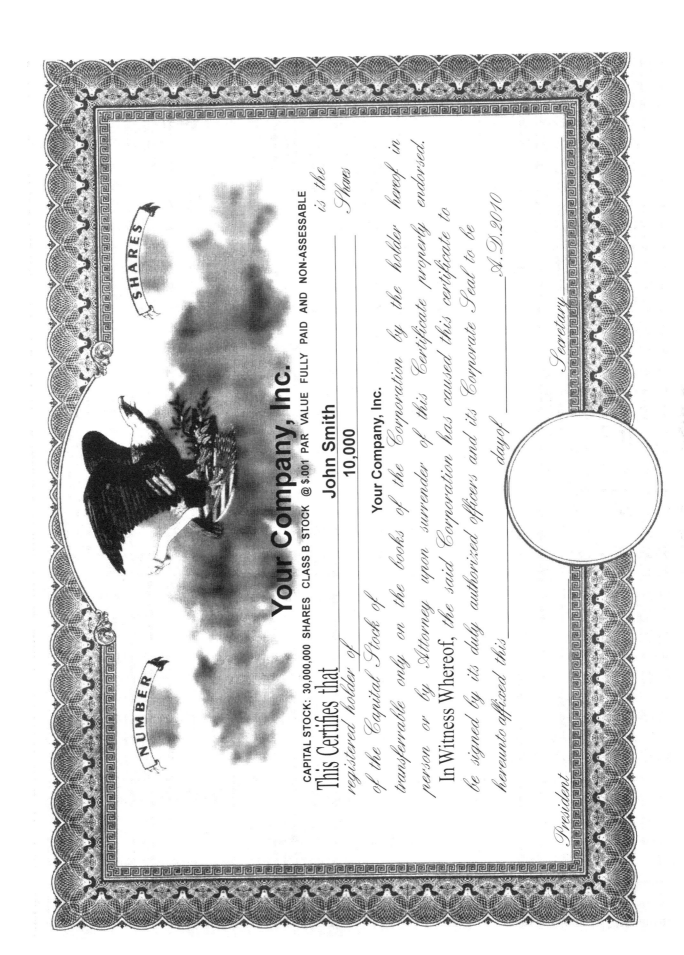

NUMBER

SHARES

Your Company, Inc.

CAPITAL STOCK: 30,000,000 SHARES CLASS B STOCK @ $.001 PAR VALUE FULLY PAID AND NON-ASSESSABLE

This Certifies that John Smith 10,000

is the

Shares

registered holder of

of the Capital Stock of Your Company, Inc.
transferrable only on the books of the Corporation by the holder hereof in
person or by Attorney upon surrender of this Certificate properly endorsed.
In Witness Whereof, the said Corporation has caused this certificate to
be signed by its duly authorized officers and its Corporate Seal to be
hereunto affixed this _____ day of _____ A.D. 2010

President

Secretary

but they may be renewed for another 15 years if the renewal is done within the last two years of the agreement. This keeps the parties in an agreement from having a 15-year term, and then extending the term the next day in order to avoid the statutory limitation.

What can a person do if the other party to a voting agreement doesn't act in accordance with the agreement, or if the trustee violates instructions? The trustee and the non-complying party to a voting agreement can be compelled by the court to vote in the way they were instructed, by specific performance. The damaged Shareholders could also seek to be compensated for any damages resulting from the wrongful votes.

Additionally, it is possible the result of the offending vote or votes could be set aside, particularly where the corporation is aware of the requirement that the shares be voted in a certain way and they were voted differently. The options available to the shareholder would depend on the state where the corporation is located.

Stockholders should specify in any voting trust or voting agreement what recourse the parties have in case the agreement is violated, including whether the vote is invalid, money damages, specific performance and payment costs and attorneys' fees to the prevailing party.

Buy Sell Agreements

Shareholders in a closely-held corporation should always have a buy/sell agreement. This is an agreement between shareholders in which certain events compel a Shareholder to sell shares either to the corporation or to other shareholders. There are basically two types of buy/sell agreements:

1. An entity purchase: In this case the "entity" (corporation) buys the shares from the Shareholder.

2. A cross-purchase: Here other Shareholders buy the shares.

We recommend the entity purchase since it is simpler, involving a transaction between two parties rather than multiple transactions between Shareholders. It's also cheaper in terms of legal fees.

There are six circumstances that should trigger buy/sell agreements. The first two are found in most such agreements, but the last four are also important.

1. Lifetime transfers: If one of the Shareholders wishes to sell some or all of his or her stock, then the corporation or its Shareholders should have first option to buy.

2. Upon the death of the Shareholder.

3. Upon the divorce of the Shareholder. This not only prevents at least half of the shares ending up in hostile hands, but also prevents disputes

between the divorcing parties about the value of the shares.

4.   On retirement. This would only apply in corporations in which the shareholders are active managers in the business and avoids a situation in which a formerly active Manager opts for the beaches of Hawaii and leaves the running of the corporation to those left behind.

5.   Disability. Again, for shareholder/ employees to avoid a situation in which a major participant is suddenly unable to perform duties but still maintains a large shareholding.

6.   Discord. If irreconcilable differences arise between shareholders, then as a last resort a buy/sell agreement should be invoked.

There are basically four different methods of establishing a fair price for buying out a shareholder:

1.   Periodic revaluation. The shareholders get together and mutually agree on the current value of the corporation.

2.   Appraisal. An outside appraiser is brought in to value the corporation.

3.   Formula. An agreed calculation (assets plus estimated future earnings minus liabilities divided by the number of shares) produces the share price.

4.   Book value. The price is based purely on the book value of the net corporate assets.

We recommend periodic revaluations (providing agreement can be reached among shareholders). The problem with appraisals is that the price can vary widely among appraisers and each appraisal can cost several thousand dollars. Formulas may become outdated as the corporation's circumstances change. Book value is likely to yield the lowest price and should be invoked only as a penalty clause — for example, with the discord provision — to motivate shareholders to resolve disputes amicably.

It is unreasonable to demand immediate payment for shares in a buy/sell agreement. We recommend an approach which provides between 10% and 30% as a down payment with the balance to be paid off over anything from three to eight years, with interest paid on the outstanding balance.

Selling Stock — Going Public & Other Issues

There are many diverse and complex laws and regulations that apply to selling stock or securities. Of course, we want to tell you right up front that applying statutes to your particular facts is the practice of law. Obviously, we don't have your facts and we don't practice securities law. But we would like to pass on some helpful information about selling stock.

Do not be apprehensive if you want to sell your stock in order to sell your corporation. That is not what we are discussing here. We are discussing a corporation selling its stock to raise money for capitalization. One of two kinds of regulations may apply:

1. An interstate public offering regulated by the Securities Exchange Commission (SEC).

2. An intrastate offering regulated by the state in which you make the sale.

Make no mistake about it — the offering or sale of stock or securities is serious business. You cannot simply go up one side of the street and down the other peddling stock. You cannot run an ad for the sale of stock in a newspaper or other publication. That is a public offering. You cannot address a meeting or seminar at which you offer to sell stock or securities. You cannot do any of those things without the proper approval of the proper state or SEC. There are thousands of other things you cannot do — those are just a few representative examples.

We cannot over-stress the importance of exercising caution and prudence by making a complete and careful investigation before proceeding as a Corporate Officer, Director or agent to attempt to sell stock. This is certainly one time and place where you definitely need the counsel of a competent securities and corporation lawyer in your state.

You may make a preliminary investigation by calling the closest federal SEC office or the proper regulatory commission in your state. However, even after you have basic information and knowledge, you still will be most certainly well-advised to consult with a corporation and securities attorney. This subject is so complex that even complying with one agency may leave you in trouble with another one. There can be many hidden traps.

Believe us! There have been many overzealous, ambitious, aggressive, innocent, well-meaning people who have gotten themselves into some very serious, long-term, expensive trouble (and in some cases into the penitentiary) by attempting the sale of stock.

We have discussed in generalities the laws that regulate the issue of stock by the corporation. If you have not understood that discussion, please go back and review it before proceeding.

The laws and regulations that govern the issuance and sale of stock by a corporation to the public are multiple and complex. They are usually time-consuming, burdensome and expensive to comply with.

However, the private sale of stock from one individual to another is an entirely different matter. The individual has acquired his or her stock from the corporation. It is now his or her stock. The stock does not belong to the corporation, it belongs to the individual.

An individual can sell stock to whomever without being encumbered by laws, rules and regulations. If you own stock in a corporation, you can sell it generally to whomever you wish. The corporation cannot.

Example: *Let's say there is a small, privately held-corporation with five stockholders. Now, obviously those five stockholders can continue to buy as much stock as they wish from the corporation so long as it is properly authorized and approved by the Board of Directors.*

Let's say those five stockholders can buy stock from the corporation at $8 per share. Say one of those stockholders buys 1,000 shares at $8 per share. Say that he then sells his stock to another individual at $10 per share. That is motive enough for his selling that stock. Then let's say he turns around and buys another 1,000 shares at $8 from the corporation, and then as an individual sells his own private stock to someone else.

The first thing you know, the corporation has a considerable amount of stock outstanding and is capitalized, but has never sold its stock to anyone but the original group of five stockholders.

When the people acquire the stock they purchased in a private transaction, they present that negotiable instrument to the secretary of the corporation and the stocks are then transferred on the books and records of the corporation from the individual to the new owner.

This corporation might eventually wind up with hundreds of stockholders, but it has never solicited anyone for the sale of stock, it has never sold any stock to anyone but the five original stockholders, and as we see it, it certainly is not in violation of any regulations. It has never registered as a public company because it has never made a public offering or sale of its stock.

In some situations there are restrictions on transfer of privately-held stock that require the stock to be held by the individual for a specified period of time. Additionally, some states have restrictions on how many sales a shareholder can enter into during a specified period (e.g., two sales in a 12-month period). Obviously, these types of restrictions vary from state to state; so even as an individual, you would be well-advised to review your stock sales plans with a knowledgeable securities lawyer in your home state.

Summary

There are several different types of corporations and types of stock that a corporation can issue. Knowledge of these different types of corporations and types of stock can greatly enhance your ability to use the corporate structure to your benefit.

The rules for issuing the corporate stock can either be straight-forward for initial shareholders or very complex when seeking potential shareholders as investors. Be very careful when seeking investors as the Securities Exchange Commission has very strict rules for soliciting these potential investors.

You have a couple of options should you wish to take your stock public, but again be very careful when taking steps to accomplish this. Know who you are working with and make sure they are licensed to complete the transactions necessary to take you public.

STOCK LEDGER STATEMENT

This statement made by __Your Company, Inc.__ , maintained and kept on file at its registered office in Nevada in compliance with Section 78.105 (d) of the Nevada Revised Statutes.

The name of the custodian of our stock ledger or duplicate stock ledger is:

John Smith
(Name of person in possession of Stock Ledger)

Whose complete address where said ledger is kept is:

1234 First St.
(Physical address — Street, etc.)

San Diego,   CA   92127
(City)   (State)   (Zip Code)

858-555-1234
(Telephone Number Including Area Code)

This statement is current until altered, changed, amended or revoked and our Nevada Resident Agent so notified by next Original revised statement or revocation.

DATED THIS 5th day of January , 2012 .

CERTIFIED TO BE THE STATEMENT OF:

Your Company, Inc.

By: _My Secretary_

NOTES

18 Professional Companies

- *Professionals Beware*
- *Too Much Passive Income*

So, you've gone the extra mile. You've earned that advanced degree, you are now a professional and you're thinking about personal protection from the risks you take in your practice, or you've worked hard all of your life and you've finally built up an investment portfolio that's worth protecting...think twice before you incorporate!

The government knows your potential earnings and wants to make sure they get their "fair" share.

What Are "Personal" Service Corporations?

A Personal Service Corporation (PSC) is a corporation whose principal activity is the performance of certain personal services that are substantially performed by employees who own more than 10% of the outstanding stock.

What personal services are we talking about here?

- Health & Veterinary Services
- Law
- Engineering (Including
- Surveying & Mapping)
- Architecture
- Actuarial Science
- Performing Arts
- Consulting

There are two tests to apply to determine whether a corporation is a Personal Service Corporation: a Function test, and an Ownership test. These are tests you'll want your corporation to flunk.

Function Test: The function test is met if substantially all (95% based on compensation costs) of a corporation's activities involve the performance of services in the fields of health and veterinary services, law, engineering (including surveying and mapping), architecture, accounting, actuarial science, performing arts or consulting.

Ownership Test: Specifically, this test requires that "substantially all" (at least 95%) of the value of the corporation's stock must be owned directly (or indirectly through one or more partnerships that do not have a corporation as a partner,

S-Corporations, or qualified PSCs that are not tax shelters) by 1) current or retired employees; 2) the estates of current or retired employees; or 3) persons who acquired the stock by reason of the death of such employees (but only for a 24-month period that begins on the date of the death of such employees).

In order to pass the test, the employees owning stock must perform services for the corporation in connection with activities involving one of the fields above. Indirect holdings through a trust are taken into account. For purposes of applying the ownership test, community property laws are disregarded, and stock owned by an ESOP or a pension plan is considered to be owned by the beneficiaries of the plan.

At the election of the common parent of an affiliated group, all members of the group may be treated as a single entity if 90% or more of the activities of such group involve the performance of services in the same qualified field. Stock is considered to be held indirectly by a person to the extent that he or she owns an interest in a partnership, S-Corporation, or qualified personal service corporation that owns such stock. For purposes of applying the ownership test, stock attribution rules, other than those already mentioned above, are to be ignored.

NOTE: The ownership test would not be considered to be met if non-employee

children owned more than 5% of the stock, despite the fact that their father might be an employee of the corporation.

If the corporation meets both of the above tests, then it is considered to be a Personal Service Corporation.

Disadvantages Of Personal Service Corporation Status

With one notable exception, status as a PSC is not beneficial. A PSC is exempt from the rule denying the cash method of accounting to corporations with more than $5 million in gross revenues. Now, the downside of Personal Service Corporation status:

1. Denies benefit of lower graduated corporate tax rates; all taxable income is taxed at the rate of 35%;

2. Postpones deductibility of payments to an employee-owner until the tax year in which the payment is income to the employee-owner, for accrual corporations;

3. Allows the IRS to reallocate income and deductions between the corporation and employee-owner where PSC is formed for tax avoidance motive;

4. Generally requires the corporation to have a calendar

year;

5. Limits loss deductions to the investment amount at risk; and

6. Limits deductions for passive losses.

Planning Tips Around Personal Service Corporation Status

The chain of stock ownership by attribution under code section 318 is only as strong as its weakest link. Severing the weakest link by having the employee-owner own 10% or less of the stock, with the balance owned by in-laws, brothers, sisters or individuals as listed above, will escape status as a Personal Service Corporation. Or, conversely, see that non-employee owners own more than 90%, or see that certain employees not connected to personal service activities own more than 90%. Also, if 80% or more of the corporation's compensation costs are paid to non-owner employees, who also perform services, then the corporation is not a Personal Service Corporation. Since S-corporations are not subject to PSC provisions, an S-corporation election will terminate status as a Personal Service Corporation as well.

Suffice it to say, that again, I like limited liability companies here in a lot of the circumstances or limited liability partnerships in the cases where certain state's laws do not allow an LLC to be a law corporation or an accounting corporation. But you can still have a corporate manager. And the corporate manager does not get income derived from the personal service activity. It gets income from managing the LLC or the LLP.

What Is A Personal Holding Company?

In 1934 the Personal Holding Company surtax provisions were added to the Internal Revenue Code. Wealthy individuals who placed their stocks, bonds, and other investments into controlled corporations to take advantage of the corporate tax brackets, which were lower than the highest individual tax brackets at that time, were referred to as "incorporated pocketbooks."

Put simply, a Personal Holding Company is a regular corporation, not an S-corporation in which five or fewer individuals own more than 50% of the stock which derives more than 60% of its income from personal holding company income sources as described below.

By Internal Revenue Code definition, a Regular Corporation is a Personal Holding Company by meeting the following tests:

1. If at any time during the last half of the tax year more than 50% in value of the outstanding stock is

owned, directly or indirectly, by or for not more than five individuals (including stock ownership by attribution under code section 544 which includes stock owned by brothers, sisters, spouse, grandchildren, and partners, and unlike code section 318 or PSCs, all lineal descendants, all ancestors, brothers, and sisters), and,

2. At least 60 percent of adjusted ordinary income for the tax year is "personal holding company income."

What Is Personal Holding Company Income?

As distinguished from an operating company's normal operating income and capital gains, Personal Holding Company Income includes:

1. Dividends, interest, and royalties (many exemptions apply here if interest or royalties are the primary trade or business of the corporation);

2. Rents, unless rents are greater than 50% of adjusted gross income, and a 10% test is met regarding dividends received (if no dividends, then no problem—your corporation is not a personal holding company;

3. Mineral, oil, and gas royalties, unless a similar 50% and 10% test are met as in (2) above (again, if you have no dividends, you have no worry);

4. Copyright royalties, unless a similar 50% and 10% test are met (again, no dividends, no problem);

5. Produced-film rents;

6. Payments received from a 25% or greater Shareholder for the use of personal property;

7. Payments received from personal service contracts for services performed by a 25% or greater Shareholder, who is specifically named in the service contract by the other party to the contract, and whose services are so specialized that no other person or substitute can be named to perform the services on behalf of the corporation;

8. Income derived from loan interest (unless a small business lending company exemption is met as could be the case for Warbucks. That exemption applies if generally the corporation has qualifying business expenses equal to at least 15% of the first $500,000. The company must

receive 60% or more of its income from an active and regular lending or financing business. No more than 20% of its ordinary gross income can be from sources such as dividends, rents, royalties and so forth; or,

9. Any gain derived from the sale of any interest in an estate or trust.

Disadvantage Of Personal Holding Company Status

The penalty for being classified as a PHC is a 35% additional surtax over and above the normal corporate tax rates on undistributed "Personal Holding Company Income" on tax years beginning January 1, 1993.

What To Do If You Might Fall Into The Personal Holding Corporation Trap

Your first line of defense here, if you think you have a problem, is to try to meet an exemption. This is usually a good possibility if your business is in copyrights, oil or gas royalties, making loans, renting real or personal property or providing personal services. Secondly, there are strategy options that you have available to "get out of the pickle."

Planning Tips To Avoid Personal Holding Company Status, Meeting An Exemption

1. Consider an S-Corporation election, since an S-Corporation is not subject to PHC tax provisions or, use an LLC instead of a corporation..

2. Reduce the amount of PHC income below 60%. For instance, dividend income can be reduced by investing only in growth stocks instead of yield stocks. Interest income can be reduced through shifting investments to exempt state and municipal obligations.

3. Increase operating income above 40%.

4. When using personal service contracts avoid naming a 25% or greater Shareholder as the individual to perform the service. If this is still not possible, add a provision to the service contract that allows the corporation to name a substitute providing the named employee-owner cannot perform the service. (NOTE: Professional retainer agreements are personal service contracts.)

5. If possible, spread ownership among at least 11 unrelated Shareholders so no five own greater than 50%.

6. Structure your affairs to meet an exemption if income is derived from royalties or interest.

Many times when we discuss corporation strategy options with attorneys and accountants, there is weeping and wailing regarding passive income and the personal holding corporation trap. We fail to see any problem here, ever, in any situation, if the Shareholders involved have enough business savvy to operate a simple corporate strategy as and when necessary. The strategy is a simple one involving two corporations.

The solution is whenever you are approaching an undesirable percentage of passive income (60%), cause the other corporation to do some business with the passive income corporation.

Purchase certain items or services through or from it, in order to alter the passive income percentage. That way you are pumping active income into the corporation. Pump enough active income into the corporation so that it is no longer in danger of being construed as a personal holding corporation.

Let's say the other corporation purchases $50,000 worth of items and services from the passive income corporation. That means $50,000 has gone from the other corporation to the passive income corporation. Now the passive corporation will purchase certain items and services from the other corporation.

The other corporation has its $50,000 back in the bank. The passive income corporation is no longer passive income,

because it has enough active business to alter that percentage. The entire transaction was a wash. There are no other taxable consequences or liabilities.

Just a little ingenuity and effort and some legitimate business transactions provide a simple solution to what some consider an impossible problem. (We might add: A Happy Solution!)

If Personal Holding Company status cannot be avoided, the penalty can be avoided by reducing taxable income to zero or below by increasing expense deductions which can include salaries to employee-owners. Also, don't forget perks like pensions and medical reimbursement plans.

An Exemption to the PHC Rule

One of the exemptions to being a personal holding company is the small business lending company exemption. If Warbucks is in the business of making loans with a maturity date of 144 months or less — meaning twelve years, which in the case of the demand note we're okay since that's considered a current obligation. If Warbucks is in the business of making loans for the maturity of 144 months or less, and it spends 15% of its first $500,000 on necessary and ordinary business expenses — which can include your director's fee, your travel, W2 salary to you, to your family, etc. — it spends 15% of its first 500,000, and 5% of the excess of above 500,000, you meet the qualifications of being a small business lending company, you're not a PHC.

So what do you need to do? You need to remember before the end of the tax year with Warbucks, if you're using the regular corporation, to pay out 15% of the first 500 grand — and 5% above that 500 — grand for necessary business expenses to insure that you have the necessary and ordinary business expense to meet the small business lending company exemption. Otherwise, they're going to rack you on federal taxes.

Now, another way around is, of course, an S Corporation, but we don't want to use an S Corporation for Warbucks because that's a pass-through entity. Income and losses of an S Corp pass through to the individual shareholder. Well, gee. What would that do? That would take the income from our home state company to the Nevada company right back to us in our home state, subjecting it to tax in our home state. Now an S-Corp's a way around, but you probably don't want to do that.

Limited Liability Companies & PHCs

You can have a limited liability company be Warbucks if you are not concerned about privacy. And while it's true that a limited liability company is going to be a pass-through entity, and any of its net income will pass through to us if we personally hold ownership in that LLC, we can have a corporation become it's member/manager. So we could have a corporation that manages the LLC and

charges the LLC fees to manage it. So we have the money that comes from our home state company to our Nevada limited liability company. The amount that we want to retain in Nevada income tax-free — state income tax-free — we pay to the Nevada corporation as the manager of the limited liability company. Voila, that is no longer interest income. That is income earned from managing the LLC. So we don't have a PHC in that Nevada corporation.

Remember how we talked about LLCs being neat tools as income diverter valves. They really are. And I really like an LLC. For those of you that want to go to a little additional level, I like a limited liability company as the Warbucks corporation because it allows you so much flexibility. With an LLC as the Warbucks corporation, you never had to worry about a personal holding company because it's not a regular C Corporation. You use the regular C Corporation as the manager of the limited liability company, and it never earns passive income. It's all active income. And you can put money in that corporation and retain it in Nevada where it's tax free. You get the asset protection, you get the state tax savings, and you don't have to pay out the 15% of the first 500,000 for business expenses.

Remember that Warbucks can also mix the services it offers and by selling enough copyrights, intellectual material, and other services you can easily bring the income mix to less than 60% circumventing any concern over it being considered a personal holding company.

Summary

Both Personal Service Corporations and Personal Holding Companies mean a higher tax liability if your corporation is classified as either one. Personal Service Corporations pay a flat tax of 35% and Personal Holding Companies have a 35% additional tax on any undistributed earnings. By knowing the exceptions to the rules you can circumvent these potential problems.

A situation where your business may be considered a Personal Service Corporation you can take S-Corporation election or use an LLC instead and work with your Warbucks corporation to retain money in your business endeavors for future growth, asset protection and the tax savings it can offer you.

If you arrange your business affairs where your corporation may be defined as a holding company, such as several possible Warbucks scenarios, you can use an LLC with a corporate member manager that charges most if not all of the profit as it's Management fee. This service is active in nature so the income it produces would not result in a classification of the corporation as a Personal Holding Company.

NOTES

Appendix

APPENDIX A

TYPES OF ENTITIES

Corporation: A corporation is considered a separate legal entity; because of this, the owners of the corporation (known as shareholders or stockholders) are not personally responsible for the losses of the business. Creditors of the corporation may look only to the corporation and the business assets for payment. The individual shareholders are not personally liable for the losses of the business if the corporation is properly established and maintained. Although a corporation usually has more than one owner, it is possible for only one individual to create and own 100 percent of the corporation.

A corporate can be formed in its home state or any other state. The corporation is regulated by the state it was formed in. This can be very beneficial if you form your company in a preferred state like Nevada or Wyoming.

S-Corporations: A corporation can elect to be treated as an S-corporation for tax purposes. This means that without first being taxed at the corporate level, all income or losses are passed through to the individual shareholders. Essentially, an S-corporation is treated like a partnership for tax purposes, but it has all the limited liability protection of a regular corporation.

S-corporations, however, don't have many of the fringe benefits that regular corporations do, such as certain pension plans and full deductibility of passive losses against active income. An S-corporation can, however, help you to reduce self-employment taxes while avoiding double taxation.

Limited Partnership: A limited partnership is taxed like a partnership yet it has many of the liability protection aspects of a corporation. There are two types of partners in a limited partnership: the limited partners, who invest in the partnership but have no control, and the general partner (or partners), who controls the partnership. The asset protection property of a limited partnership is held by a charging order. Which means if a limited partnership is sued a judge can issue a charging order allowing the plaintiff rights to the partnership interest. That means that the creditor only gets what the general partner decided to distribute, which is often nothing. Making the limited partnership a very powerful asset protection tool when utilized with other business structures.

Limited Liability Company: Limited Liability Company, as its name implies, provides limited liability for its members-owners, like a limited partnership provides for its limited partners or a corporation provides for its shareholders.

Unlike a corporation, LLCs provide members the power of controlling other members' ability to transfer the ownership or voting power of their membership. An LLC can be structured to be taxed as either a "pass-through" entity or as an association that pays its own taxes.

LLCs have far fewer restrictions on membership than an S-corporation has on shareholders. LLCs also allow members to participate in management of the LLC without losing their protection from liability, whereas a limited partner in a limited partnership does not have this benefit.

The main disadvantage of LLCs is that their use is relatively new in the United States and so there is no uniformity in the laws governing LLCs between the individual states. Also, because they are new, there is little case law to help you make decisions based on your state's past decisions concerning LLCs

Private Corporation: A corporation that is owned and controlled by a private group of people, as opposed to the general public. This term distinguishes a corporation that is owned by individuals, for a business purpose, from the corporations that are used for governmental purposes or those whose stock is sold to the public (cities are actually "municipal corporations"). A corporation that is owned by a small group of people (10, for example) might be considered a private corporation; whereas, a corporation whose stock is traded in the public market (New York Stock Exchange, over the counter, etc.) and has thousands of Shareholders would be considered "public."

Public Corporation: A corporation whose stock is traded on the public market. This can also refer to a governmental corporation for public purposes.

Closely Held Corporation: This term is generally used with regard to federal taxation and means a corporation in which five or fewer Shareholders hold 50% or more of the stock in the company. Also, it is commonly used in a less technical and accurate way to describe any company held by a single Stockholder or a closely knit group of Stockholders.

Close Corporation: It is good to know what a close corporation is so you can avoid involvement with one. It is a creature that only some states allow to be formed. The close corporation is designed so that a few people can form a corporation and operate it without the normal formalities of a regular corporation, such as certain minutes of meetings, resolutions, and the like. Although this might sound appealing, upon further consideration it usually proves to be the road to disaster.

APPENDIX B

Why Form A Business Entity In Nevada ?
Directors And Officers Protected

<u>NRS 78.138</u> protects Directors and Officers from personal liability for lawful acts committed on behalf of the corporation or by the corporation.

Although Delaware and a few other states have enacted similar legislation, the Nevada law is much more thorough, all-inclusive and comprehensive. The message to corporations and their Directors and Officers is designed to say loud and clear, "Go West, entrepreneurs, go West!" to Nevada for incorporation benefits.

Advocates said that because of the concern over big awards or settlements that can result from shareholder lawsuits, corporations have had difficulty in finding qualified people to serve as Directors.

Because corporations draw their powers from the laws of the state of their home domicile (the state in which they are incorporated), it is believed that knowledgeable attorneys and entrepreneurs will place their home domicile in Nevada and, if necessary, qualify to do business in the state(s) where they wish to do business in order to have the protection of the Nevada home domicile.

Why Nevada Corporations?

The corporation laws of the state of Nevada have many advantages over similar laws and are far more liberal than laws in any other state in the Union. This policy has been felt to be advisable by our Legislature for many years to encourage prospective incorporators to come within this jurisdiction. Some of the compelling reasons, benefits and advantages that make it good business for you to incorporate in Nevada follow.

- No franchise tax — even though you do business in another state, your franchise taxes may be reduced or eliminated in many situations as a result of your Nevada corporate status

- Nevada has no corporate income taxes whatsoever.

- Nevada has a constitutional ban on personal income tax.

- Shares can be sold or transferred with no state tax consequences.

- No succession tax. This added type of inheritance tax is found in some states but not in Nevada.

- Stockholders and Directors are not required to live in or hold meetings in Nevada. In fact, such meetings may be held anywhere in the world. Of course, travel expenses are usually reimbursed by the corporation and fully tax deductible.

- Nevada allows corporations to determine what kind of stock will be issued.

- Nevada law allows bylaws to be changed by Directors.

- Initial or minimum capital is not required.

- Anonymity, privacy, secrecy of owners or stockholders of a Nevada corporation: Nevada is the only state in the union which refuses to share tax and other official data with the Internal Revenue Service.

Nevada corporations have freedom to do business practically any place on the globe where such activity is legal. And the corporation is free to engage in almost any business activity from buying to selling real property.

- Minimal disclosure and reporting requirements: Only names and addresses of Officers, Directors and resident agents are required on an annual basis. Meetings can be held anywhere, at the option of the Directors, a feature of Nevada law that can be very valuable to you.

- Nevada welcomes new

corporations. Incorporation is completed with a minimum of delay and a maximum of cooperation.

- Directors may, by majority resolution, designate one or more committees with a Director or Directors on said committee(s) to manage the business and have full power.

- Nevada allows you to conduct business at one or more offices and hold, purchase, mortgage and convey real and personal property in this state, and in any of the states, territories, possessions and dependencies of the United States, the District of Columbia, and any foreign country. (NRS 78.070(4))

- Nevada corporations can guarantee, purchase, hold, take, obtain, receive, subscribe for, own, use, dispose of, sell, exchange, lease, lend, assign, mortgage, pledge or otherwise acquire, transfer or deal in or with bonds or obligations of, or shares securities or interests in or issued by, any person, government, governmental agency or political subdivision of government, and to exercise all the rights, powers and privileges of ownership of such an interest, including the right to vote. (NRS 78.070(2))

Nevada: Annual Reporting Requirements And Fees

The current reporting annual requirements in order to maintain your corporation in good standing in Nevada are:

- You must file each year, on the anniversary date of your incorporation, a one-page list of Officers and Directors, containing their name, address and the name and address of your resident agent.

- Annual state business license

- Resident Agent

Laughlin Associates can act as your Resident Agent. We only charge $135.00 per year after the first year (the first year is included in your Deluxe Corporate Package). As a part of our Resident Agent Service, we notify you each year when the annual filing is due, and send the necessary forms to you for the approval and signature of your president. You send it back to us and we execute our part and file the annual document for you with the Secretary of State. Just part of our personalized service to protect you and make sure your company stays current.

WHY NEVADA CORPORATIONS?

SUPERIOR NEVADA CORPORATION ADVANTAGES AND BENEFITS TO YOU:
SELECTED TAXES IMPOSED BY WESTERN STATES

State	Franchise	Corporate Income (Percent)	Personal Income (Percent)	Sales (Percent)
NEVADA	NO	NO	NO	6.85+
ARIZONA	YES	6.968	2.59-4.54	6.6
CALIFORNIA	YES*	8.84	1.0-9.3	7.25 +
OREGON	YES	6.6	5-9	NO
UTAH	YES*	5	5.00	5.95-7.70
COLORADO	YES	4.63	4.63	2.9
IDAHO	YES	7.6	1.6-7.8	6
MONTANA	YES*	6.75	1-6.9	NO
WYOMING	NO**	NO	NO	4
WASHINGTON	NO	NO***	NO	6.5
NEW MEXICO	YES	4.8-7.6	1.7-4.9	5.125

* Corporate income tax
** Filing fee based on corporate property and assets located and employed in Wyoming.
***Gross receipts tax imposed

APPENDIX C

Nevada Headquarters Program
5p's Of The Nevada Headquarters Program

Profits, Privacy, Protection, Proof, And Prestige

Your privacy can be preserved and enhanced. You can have bulletproof protection for your assets, your loved ones and your future. Your profits can be increased. Plus, you can prove that everything you have done to achieve these vital goals is legitimate, aboveboard, and legal. You can have it all with the Nevada Headquarters Program.

When you incorporate in the tax-free state of Nevada, you incorporate in the state with the best pro-business corporation and tax laws in the United States. You incorporate in the only state that does not share your confidential tax information with the Internal Revenue Service. You incorporate in a state that has absolute nondisclosure of the Shareholders or owners of the corporation. You incorporate where you have privacy.

Why Not Achieve The Full Potential That Incorporating In Nevada Offers You?

You see, many people are deceived

into believing that by simply forming a Nevada corporation they can avoid their home state income taxes and have the privacy that incorporating in Nevada offers. That is not true.

The main factor that determines where your Nevada corporation does business is the location of its office, its headquarters, and its base of operations.

Proof

With your Nevada Headquarters Program your corporation has a real office. That office is staffed with real people operating under contract to you or your corporation. When those people provide services on behalf of your corporation, they become your corporation's contract employees. That provision is in the Nevada Headquarters Program Agreement. The Nevada Headquarters Program proves you have a real office for your corporation in Nevada.

Do Not Be Deceived Into Perpetrating A Sham

Many try to use abbreviated office services, mail drops, answering services, and other services to make it "look" like their Nevada corporation has an office, employees, and conducts business in the state of Nevada. That's like living in a campsite and claiming you own a home. It's not true or real. It won't work. It's a sham and a fraud.

You are serious about your business operation, and you certainly want to prove it is legitimate. You want it to be real. You want it to be legal.

Webster's dictionary defines a sham as a hoax purporting to be real. If you get a mail drop and abbreviated office service (or any one of the things that people do to make it "look" like their corporation is doing business in Nevada) you have a sham. You are saying it's a real office. You're saying it's a real business operation. But the facts prove otherwise.

On examination by your state's tax board, one attorney poking around, one investigator checking the situation out, or one customer checking on your credibility and it's all over. Your sham is exposed and so are you. You are exposed to your corporation's tax-free status could be set aside. You are exposed to a plaintiff's attorney successfully arguing that you promoted a fraud or created an injustice.

Meeting The Tests Of A Corporation

Doing Business In Nevada

Proving that your Nevada corporation operates and does business in Nevada is essential to corporation strategies that lawsuit-proof your business, eliminate or reduce state income taxes and protect your privacy. The proof is imperative. The following proofs and tests must be met:

The corporation should have an actual business address.

- The corporation should have its own telephone listed in its name at the office address. This telephone service should be documented by actual monthly telephone bills and the corporation's canceled check for payment of same.

- The corporation should have a business license issued to it by the City of Carson City to do business at the above address.

- The corporation should have people at the Nevada office to take care of its business, to answer the phone, to greet and handle any callers, and to receive and to disburse mail, messages, etc.

- The corporation should open and maintain its own bank account.

Once you subscribe to the Nevada Headquarters Program your business can very efficiently conduct real, legitimate, provable operations in the state of Nevada. With the Nevada Headquarters Program you now have an office, a bank account, a business license, and a telephone in your company's name. That number is available to anyone who dials Directory Information.

What You Get And How The Nevada Headquarters Program Works

Business Address. With the Nevada Headquarters Program you'll have an actual business address under your agreement with us. You'll have your own unique business address in the Laughlin Building and you will have an agreement to prove it.

Telephone. You'll have a telephone listed in the name of your corporation. Your corporation's name will be published in the Carson City telephone directory. The number will be available from Directory Information. That telephone is answered by a live operator in your company name. You'll also have a Yellow Page listing that shows your corporation is a public holding out to do business. This is an important legal point and often a legal necessity.

When your telephone line rings, the person answering the phone knows at a glance of the screen how to answer the telephone and also knows your specific instructions about how to handle the call. They'll know such information as who is with your company, what your company's products and services are, and what information they are supposed to give out concerning the people with your company.

Your Contract Employees. You'll have contract employees in your office.

Business License. We assist you in obtaining a business license at your Nevada business address for your corporation. Anyone can quickly determine that you are licensed to do business in Nevada simply by a quick check with the local licensing bureau.

Bank Account. You'll receive assistance in opening a bank account for your corporation.

Mail Service. You have complete mail service, both inbound and outbound, handled by your contract personnel. That means mail is forwarded to you from your corporation according to your instructions, or your mail can be held at your office.

How Your Visitors Are Handled. Further, your office is completely staffed at all times during normal business hours. Instead of a dead office or a front, you have a real office with real people in it who are contracted to take care of your business when and as needed. Your Nevada Headquarters manager is on duty at all times.

FAX Service. You are also able to include our fax number on your business cards and advertising materials. This can be a real plus and prestige item for immediate transactions and high level priorities.

To sum it all up, the Nevada Headquarters Program gives you proof of a real Nevada base and operation. That proof translates into profits through tax savings, privacy by doing business in Nevada, and protection through strategies now available to you. Add in the prestige afforded by the professional atmosphere and the package is complete.

With your Nevada Headquarters Program, your Nevada corporation can operate in tax-free Nevada independently and separate from you. You get the asset protection and tax savings that your Nevada corporation can offer. You realize the full potential of doing business in Nevada. You enjoy more money in your pocket, and you are safer and more secure. The best part is that with your Nevada office and staff everything can be done in and through the Nevada office.

You can see how the Nevada Headquarters Program can turn your Nevada corporation into the tool that will provide you with profits through state tax savings, asset protection, business privacy, and proof of legitimacy. The prestige that goes with the territory is a bonus. Our consultants would be happy to discuss strategies and ideas with you that you can tailor to your own specific situation.

Appendix: D

WARBUCKS/RED, INC.

What can your Nevada or Wyoming corporation do without having to pay taxes to your home state?[1]

The Supreme Court recently clarified some ambiguous provisions of a long standing public law. This clarification will give you great guidance if you choose to use your Nevada or Wyoming corporation for state income tax planning. 15 U.S.C. §381 sets forth when states can, and when states cannot, assert taxing authority over an out-of-state (Nevada) corporation. Essentially, §381 states that a state cannot assert taxing authority over an out-of-state (foreign) corporation unless that corporation has a sufficient nexus with that state for it to do so. So what's a sufficient nexus? This question was cleared up in Wisconsin Dept. of Revenue v. William Wrigley, Jr., 112 S. Ct. 2447 (1992).[2]

According to §381 (a), an out-of-state (foreign) corporation can engage in any conduct which constitutes the "solicitation of orders". The Supreme Court, per Justice Scalia, expanded this rule to any activity which is entirely ancillary to requests for purchases — in other words, to include those activities that serve no independent business apart from their connection to the soliciting of orders. Therefore, any activity which is directly the solicitation of orders, or is entirely ancillary to the solicitation of

orders, is immune from taxation by the state in which the activity takes place.

The Wrigley court cited several examples of what activities would be protected from state taxation under §381, and what activities would not be. Activities such as recruiting, training and evaluating an in-state sales force, providing that sales force with company cars and sample products, and the use of hotel rooms for sales-related meetings are considered ancillary to the solicitation of orders, as they do not have any business purpose apart from the solicitation of orders. However, other activities within a state, such as product repairs, storing products in the state for the purpose of selling or replenishing a retailers stock, or maintaining an office in the state cannot be construed as ancillary to the solicitation of orders, and thus destroy any §381 immunity from taxation in that state which your company may have enjoyed. The court made a special point about the maintenance of an office in the taxing state, when it stated, "Even if engaged in exclusively to facilitate requests for purchases, the maintenance of an office within the state, by the company or on its behalf, would go beyond the solicitation of orders... It seemingly represents a judgment that a company office within a state is such a significant manifestation of company "presence" that, absent a specific exception, income taxation should always be allowed". Wrigley, 112 s. ct. at 2457.

Appendix D

So, basically, your corporation can do anything with regard to the solicitation of sales of your products or services. What you cannot do is go beyond the solicitation of sales, or have an office base within the taxing state, unless you want to be taxed by that state. A Nevada or Wyoming corporation with a headquarters in one of those states can truly be your golden opportunity when it comes to saving your hard-earned money.

NOTE: The Supreme Court has now said what we have been saying for years. The tax strategy that we suggest WORKS. It is simple, LEGAL, honest and efficient. If anyone wants to question the legality of what we propose, they should take it up with the U.S. Supreme Court!

GREGORY v. HELVERING, 293 U.S. 454 (1935)GREGORY v. HELVERING, 293 U.S. 454 (1935)

"The legal right of a taxpayer to decrease the amount of what otherwise would be his taxes, or altogether avoid them, by means which the law permits, cannot be doubted."

RAYMOND PEARSON MOTOR CO. v. COMMISSIONER, 246 F.2d 509

"Taxpayers are not required to continue that form of organization which results in the maximum tax."

MOLINE PROPERTIES, INC. v.

COMM., 319 U.S. 436MOLINE PROPERTIES, INC. v. COMM., 319 U.S. 436

In 1943, the United States Supreme Court said:

Whether the purpose (of incorporating) be to gain an advantage under the law of the state of incorporation or to avoid or comply with the demands of creditors . . . so long as that purpose is the equivalent of a business activity or is following by the carrying on of business by the corporation, the corporation remains a separate taxable entity . . . .

A LEGAL IMPENETRABLE NEVADA ENTITY FOR YOU: THE ONE PERSON CORPORATION

Often times when the one-man corporation is discussed, it is alleged that the corporate veil may be easily pierced or set aside. NOT true under protection of the Nevada law. This is the case whether you are talking about a one-person or a 20-person corporation.

The corporate veil is that shield separating Directors, Officers and Shareholders from the corporate entity. The principle of piercing through the corporate veil and holding Directors, Shareholders and/or Officers responsible is known as the "Alter Ego Doctrine." The Doctrine simply means there is no corporation. The corporation is not an entity separate and distinct from the Directors, Officers and Shareholders. It is, in reality, only a sham that exists as a mirror image or "Alter Ego" of the individuals composing the business. It is these individuals and not the corporation that are held liable.

The most effective and simple insurance or guarantee to protect the corporate entity is for a corporation to observe corporate formalities.

Nevada offers further insurance and piece of mind to those who wonder how strong the corporate veil really is. In Nevada, it's very strong. In Nevada, Shareholders, Directors and officers can find the ultimate personal liability protection and sleep like babies. The fear of personal liability has become almost non-existent in Nevada.

The Supreme Court of Nevada has refused to apply the Alter Ego Doctrine in the landmark case Rowland v. LePire, 99 Nev. 308, 662 P.2d 1332 (1983). Rowland, following earlier cases, set forth the requirements for piercing the corporate veil in Nevada under an Alter Ego theory.

These requirements are:

1. The corporation must be influenced and governed by the person asserted to be its alter ego.

2. There must be a unity of interest and ownership, that one is inseparable from the other.

3. The facts must be such that adherence to the fiction of a separate entity would, under the circumstances, sanction a fraud or promote injustice.

To put this more simply, the person or persons running and owning the corporation will be deemed its alter ego if their interest and that of the corporation cannot be separated, and, if maintaining the corporate entity would be unjust or create a fraud (the key factor in determining whether to pierce the corporate veil).

To realize how much this ruling benefits you, you should understand the facts and circumstances surrounding Rowland. The corporation did not have a minutes book, nor was there any evidence supporting the proposition that any minutes were ever kept. The corporation was under-capitalized, and no formal Directors or Shareholders meetings were ever held. In fact, the Nevada court even came right out and said, "There was little existence of the corporation separate and apart from Martin and Glenn Rowland."

Simply stated, the court found a situation in Rowland where corporate records and formalities were almost nonexistent. They found a situation in which the corporation was almost indistinguishable from the people behind it. Yet, through all of this, the court refused to pierce the corporate veil.

Appendix D
Why?

Because the Supreme court found sufficient grounds even in this case to find that the corporation did, though barely, have an identity apart from its owners. The corporation was almost indistinguishable from the people behind it—but not quite. Even though the corporation in Rowland was under-capitalized and maintained little adherence to the separation of the corporate entity from its owners, the court reasoned that the maintenance of a checking account, a general contractor's license, bonding, and workers compensation insurance in the name of the corporation were sufficient to establish, though minimally, a separate corporate entity. This is what is meant by a "pro-business" Nevada judiciary.

Besides, in Nevada someone seeking to pierce the corporate veil has a large burden to shoulder. Not only must the person show that the corporation is indistinguishable from the people behind it, but must also show that the corporation, as a separate person, would create a fraud or promote injustice.

The court reasoned that, "It is incumbent upon the one seeking to pierce the corporate veil, to show by a preponderance of the evidence, that the financial setup of the corporation is only a sham and caused an injustice."

Furthermore, in many states under-capitalization of a corporation alone would be sufficient grounds to pierce the corporate veil. This is not the case in Nevada.

In Rowland, the court went on to say that in Nevada under-capitalization is not by itself grounds to pierce in the absence of fraud. Under-capitalization is merely a factor in determining whether to apply the Alter Ego Doctrine. Rowland at 1337.

Yes, the corporate veil is safe in Nevada. Rowland v. Lepire is representative of numerous cases demonstrating that fact. Case law mentioned in Rowland that supports the proposition of a "hard to pierce" corporate veil in Nevada is as follows: Mosa v. Wilson-Bates Furniture Co., 94 Nev. 521, 583 P.2d 453 (1978); McCleary Cattle Co., v. Sewell, 73 Nev. 279, 317 P.2d 957 (1957). In North Arlington Med. v. Sanchez Constr., 86 Nev. 515, 522, 471 P.2d 240, 244 (1970).

This line of reasoning was followed in Aetna Casualty and Surety v. RASA Mgt. Co. Inc., 621 F. Supp. 892 (D. Nev. 1985). The United States District Court for the District of Nevada simply stated it was insufficient to allege sole incorporator, shareholder, and director, in order to apply the Alter Ego Doctrine. Aetna at 894.

In the end it is clear to see that in Nevada the corporate veil remains strong, and thus you are safe.

Now, don't go off into the peaceful bliss of corporate fantasy land and think that you can get away with sloppy, unorganized or nonexistent corporate records and formalities. Formalities are those things that prove the corporation acts as a separate person apart from its Shareholders, Directors and Officers. Formalities and records refer to things like minutes, resolutions, etc.

This section shows you the protection afforded to you and your corporate entity in the Nevada courts. It is not meant to say that you can neglect good corporate record keeping. All authorities are not so forgiving as the Nevada courts. The Feds and other jurisdictions may have pierced the corporate veil, so be careful to keep good corporate records even though you have your corporation in the safe haven of Nevada.

To summarize, the corporate veil is safe in Nevada, the safe haven, though that's no excuse to handle your corporation in any way but the right way.

Tax Avoidance Legal For One Party In Two-party Exchange

The Federal Court of Appeals for the Second Circuit has ruled that it is legal if a business arrangement between two parties involves tax avoidance for one of the parties as long as the second party enters into the agreement for legitimate, non-tax avoidance reasons.

This means that if you can come up with a business relationship that benefits yourself from a tax standpoint while making good business sense for someone else for non-tax reasons, the IRS cannot challenge the arrangement as "merely a device" to avoid taxes.

The case (Newman, CA-2, 1/23/90) involved a taxpayer who had purchased a tractor-trailer and had an agreement with the trucking company that operated the truck as a contract between an employer and an independent contractor rather than a lease.

The IRS challenged the plan, arguing that it was a disguised lease and that the arrangement was merely for tax avoidance.

The Second Circuit Court, however, honored the form of the agreement based on a Supreme Court Case (Frank Lyon Co. 435 U.S. 561, 1978) which held that agreements intended to have economic substance as opposed to mere tax avoidance should be allowed. The court established four tests for agreements claiming to have economic substance. They must:

1.   Be made for non-tax business reasons.

2.   Have economic substance.

3.   Be between independent parties acting at arm's length.

4.   Be honored in form and
        substance by the parties to the
        agreement.

With regards to these tests, the Circuit
Court ruled:

1.   The trucking company was
        motivated by non-tax business
        reasons, even if the taxpayer was
        not.

2.   The taxpayer's liability for
        operating costs and risk of
        losses showed the agreement
        had non-tax economic substance.

3.   The trucking company and the
        taxpayer dealt at arm's length.

4.   The trucking company
        complied with the form of the
        agreement.

NOTES

Instant Glossary

Alter ego doctrine — This principle allows the courts to refuse a corporation's right to shield its owners from the liabilities associated with the corporation. It stipulates that a corporation formed merely for personal advancement rather than sound and legitimate business purposes — cannot be considered a corporation.

Annual meeting of directors — This is a yearly meeting of the directors of a corporation to show ongoing management of the corporation. These meetings are usually mandatory and help to prove the corporation is currently viable.

Annual meeting of stockholders — This is a yearly meeting of the stockholders of a corporation to show ongoing management of the corporation. These meetings are usually mandatory and are mainly used to elect directors for the next business year.

Articles of incorporation — Articles represent the contracts that hold the corporation together and set the guidelines for the business purpose and how the corporation will be structured.

Bearer shares — Stock of a corporation that is owned by the holder of those shares. These are hard to track and make it hard to call meetings or take a vote in a corporation.

Bylaws — These are rules adopted by an organization chiefly for the government of its members and the regulation of its affairs.

Charging Order – A "Charging Order" is what is issued to a judgement creditor who has won a lawsuit against a party who only owns a percentage of shared interest property. (They can't take the stuff because it doesn't belong entirely to you – but they can take the proceeds or the profits that you enjoy from that property.)

Corporation — A body formed and authorized by law to act as a single person although constituted by one or more persons and legally endowed with various rights and duties including the capacity of succession.

Deed of trust — A document that evidences a lien on real property, not unlike a mortgage.

Director — An individual selected to sit on a board that transforms the goals of the stockholders into action plans.

Employee — An individual hired by a business to fulfill the common duties of the business through an employee contract.

Fiscal Year — An accounting period of 12 months.

Foreign corporations — A corporation that is formed in another state or jurisdiction that qualifies to do business in another state.

Formalities — The procedures that must be followed to allow a corporation to run as a separate entity.

Fraudulent Conveyance — A transfer of property intended to place assets out of reach of rightful creditors.

Freestanding Resolution — A motion passed on the spot by the Board of Directors to resolve an issue. The ability to make freestanding resolutions is given to one director, or when there is only one director to make the resolution. This is a more expedient and less formal way of making major decisions in a corporation. These freestanding resolutions still need to be entered into the corporate minutes as past business of a corporation for the next meeting of directors.

Judgment Creditor — The winning plaintiff in a lawsuit to when the court decides the defendant owes money.

Limited Partner — A partner in a venture who has no management authority and whose liability is restricted to the amount of his or her investment.

Partnership — a: A legal relation existing between two or more persons contractually associated as joint principals in a business **b:** the persons joined together in a partnership, a relationship resembling a legal partnership and usually involving close cooperation between parties having specified and joint rights and responsibilities.

Preferred State — A state in which the laws and regulations that govern business are established to encourage economic growth in favor of business.

Red Inc. — A fictitious term used to describe your home state corporation; the state in which you are currently doing business.

Registered Agent — One who is readily available for service of legal process; duties vary from state to state.

Registered Shares — Shares that have been issued and the current owners names and addresses are recorded.

Resolution — A written consent to action by the Board of Directors.

Shareholder — An owner of stock in a corporation.

Warbucks Nevada, Inc. — A fictitious term used to describe a Nevada corporation that is making money in the tax-free state of Nevada.

Writ of Execution – A "Writ of Execution"

can be issued to a judgement creditor
who has won a lawsuit so that they may
step in and take what they need from
you in order to satisfy the judgement
awarded to them through the lawsuit.
(They can come in and take your stuff.)

FORMATION PACKAGE

Corporation or LLC Package
Laughlin Makes Incorporating EASY!!

- Company Name Search - to ensure your choice is available

- Filing of the Articles of Formation/Organization

- 12 Months of Registered Agent Service

- Customized Complete Deluxe Corporate Kit, Seal and 20 Stock Certificates

- Corporate Bylaws and First Meeting Minutes

- Federal Employer Identification Number (EIN) - assistance with filing

- Assistance with Subchapter S Election Form 2553 (form only)

- Kit Review - A hands-on review and walk through of your corporate kit

- Unlimited Phone Support

- Subscription to the Power of INC. Newsletter

- Priority Handling

- Shipping Via UPS 3 Day Service

- First Year Federal Tax Return

- Limited Liability Company Contains Alternative Forms:
  - Operating Agreement
  - Membership Certificates
  - Membership Ledger

Laughlin will incorporate or form a LLC in all 50 states!

THE NEVADA HEADQUARTERS PACKAGE

Nevada has consistently proven itself as a premier state for businesses to incorporate in. Laughlin pioneered the Nevada Headquarters program over 40 years ago so that our clients could take full advantage of all the benefits Nevada provides, in particular reduced taxes and rock solid asset protection.

Your Nevada Headquarters program establishes a complete corporate base including the following:

Business Address. With the Nevada Headquarters Program, you'll have an actual business address.

Business License. We assist you in obtaining a business license at your Nevada business address for your corporation. Anyone can quickly determine that <u>you are licensed to do business</u> in Nevada by simply checking with the local licensing bureau.

The Agreement. You'll receive a written, binding <u>agreement</u>. This is an ironclad contract that <u>is worded to give you documentation</u> that you have a real operating office with contract personnel that meets the legal criteria.

Telephone. Your telephone will be answered by a live operator and your calls are handled according to your specific instructions.

Contract Employees. You'll have contract employees working in your office including an in-house office manager.

Mail Service. You have complete mail service, both inbound and outbound.

Strategic Consultations. Our consultants have at their disposal a network of attorneys, CPAs and other professionals who can help find the solutions you need. By phone, or in person, your account executive will help you develop your corporate strategy.

1-800-648-0966
www.laughlinusa.com

TURNKEY PACKAGE

If you need asset protection right now, we have the solution. With our Turnkey Corporate Package you will receive everything included in our Corporate Privacy Package, but with your Nevada Corporation already formed, business license already in place and all of the corporate paperwork already taken care of. Everything is operational at the point of purchase.

The Turnkey Corporate Package includes:

- **An exisiting Nevada corporation**
- **The Nevada Headquarters Program** - initial paperwork already completed
- **Professional Nominee Service**
    - Contract officer represented on the list of officers filed with the Nevada secretary of state.
    - Preparation of the first minutes
    - Client appointed Vice President with full powers
- **Corporate Record Keeping**

Call 1-800-648-0966 for pricing

1-800-648-0966
www.laughlinusa.com

CORPORATE VEIL PROTECTION SERVICE

- Initial review of your corporate status with your compliance coach. Our quick and easy online questionnaire outlines which documents your company needs now.

- Unlimited custom corporate documents including minutes, resolutions and amendments.

- Unlimited access to a personal corporate coach by phone or e-mail anytime to receive quick, knowledgeable answers to your questions.

- 12-month customized calendar of recommended documents.

- Corporate benefit kit; includes a priceless library of resources.

- Ongoing monitoring service and auditing of your corporate records, and continual contact and review of your corporate status.

- Subscription to "The Corporate Veil" monthly newsletter - Get the information you need to run your business. We provide you with timely resources to keep you informed and up to date on current business trends.

- Digital Record Book - Any documents produced in the program are maintained and stored for you records.

- Assistance with state filings - It's imperative that you keep your company current with its annual filings and reports in the state where it was formed. Failure to do so will leave your company in bad standing. We will notify you when state filings are due to assist you in keeping your company current and avoid late penalties.

- Record Reconstruction - It doesn't matter if you have been in business for years. We get your corporate records caught up for one low price.

- Business Success Webinar Series - Learn powerful business strategies from a variety of business professionals from the convenience of your own office. These dynamic webinars will focus on you, the business owner, and how you can leverage your business for maximum growth.

$125,000 Corporate Compliance Guarantee. We will guarantee the integrity of your Corporate Veil up to $125,000.

www.corpveilprotection.com

SEMINARS

Our extensive expertise in the areas of incorporation, asset protection, minimizing taxes and estate planning allows us to develop educational workshops that are tailored to meet the needs of your unique group.

Our workshops are led by industry experts that range from CPAs and attorneys to small business development consultants, asset protection specialists and estate planners. These individuals have taught thousands of business owners, medical professionals, contractors, real estate investors and many more to successfully implement corporate business strategies.

BUSINESS OWNERS BOOT CAMP

Owning your own business is the hardest job you'll ever love. But, to drive your business forward, you must have a basic understanding of how the pieces come together. This powerful 2-day workshop will provide you with an intense overview of taxes, human resources, marketing and financial planning.

ASSET PROTECTION AND TAX REDUCTION

As attacks on small business continue to rise, it's critical that you level the playing field. Learn how to protect the things you've worked hard to build and to ensure you are getting the tax advantage to which you are entitled.

HOW TO USE A CORPORATION AND LIMITED LIABILITY COMPANY WORKSHOP

These condensed information-filled seminars are taught in a live format with the ability for attendees to ask questions specific to their businesses. These one-day seminars take place throughout the country and are directed at new corporate owners. They provide a brief understanding of how to set-up and manage a new corporation.

Additional Topics:

- Ownership Has Its Privileges
- Your Paper Shield
- Leave A Lasting Legacy For Your Family
- Taxation Basics For The Business Owner
- Legal Tax Reduction Can Be Yours
- Deduct, Document and Defend
- Risk vs. Reward

1-800-648-0966
www.laughlinusa.com

9120 Double Diamond Pkwy.
Reno, NV 89521
Phone: 775-525-2892 1-800-648-0966
FAX: 775-525-2898
E-Mail: info@laughlinusa.com
Web: www.laughlinusa.com